Creating Shamsiyah

By

T.L. McCown

For additional information or to order T.L.'s first book, "Shifting Sands: Life in Arabia with a Saudi Princess," please visit www.tlmccown.com

Copyright © 2007 by T.L. McCown
Printed in the United States. All rights reserved.

ISBN # 978-0-9779407-3-8

Father's Press, LLC
816-600-6288
www.fatherspress.com

ॐ*Dedicated*ॐ

To my amazing family

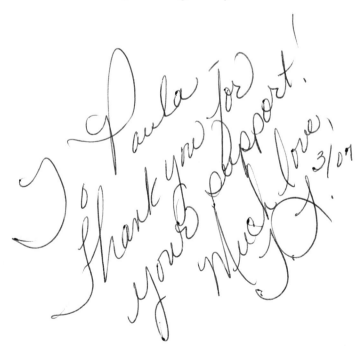

Introduction

When I think of the steps I saw the Saudi women make during my time in Kingdom and I think of where they are today, I applaud them. Through her vision, my Princess carried the torch of her antecessors with the understanding that Saudi women, like their sisters of years past, hold an important place in society. When I speak of their "feminist movement," the term in should in no way be equated with the suffrage or movement of any other country. What is happening with the Saudi women is theirs and theirs alone. From what I witnessed in the beginning, the steps they took on their path of personal development honored their religion and embraced their traditions, and I believe this will continue, as is their way.

I do not claim to be a scholar of Islam, and I do not wish to demean the Islamic religion with the writing of this book. I do not know or claim to know everything there is to know about the Saudi people. I doubt many Americans could make this claim. When the decision was made to write about my experiences, I made a promise to myself that only what I experienced would be included in the pages. As is life, there are always two sides to every coin. Hence, I leave judgment and opinion to the reader.

To assure individual safety and to satisfy my need to keep the privacy of the princess and other friends, all names have been changed, including my own. Consequently, the pictures I include are limited to protect privacy as well. However, every event that follows is true.

Not all of the words I share about the Kingdom are pleasant, but I would assume if someone wrote about America or other countries, the same would be true. If I offend, I apologize to my Arab friends. I only want to share what I believe will have historical value as to who placed *The Shamsiyah*.

ॐContentsॐ

Chapter 1	Escape..	1
Chapter 2	En Route..	11
Chapter 3	The Journeys Began...........................	21
Chapter 4	The South of France...........................	45
Chapter 5	Weaving the Friendship......................	69
Chapter 6	The Year of the Dance........................	87
Chapter 7	Second Time Around..........................	105
Chapter 8	The Vision..	131
Chapter 9	Redefining..	165
Chapter 10	Transforming the Dream....................	201
Chapter 11	Unveiling the Dream..........................	229
Chapter 12	Destiny Foretold.................................	251
Chapter 13	Recharging...	283
Chapter 14	Coming of Age...................................	313
Chapter 15	Fate Unveiled.....................................	341
Chapter 16	Reconnecting.....................................	361
Chapter 17	Pushing the Envelope.........................	385
Chapter 18	Ma'as Salaama...................................	419

Appendices

| A – Glossary of Arabic Terms............................. | 439 |
| B – Photographs.. | 445 |

Chapter 1
Escape
June 2001

My heart raced faster than it usually did in the 110 degree heat as Saleem loaded our bags into the van. In the dark of the night, the stifling heat seemed unreal, but it was real. It was Saudi Arabia in late-June. As I watched, Saleem seemed to move in slow motion, although I knew that he was doing his best. He was helping me in his own way.

The children ran around the pile of sixteen pieces of luggage and carry-ons, giggling with glee and anticipation of the fun to come the way they always did right before we traveled. For me, it was different. I just wanted to be on the plane. I wanted to be safely out of the Kingdom.

Finally, the slamming van door broke my daze as Saleem announced that we were ready. Taking one last walk through our villa, I looked around. Only the company-issued furniture and household items remained either against the wall or neatly folded on the kitchen bar. Our personal things, our memories, were gone. As I walked from room to room, I knew this would be the last time I would see my Saudi home, so I moved slowly, burning my memory for a lifetime.

Somberly, I closed our front door for the final time. With my *abaya* flying behind me in the hot, lofting breeze of the night, I turned and joined my two small children, Mason and Michelle, their nanny, and my trusted friend and driver, Saleem, in the van.

My gaze was broken with each gear shift of the van, as it gained speed to exit the machine-gun guarded gates. The manicured palms lining the main thoroughfare of the compound passed in a blur with each blink. As the van rocked toward the gate, I felt the hot air flow past me, streaming through the open window. I needed to feel the wind in my face, even though the air conditioner would have been more comfortable.

Packed so tight that none of us could move, the van rolled along the highway as Saleem's favorite Arabic music resonated in the background. The drive to the new airport in **Dammam** took much longer than the old airport run in **Dhahran**. We seemed to drive endlessly through the black of night, rarely passing another car. It was "o'dark thirty," thirty minutes past midnight, and the stars twinkled in the heavens over the desert as they had done for me a thousand times before. "Soon," I thought, "soon we'll be out of here." The time could not pass quickly enough to calm my racing heart.

The enormity of the new **Dammam** International Airport did not strike me until I emerged from the over-packed van. Although I had entered and exited the Kingdom through it many times, I had never taken a moment to notice its beauty. The highly polished brown marble walls and floors twinkled because they were so clean. The Saudis had spared no expense for the latest airport technology, such as scanners, flat screen TVs and all the other technology created and sold by the Western world to create a first class transportation hub. The airport's beauty and size had never occurred to me because I was usually hurrying though to board a flight for my next adventure. Only this time I did notice because I knew I would never see it again. I wanted to burn my memory so I would never forget the life I had lived for the past ten years. I had to remember the things that were accomplished because in the future, historians will want to know. This time I wasn't fluttering in and out of the Kingdom in royal style with my Princess, expecting everything to be first class. Rather, I was quietly leaving, with kids and baggage in tow, through the dark of the night. Leaving as if the past ten years had never happened and the things that I had accomplished had never occurred.

While I gazed about trying to absorb even the smallest of details, Saleem negotiated with the man from Pakistan to take our baggage to check-in for a fair price. Typically, I like to handle matters such as these because I just love to barter. Yet this night, I had no stomach for it and I knew my driver and trusted friend could handle it.

Over the decade, Saleem and I had developed an unusual relationship. It was a relationship that operated on numerous levels with one clear, yet fuzzy line. On the one hand, I was the Madame, the *modarisa*, and he was the driver, there to drive me, to serve me. Our distance always remained as such while we understood and mutually respected the others' position in the hierarchy dictated in the Kingdom. Yet, on the other hand, Saleem was my friend in his professional, protecting way. Year after year, he was always there for me. He had an uncanny way of knowing when I was emotionally or culturally on shaky ground, and he was there to make things right. He would fill me in on Arab culture etiquette when he saw that I didn't know or share the latest rumors from the drivers' lounge at the palace. As we would ride down the street on our daily afternoon runs to and from the palace, he would teach me Arabic from behind the wheel as I graced the backseat alone. Because he had always been there, I knew he would be there for me this night.

Inside my footsteps echoed against the massive marble floor, making me feel subconscious as if everyone were looking at me. When we approached the ticket counter for our boarding passes, I stepped slower to gain my composure. "Only a few more challenges and we would be airborne," I reassured myself acting as confidently as I could.

As I should have anticipated, the check-in portion of our journey was exhausting. "For ten years it had been that way so why should this night be any different?" I thought with exasperation. "Oh, Teresa, get a grip," I urged myself. To my despair, these attempts to reassure myself were truly ineffective, yet I had to continue.

While the children jumped and played around our heap of luggage, I tried to understand what the ticket man wanted. My head pounded as he took an eternity to telephone the proper authority to answer whatever question he had on his mind. My anxiety rose with every passing moment as I waited direction.

After what seemed like hours, he explained that our tickets only reflected payment for two checked bags each rather than three. I would have to pay for the overage of weight. Calmed, I handed him my credit card. Normally, it would have irritated me that the company did not handle a detail that they were supposed to handle, but this time, it was a relief.

When we approached the security check point, the inevitable became unavoidable. Momentarily, my fear escaped me and my heart sank. Understanding the obvious as well, Saleem stood near with his hands in his pockets the way he always did when he felt awkward. Looking down, he stood there, my friend of so many years. My heart felt pain as I knew I would never see this wonderful man again.

As I stepped closer to him, he withdrew his hand from his pocket, and in his closed fist was a tattered piece of scrap paper. He handed the paper to me and threw on his big Kenyan smile. "I can drive for you in America," he suggested as I took the offered paper. Looking down, I saw his address in Kenya, written in penmanship equal to a typical third grader. I briefly wondered if he thought that he would not be in Kingdom once *Amity* learned that he had been the one to bring me to the airport. I wondered if he felt the fear that I felt.

"Oh, Saleem," I uttered, trying to make the goodbye easier. "I can drive in America." I reminded him with a soothing voice and caring smile. Pausing with my response, he shuffled his foot like an unsure, younger man as he offered another idea.

"I can drive for Mama Ann and help Baba John," he said humbly.

Not wanting to shatter his hopes, I agreed and assured him that I would be in touch should Mama or Daddy ever need his help. "Maybe you can come to America one day," I encouraged, smiling and nodding my head in agreement. Knowing full well that these were only dreams that probably would never happen, we both continued to smile and nod to make the end more palatable. I wanted to hug his neck to thank him for all that he had done for me, but I could not. No bodily contact is allowed between a man and a woman in public in the Kingdom of Saudi Arabia, even if it is only a platonic hug of gratitude. Given our situation, I could only smile as we inched away from him toward the security clearance line. As we started to turn the corner, he was still there. Looking back to the very last possible moment, I saw Saleem for the final time, standing with his hands in his pockets, smiling as he always did even when he didn't feel happy.

It is only in security and passport control that you will see a Saudi man working in an airport in the Kingdom. All of the perceived unimportant jobs are accomplished by *Third Country Nationals* (TCNs). It is the positions of authority, the positions of control that the Saudis maintain. Fortunately, clearing security was a piece of cake. Yes, it was worrisome because we had to unzip all of our carry-ons for inspection and pass through the women's security section for further security checks under our *abayas*, but for the most part, it was fairly uneventful.

Unfortunately, my time of relief was short-lived as we rounded the next corner toward passport control. Four carry-ons and two young children were enough of a challenge in an international airport on a normal night, even with a nanny in tow, so the additional worry only made things seem even more frantic. We had only begun our journey, and I was already worn out. Again, I had to muster my composure. This would be the big hurdle. Passport control would determine our departure from the terminal: on an airplane westward bound or in a "gymcee,' as the Saudi refer to a suburban, to police headquarters. The moment of truth was near.

Had she sent word to stop us? Were they going to arrest me or simply take me to the palace? Was she really angry enough to go to that extent? Surely my dear friend would not purposefully put my children and me in harm's way! My mind raced with a hodgepodge of thoughts as I approached the uniformed Saudi man in passport control—the other airport position of power.

"Passport," he demanded as he held his hand out firmly.

Flashing a counterfeit smile of sincerity, I gave it my best shot. I had to pull this one off, not only for my sake but for the sake of my children. Consequently, I threw on the Southern charm that had never failed me before, even when carrying something in my luggage that was listed on the Kingdom's "Prohibited List" after a holiday.

Understanding how the Saudis revere family, I threw my next trump card: Michelle on the counter with her big, blue eyes, blonde hair, and magnificent personality. Truly, this one would never fail to distract from the most serious of situations. Then, just to be sure, I pulled Mason into the picture and made a big deal of his saying **Marhaba** to the man who held our fate in his hands. Relentlessly, I continued with my chattering and charm, remarking about family and children as he sequentially punched our visa numbers into his computer. I did my very best to peer over his shoulder and read what the monitor revealed about me, but to no avail. All I could see were the markings of the Arabic tongue. He said nothing while he typed. He showed no emotion. After what seemed like an eternity, he looked up at me. He looked straight into my eyes the way the Arabs do as if they are looking into your soul.

As my charade continued, my hand fumbled within my shoulder bag for our papers, our forged travel papers, knowing that he would request them next.

"Papers," he demanded in a voice that shook me from my rambling. Again, I looked straight into his eyes. He assumed that I was questioning his request when, in fact, I was trying to analyze his intent. "Papers," he demanded again with his hand outstretched, but only slightly as he would never stoop to give it any additional effort than required. Afraid he would notice my hand shaking and sense my anxiety, I handed the papers to Michelle for her to pass to him. I then began to ramble again about children and family. All insignificant comments designed to distract him and convey my helplessness as a woman, seeking pity every step of the way, which had been a successful ploy in the past as well.

He starred at the papers as I continued to talk. Detached, he glanced up and glared at the nanny and then, without a comment, returned his attention to the papers. Suddenly, his loud stamp seemed to echo off of the marble surroundings as he manually pounded exit only visa stamps into each of our four passports. When he laid them in my outstretched hand, my heart leapt, but only for a moment. Perhaps we were home free. Herding the children forward while giving the officer a sincere smile this time, I uttered **Shukran** earnestly over and over again as we scooted through the tight passage way as swiftly as possible.

The children had no problem keeping up with my hurried pace as we worked our way down the long corridor to the gate. For them, it was fun to run along side of Mommy and to jump on and off the luggage trolley. Yet for me, it was the last hurdle to freedom. Although I felt as if the worst was over, my fear still loomed. I knew that it would not totally leave me until we were safely out of Saudi airspace.

Once on the plane, I looked around suspiciously as the nanny heaved the heavy carry-ons into the overhead compartment. Unknowingly, I was neglecting my regular routine of helping the children settle into their seats – their personal space for the next fourteen hours. Our safety took precedence.

Nervously, I took my seat by the window still clad in my *abaya*. Although I heard the children comment about this and that, I cannot recall the details because my attention was elsewhere. Soon, the engines began to roar and the flight attendant announced to cross-check the doors. I knew we were almost home free and my heart began to beat more rhythmically. As I felt the force of take-off push against my chest, my hand unconsciously touched the glass. For one last look, I pulled myself up against the forward thrust of the plane to see out of the window as we made our assent. I saw the defined area of the city lights skirted by the darkness of the barren desert. As we rose higher and higher, the city lights became more distant and took on the shape of celestial bodies. They twinkled for me as stars do. Again, my hand went to the window as if I were trying to hold on. And then, I felt it. A single tear ran down my cheek, as I said the final goodbye to my home and the way of life to which I had become so accustomed.

Chapter ٢
En Route
June 1992

The water droplets streamed erratically backward on the glass as the jumbo jet rumbled forward. While the others slept, I sat quietly, exchanging periodic smiles with the flight attendant when she would pass. Even though I was starring at the small, oval window, the sight of the rain barely drew my attention. I didn't appreciate the beauty of water then because I had not lived in the Kingdom for very long. Yet, the day would come when I would pray to see rain.

Becoming memorized by the continual roar of the engines, I was relaxed yet inwardly overwhelmed with emotion. I still could not believe that I was on my way to Paris, France, seated in first class with my new employer, a royal Saudi princess and her children. I had been fortunate to grow up in a wonderful, loving home, nestled in a small Georgia town. However, I was experiencing something I had never thought possible. It was like I had stepped into an unbelievable fairy tale only a few months prior.

In November of 1991, I mobilized to the Kingdom of Saudi Arabia to join my husband, David, who had accepted a two year defense contract with a prominent American company. Wanting adventure, we walked away from our average American neighborhood and our average American jobs to fly half way around the world to live and work in the remote sands of the Arabian Peninsula and the soul of the Middle East. Never in my wildest dreams could I have imagined the events that would follow – the decade to come.

My first four months in Kingdom had been exciting yet difficult. I had experienced the full force of cultural shock and managed to pull through. My new world was exciting. I was still in awe of the plush accommodations we were provided after a short time in temporary quarters. The first villa we were assigned in the Kingdom was over 3,000 square feet, decorated with designer furnishings, and equipped with everything needed to set up house, even down to the wire whisk.

Our walled community, known as the compound, was gorgeous with manicured palm trees and shrubs immaculately kept by hundreds of **Third Country Nationals** (TCNs.) My new world behind the fifteen-foot so called "privacy wall" included a swimming pool with an overlooking snack bar, a bowling alley, a theater for dances and plays, a small grocery store, a library, a weight room, racquet ball courts, saunas, tennis courts, and a dinning facility that would rival any five-star restaurant.

In such a world, I often questioned how anyone could manage to become depressed, but it happens. It happens when you realize that you are no longer free and able to do things that before required no thought. It happens when you can't make a pumpkin pie because you can't get nutmeg since it is considered an aphrodisiac and deemed illegal. It happens when you realize that you cannot drive and you are completely dependent on someone else to take you anywhere you want or need to go, even the emergency room. It happens when you fumble through your handbag for a copy of your husband's *igama*, which validates your right to exist, and becoming frustrated as you wrestle with the yards of black fabric that make up your veil stuffed inside, which you must keep with you just in case you are approached by the *Muthawen* – the country's "religious police." The list goes on.

To overcome the challenges of my new life in the Kingdom, I soon decided that my very mental survival depended on activity. It only took two months for me to tire of the life of leisure and the continual coffee mornings, craft bazaars, and ladies club meetings. I had to get a job. I needed to do something that would occupy my mind as well as my time. After looking at the limited options available to me, the only one remotely feasible was to begin teaching English to Saudi children. Because I was in the Kingdom with my husband, I was not legally supposed to work. However, neither were the other 300 plus women on the compound who had some sort of business going.

Even though my master's degree is in communication and not English as a second language, I knew that I could teach Arabic speaking children to understand English given the opportunity. With my goal set, I refreshed and printed my resume and gave it to David to distribute at the airbase. Because I was not supposed to work, there were no other avenues to secure employment other than word-of-mouth. Supportively, David distributed my resume to some Saudi men he knew well at work while I sat anxiously in our villa. Weeks passed with no inquiries.

My depression soon reappeared stronger than before. It became so bad that I began to rearrange our furniture on a daily basis for something to do rather than attend another women's gossip opportunity. Forcing myself out of bed each morning, I would pull open the huge, heavy curtains, designed to keep out the sand during the seasonal *shammals*, only to find the sun shinning bright with the pale blue sky sporting little puffy clouds screaming it was another pretty day.

Fortunately, one of those redundant pretty days finally brought a surprise my way when the phone rang early one March of 1992. It was David. An American man speaking on behalf of a Saudi family who was interested in me as the tutor for their five children was in his office. Finally, I had an opportunity.

My thoughts were broken by the monotone roar of the engines and the aches of my body. Stretching to relieve the stiffness my back felt from lack of moment, I looked around the first class cabin and surveyed each of my new Saudi friends, later to be affectionately called my Saudi family. Other than the few who had obviously gotten their tickets before the palace house manager bought ours, our group consumed first class.

Over to my right was Madawi, the princess. Her shoulder length, silky, raven hair fell naturally around her long neck as she rested with her big, black eyes closed. Carrying almost six feet in height, Madawi had a stately gate and could have easily been a model in any other country in the world. As the daughter of a king, you would not expect her to be so personable and so real, but Madawi is which makes her all the more the epitome of a "princess."

On the opposite side of the plane occupying one of the bulk- head seats was Fahad, the oldest child of Madawi and the Colonel and the only male of five. The dashing fifteen year old was just on the threshold of manhood, still seeking his identity and focus for the future. In the two short months I had been with the family, it had become obvious he wanted to learn from me, yet not allow anyone to know that he did. He was creative, thoughtful, and caring, yet continually looking for a balance between his personal dreams and the expectations that his position as prince had forced upon him.

Nora, the oldest daughter, snuggled beside Madawi in the window seat with her head on her mother's shoulder as any fourteen year old would do. There was an obvious blend of mother and father in Nora. Tall and slender like her mother; Nora could draw the attention of a room simply by walking through it with her mannerisms mimicking the stately, feminine qualities of her mother. Yet, her facial features and hair were definitely her father's. To watch Nora's face through a soccer match revealed identical facial gestures like her Baba would make when he would watch a game with her. Even though the shyest of the girls, Nora had what she needed to succeed in life, only refinement remained.

  A whispering ruckus drew my attention from the sleeping princesses toward the back of the cabin and another one of my royal pupils. Fatma, Madawi's middle and fiery child, was bickering with Mama Ginny, the family's matriarchal Filipino nanny, about what she wanted to buy from duty free shopping later in flight. For the most part, the discussion was pointless for the most part since the outcome was already determined, yet each felt as if they should at least appear to have discussed the purchase. As Mama Ginny tried her best to offer direction with frugal purchasing decisions, Fatma had already decided the items were something she could not live without. Fatma would win and they both knew it, yet Mama Ginny felt compelled to at least try. To be perfectly honest, I think they both enjoyed this common ritual they shared as you could always feel the love between them even if you didn't see it.

  Out of Madawi's single boy and five girls, Fatma, the chubby twelve year old, was the most vivacious and spirited of them all. Blessed with her mother's silky raven hair and big, beautiful black eyes, Fatma was always looking for ways to do things differently, constantly seeking her niche. Her smile was always genuine blended with a little mischief and fun. Consequently, I had known the night I met her that she would be the one to challenge me. She would be the one to make me reach deep inside myself to find creative ways to reach and teach her. She was simply too clever to settle for the mundane.

Satisfied that the commotion was nothing of concern, I settled myself back into my seat, wiggling to get comfy for the three hours that remained. As quiet settled over the cabin once again, my survey of the family continued. My attention was drawn by little Maha stretched out consuming her entire seat plus her nanny's. The physical image of Nora and the disposition of Fatma combined defined the chubby little five-year-old. Her toothless grin won my heart from the beginning, and I believe it was Maha who was most excited to have Mrs. Teresa on board.

Snuggled angelically in her nanny's arms with her feet curled beneath her, little Bandari slept. The beautiful child of three was blessed with the best of all before her. Long, soft wavy black hair like Nora's embellished her beautiful round face graced with the family trait of big beautiful eyes. Her father's dashing smile would win your heart as her mother's compassion shown through. Fatma's enthusiasm for life blossomed in Bandari and her zest for learning followed in line with Maha's. She was the youngest in the beginning and thus on the receiving end of everyone's adoration.

My thoughts were distracted as the pilot's voice echoed over the intercom, first in Arabic and then in French, as we were traveling on *Air France*. With my college French a little rusty, I was unsure of his announcement, so I clarified with Madawi.

"It's just a short stop, Mrs. Teresa," she remarked, "and then we'll be on our way."

Short stop, I thought, but this was ticketed as a non-stop flight. With my curiosity heightened, I questioned further.

"Short stop," I paused, "where?"

"Beirut," she replied nonchalantly.

"Beirut?" I responded rather concerned, "but Americans are not allowed to go to Beirut…"

"We are not *going* to Beirut, Mrs. Teresa," Madawi answered calmly while her hands emphasized the point. "We are only *stopping* to pick up people." Her long, slender hand went up in dismissal, "*mofie mushkala.*"

Unsure of how to respond to her reply, I quietly settled back into my seat as the plane continued its descent. For some reason, I suddenly felt fear. I knew that I had heard that Americans were not supposed to go, to land or to stop in Beirut, Lebanon. Later, I learned from a friend at the American Embassy that this little unexpected stop could have gotten me a $10,000 fine, imprisonment, or both.

Sensing my uneasiness, Madawi began to tell me more about Beirut as we circled over the water nestled up to the shore. While we both peered out of Nora's small, oval window, she told me about how she and her family used to come to Beirut on holiday when she was a little girl. She fondly remembered how they would swim in the morning and then drive up the mountain to snow ski after lunch. She told me how beautiful the country had been before the war.

Still looking out of the window, reminiscing, Madawi continued. "It was the Riviera of the Middle East before the fighting," she paused, "before the bombs." Through the glass, I could clearly see what she meant. The landscape was absolutely breathtaking. I saw massive, towering tree-covered mountains that seemed to flow directly into the sea below spotted by old, ruined buildings, and debris from the explosions that had been there for years. I could not speak. There was nothing to say that would even suffice.

In spite of my rusty French, I immediately understood the pilot's request when his voice echoed over the intercom and broke her reflections. We were landing. Once the plane came to a stop, I continued to sit, buckled up, anxiously believing that we would depart at any moment. Everyone else, however, seemed relaxed and conversations sprang up everywhere while the girls jumped from seat to seat to check out each other's duty-free desires and the view each window offered.

After thirty minutes, I was overwhelmed by the rising temperature within the cabin basking under the Lebanese sun in June; I unhooked my safety belt and moved around the first class cabin with everyone else. Curious, I strolled over by the doorway, which was open and supporting the portable stairs from the tarmac. Suddenly the flight attendant stepped between me and the door, telling me something in Arabic. Although I did not understand the words she spoke, I knew that she did not want me to try and leave the plane. To show no ill will, I flashed a genuine smile and I turned to find my seat. Slowly doing so, I took the opportunity to peer over her shoulder. I saw two men on either side of the steps on the tarmac below, uniformed and holding machine guns. With this, my smile disappeared and I anxiously returned to my seat, yearning takeoff to begin.

Although relieved when we were airborne again, I remained quiet, thinking about what Madawi had said. Gazing out of the window while the plane circled to get our correct bearing, I could see the Beirut landscape again, yet this time I thought of the people. How awful it must be to have something so beautiful destroyed by something as senseless as war. Exhausted from our stop, I leaned back and drifted into a restless slumber only to be awakened by the pilot's voice again. He was welcoming us to *Charles DeGualle International Airport* in Paris, France.

Chapter ٣
The Journeys Began
June 1992

    Still buckled when the plane rolled to the gangway, our mouths were all but buckled. Everyone was talking at once. Each of us was eager to gather our belongings and get on with our adventure. Madawi, however, sat quietly and stately. Her *abaya* had disappeared because there was no need now. When the plane came to a halt, everyone got out of their seats, everyone but Madawi. This was usual for her and she knew that there was no need to rush, particularly with Alma, her lady in waiting, gathering her belongings to depart the plane.

    Once inside the airport, our entourage was whisked past the usual rigors of an international arrival and straight into a private waiting area. There was no passport control or customs clearance for us, rather tea and more waiting. Soon I saw two of the drivers, Sabre and Khalid now dressed in western clothes; go by the window, pushing enormous piles of luggage on multiple pushcarts. I counted no less than 50 pieces of luggage before they were out of sight.

    Soon a strange man entered the waiting area and spoke to Madawi in Arabic. Following her lead, we left the waiting area to find several BMWs waiting for us. Each was running, cooled and at our beckon call. It was obvious that the girls knew some of the waiting drivers, their regular drivers when they were in Paris, because they ran up and greeted each standing by his assigned car. Within minutes, we were off and my every sense was peaked as we zipped and zoomed through French traffic. I tried to see as much as possible while I braced myself and my belongings to keep from swaying all over the back seat. Eyes wide, I tried to see it all never realizing Paris would become so familiar to me.

With the sound of multiple car horns and the braking sounds of almost crashes flooding around us, we flew down the *Champs d'Elysee*, around the *Arc d'Triumph* and onto *Avenue Foch*, one of the most exclusive sites for flats in Paris. Suddenly, our motorcade took a sharp right turn and literally screeched into the underground parking lot, one car after another. Not giving their belongings a thought, the girls grabbed my hands, all four of them, and pulled me to the waiting elevator. "Come Mrs. Teresa," they called in unison while they grinned from ear to ear. "Come and see!"

When the elevator bumped to a stop on the 5th floor, the girls began to bicker as to who would get Mrs. Teresa first. Each of them wanted to show me their room, the salon, and all the rooms of the flat before the others. Calmingly, I reassured them that I would see one special room with each of them and the rest with the group.

The flat had a huge salon for the family to gather, talk, and watch TV. Off to the side was a large dinning area with an adjoining kitchen. There were four bedrooms and a small, second TV room in the opposite direction, all decorated, naturally, in Arab style. After the tour and a quick freshly-blended fruit juice with Madawi, I learned that this was only one of the flats. Princess Amal, fondly called Mama Amal by the children and mother by Madawi, had an identical flat on the 4th floor, where I would stay, and the men had another flat in the building that I never saw. Each flat encompassed an entire floor, an entire floor on prestigious *Avenue Foch*, and I would guess about 2,500 square feet each. When I was told that my room was downstairs with Mama Amal may face must have revealed my disappointment because I felt I would be more comfortable with the girls and people who I knew, or at least with people whom I shared a common language. With her incredible intuitiveness, Madawi sensed my feelings. "It's better, Mrs. Teresa, that your room be downstairs, huh," she began. "This way you can have your own bath and privacy." Not being able to argue with that I headed downstairs with the girls'.

  With the same floor plan as the flat above, the girls' pulled me down the hall to my room right next to Mama Amal's. It was a nice room with a big queen sized bed and large sliding glass doors leading to my private balcony, which overlooked downtown Paris. Upon first site, I had no idea that this little balcony would be my refuge, my special place to go and put things in perspective. It was a place where I could breathe the city air, smell the smells, and hear the sounds of "*gay Paris*" each morning before anyone else would wake.

ॐ *Creating Shamsiyah* ॐ

With the excitement of our arrival dissipating, we all began to busy ourselves with settling into our home for the next four weeks. Unpacking my things, hanging my clothes, and the like encompassed the remainder of the day. As I worked I noticed that one bag was missing. My duffle bag with the study materials I had developed for our trip to incorporate English studies with fun activities, wasn't in my room. Making a mental note to ask Madawi about its whereabouts, I continued to unpack. Although the room I had been given was nice, it was strange to me. It was plush, but at the same time had the air of a "grandma's house," which was in some sense soothing and some sense not as it wasn't my grandmother. Surrounded by older whatnots of Mama Amal's, I added my picture of David and travel alarm clock to the nightstand. It was my simple way of making the room "home." Comfortable with my arrangement of things, I headed back up to the 5th floor to Madawi and the girls.

Almost as if we had beamed ourselves from **Dhahran** to Paris, there sat Madawi in the salon with an elderly lady that I had never seen. Slightly humped over, she was buzzing around the room fixing this and that. With someone busy unpacking her personal items, Madawi was free to plan the evening and upcoming events. She was on the telephone, yet smiled when I entered and motioned for me to sit. Respectfully, I quietly approached the sofa next to her when I saw the small table by her recliner overflowing with freshly baked snacks placed there for **Amity's** pleasure. Smiling, I quietly snagged a hot *sambousha* before I slipped back onto the cushion. With the phone still to her ear, she welcomed my continued food theft with her eyes and her smile.

 I looked around the room at the various decorations and personal items, while Madawi talked and I munched. As I waited, my eyes continued to wonder and I noticed a large blue duffle bag next to the big screen TV. It was mine! The one I had missed. Once Madawi was off the phone, I totally forgot that I wanted to ask her about the picture of the Arab man, and turned my attention to the duffle bag. Proudly, I showed her the contents filled with all of my hard work. Understanding my pride, Madawi was gentle with my feelings as she explained, "Mrs. Teresa," she hesitated. "I do not want you to study English with the girls this summer." Leaning closer to me over the arm of her chair, she smiled softly and continued in a warm voice, "I just want you to be around them, for them to experience things with you, and see things through your eyes." Still a bit unsure of exactly what she meant and what my role actually was, I felt awkward but agreed. After zipping the duffle bag, I put it back in the corner of the room and never saw or touched it again until it arrived in my villa in **Dhahran** almost three months later.

 The tension of the moment was broken as the older lady buzzed through the room once again. Madawi, standing, stopped the lady and spoke to her in Arabic and then turned her attention to me. "Mrs. Teresa," she began. "I would like for you to meet

Mama Soha." In Arabic, she then spoke to Mama Soha, obviously introducing me as I understood "Mrs. Teresa" among the Arabic words. "Mama Soha," she continued, "is special to my heart. She raised me." Mama Soha and I exchanged kisses and hugs, but exchanged few words because I understood very little Arabic and she very little English. But even so, I felt relaxed with her. Her warm, yet time weathered, loving face seemed to set the tone for the people around her. I had no idea I had just met a very important woman in Madawi's life.

After a restless sleep, I woke to the early morning sunrise of Paris in the summer. Bright rays of warmth beamed through the wall of glass that faced east in my room. Soon I learned why each window in Paris was equipped with metal shades that you crank down over the glass before bed. In the summer months, Paris enjoys long days, extremely long days with the sun rising early and setting close to midnight. As I woke, I stretched and lay in the bed a bit pondering my situation. How in the world was I there? How was this gal from a small town in Georgia now in Paris, France traveling with a Saudi Royal family? I had no answers as to why, only thankful that it was so.

Unsure of what the day would hold, what we would do or when we would do it, I decided to shower and get dressed so that I could be ready for anything on a moments notice. Once dressed, I tiptoed through the quiet 4th floor flat and made my way up stairs to find only Susan, Nora's nanny since her birth, and Sabre, the driver, awake in the kitchen. They welcomed me and laughed at my early rising. Offering me coffee and French bread with cream cheese, we sat and began to talk about the upcoming day. Shortly, Sabre got up to leave, announcing that he was off to get *Amity's* newspapers before she woke. Now this got my attention—a newspaper. Since I was traveling with an Arabic speaking family, whenever we watched TV it was, naturally, the Arab news channel and I was already yearning for some English news. I gave Sabre the necessary French Francs for him to get me a copy of <u>USA Today</u> while he was out and he kindly agreed.

 A few hours passed before anyone else stirred on the 5th floor. For the rest of our stay, Susan and I spent this morning time getting to know each other, sharing thoughts and feelings. On this first morning, she was extremely helpful in telling me where to get my clothes washed, helping me make a telephone call to David, and letting me know where I could find this and that. It was during this first trip that Susan became my dear friend and she was always there to cheerfully answer any questions I had.

 Soon the noise level of the flat rose as each child meandered into the kitchen, sleepy and still in their pajamas. Of course, me and my perky self gave all the girls a hard time for sleeping so late and told them about what we had missed on our first day in Paris. "It's the early bird that catches the worm," I jested as I ate my second breakfast. Politely they smiled as if to humor me, with me not realizing they had been to Paris numerous times and had no desire to see the common tourist spots again. After we finished eating, they all disappeared and returned dressed and ready to walk the *Champs d'Elysee*—their favorite Parisian pastime.

 We spent the entire day walking and shopping. We searched store after store for the latest fashions, the most recent hit music and videos in an effort to discover the latest from the west, periodically stopping for sodas or ice cream at the various café's along the way. Never was I asked to pay for a thing. The check was always taken care of. At first, I tried each and every time to step up and pay my way, but my offer was always refused. After a while and with Susan's encouragement, I stopped trying. As we passed *Pizza Pino*, the girls pointed out the famous pizza place to me and decided that we should have dinner there. We continued to walk and walk and walk, with conversation buzzing about this new outfit and that new gadget or which movie we would see that night. By the end of the afternoon and our complete inspection of every shop along the *Champs d'Elysee*, my legs truly ached.

 It wasn't until we returned to the flat around 7:00 p.m. that I saw Madawi that day. Again she was in the salon, but this time with a young woman who was petite and pretty with long, jet black hair. When the children and I entered the salon, they were all speaking at once to Madawi, in Arabic of course, telling her all that we had done during the day and our plans for the evening. I sat, extremely happy not to be walking the *Champs d'Elysee*. After a bit, the conversation turned to me.

In English, Madawi introduced me to the strange woman. "Mrs. Teresa," she began, "this is Francis." We exchanged greetings and handshakes and turned our attention back to Madawi, each wondering the other's position in this relationship. "Francis is here to help us," Madawi continued, "to be with us." Francis was our "companion" as the Arabs describe it. Her father was French and her Mother Lebanese, hence she was fluent in Arabic and French. It was her job to let us know where the good restaurants were, help us order when we got there, and let us know about any good shows or happenings around the city. Basically, our private tour guide as a westerner would define it.

After a brief reprieve with our feet up at the flat, the girls and I returned for another round on the *Champs d'Elysee* for more shopping, a movie, and dinner at *Pizza Pinos*. I knew a bond was forming between the girls and I when they showed their concern for my having ham on my personal pizza. "But it's pig, Teresa!" they would exclaim every time the waiter left with my order that summer. It was so obvious they cared. Even so, I simply reassured them that "Mrs. Teresa would be okay and they shouldn't worry."

Each night the girls and I would return to *Avenue Foch* around midnight after an evening full of food, shopping, movies, and cafes. After our good night hugs were exchanged, I would tiptoe into Mama Amal's flat on the 4th floor, usually to find her awake and praying. I felt so bad that I might be disturbing her, but I assume I didn't because our midnight encounters never included glances or words.

In the beginning, I slept around 1:00 a.m., yet still woke bright and early each morning in spite of the lowered shutter. Obviously, I was still on an early morning western schedule in spite of my late evenings with the girls. I simply had not adapted to the nocturnal, Arab way of staying up and sleeping late. Every morning, like clockwork, my eyes would pop open. Anxious not to miss anything, I would dress, head up stairs, and begin the morning as my first in Paris. Coffee and French bread with Susan and Sabre followed by a quick read of the <u>USA Today</u> that Sabre would bring. Several hours later, the girls would trickle in one by one, rubbing eyes and looking for food. At first I thought this was due to jetlag, but I soon realized that it was simply normal for them. Once this routine became evident, I asked Susan about the chance of sight-seeing. I had been in Paris for five days and had yet to see the *Eiffel Tower* up close. Susan quickly told me that I should not wait for the girls to want to go with me and suggested that I use my morning time to go while they were still sleeping. Believing this to be a good idea, I checked with Madawi that afternoon to make sure it fit the family's schedule. After all, I was "working."

"Of course, Mrs. Teresa! You should see the sights of Paris," Madawi exclaimed at my inquiry. "I think your morning plan is a good idea" she encouraged as she munched her lunch provided on the little table by the chair. "Why don't you take Susan with you" she remarked in spite of stating it as a question. I agreed, but had no idea that she wanted her to go to "protect" me, so to speak, to make sure I did not get lost or have any hassles with the French drivers, to pay for things, and yes, even carry my purchases.

In spite of another late night with the girls, I could not help but bounce out of bed early. I dressed quickly and quietly headed for the fifth floor where I found Susan ready to go and my breakfast ready to eat. Honestly, I think Susan was excited about our first of many adventures as well. With me, she could be herself even though she insisted on being my companion and servant when she deemed necessary. Over the next week I saw Paris thanks to Susan. We went to the top of the *Eiffel Tower* and toured the *Arc d'Triumph*, not simply walk around it on our way to the other side of the *Champs d'Elysee* as we did each night with the girls. We cruised down the *Seine* river and embraced the treasures of the *Louve'* Museum. We prayed together at *Sacred Heart* church and had our portraits drawn in charcoal by the artists in *Monte Mart*. Each day we visited a new sight and topped off the adventure with a cappuccino stop at one of the many street cafés followed by a touch of shopping before our day with the girls began.

Although I was intrigued with Francis at first, I soon became a touch jealous because she always got to go with Madawi while I was always with the girls. Now this is not to say that I did not enjoy their company. I did. I had a great time with them however, every now and then, I yearned for adult conversation. It didn't take *Pizza Pino,* ice cream on the *Champs d'Elysee,* and the latest kids' flick long to get old and I needed some adult time.

One particular morning after our sight-seeing excursion, I returned to find Madawi in the salon, which was very unusual since she and Francis typically enjoyed the Parisian nights until the wee hours of the morning and slept late as a result. Since our arrival, I had only seen her when the girls and I would stop by the flat before heading out again for our evening ritual. Seeing her, I popped in the salon and sat down to visit for a moment. Francis was there also and we all talked about what we each had been up to lately. Then Madawi mentioned tomorrow would be a special day. We were going to *EuroDisney,* about an hours drive from Paris.

"It should be fun, Mrs. Teresa," she began. "I look forward to you being with the girls." Just then, it hit me. Because she never talked about the baby, I had forgotten she was five months pregnant. All along, I could not figure out what she meant each time she would mention that she wanted me to "be with the girls" this summer. My role was now crystal clear. She had not wanted me to teach English at all. She wanted me to romp and do with the girls because she could not. It all made sense now.

"We plan to leave early," she continued. "We will stay the day and we won't be home until late." Even though I had only been with my royal family a short time, I knew exactly what "late" meant when coming from an Arab, so I decided to throw a change of clothes in my backpack just in case.

    It was early, at least for this crowd, when we departed at 9:00 a.m. Three mini-vans rented for the day and the lead Mercedes rolled in tandem toward *EuroDisney*. Bashmah, who just loved hanging with Mrs. Teresa, insisted that she sit on my lap for the entire journey. Everyone was excited. While we rumbled down the French autobahn, the girls and Fahad, who I saw very little of in Paris, taught me the words to their favorite Arabic tunes and then laughed when I mangled the enunciation with my southern drawl. Through all the laughter, the time passed quickly and we were at the theme park in what seemed like a blink.

    Not having been to Disney World in Florida since I was twelve years old, I was like a kid with eyes wide open, pointing out everything that caught my attention to the kids, explaining the English term for each and throwing in a story here and there about Disney, its history, and notable characters. I was in awe as we drove past the numerous, less expensive three and four star hotels, straight down the main road to the entrance of the famous Disney castle hotel. Our motorcade whirled into the circular drive to valet. We all piled out and stepped to the side to wait Madawi's lead. Within a moment, Sabre approached with the keys to two suites, rented for the day so that we would all have a place to rest and freshen up as we toured the park.

Inside our suites, the kids went wild as did I with all the neat Mickey Mouse shaped soap and Donald Duck towels. Everything imaginable reflected the identifiable themes of Disney, even the tissue box and chocolates on the pillows. It was incredible to me because I could not remember such from my childhood visit. I felt like a kid in a candy store for the first time right along side the girls while they absorbed a solid taste of the west.

After everyone raided both mini-bars for a quick snack, we put on our tummy pouches and slipped on our sunglasses for a magical day at the park. Being that I was the newest addition to the entourage, all of the kids wanted "Mrs. Teresa" to ride with them. Realizing early that this could become an issue, I set the ground rules after we entered the gate. "I'll take turns. I'll go once with each group and then we'll start again." It was the haunted house roller coaster with Fahad, Nora, and Fatma who seemed to enjoy my screams more than the attraction itself. Again, I was unaware that this was not their first visit. Then it was off to Dumbo with Maha and Bandari with Bandari clinging to me for dear life as we whirled around, fighting centrifugal force and our hair in our faces. As we laughed with delight, I knew I was in a magical world – not just *EuroDisney*.

As the day went on, we walked, spun, ate, and laughed more than any group should in a day. While Maha and Bandari rested in our suites during the heat of the afternoon, I continued with the older kids. It was ride this ride then onto the next as fast as our feet could take us. At one particular point in the day, I graciously backed out of joining them on one extremely fast-paced, rough ride, blaming it on age and the need for a short break.

In doing so, I joined Madawi on a nearby bench, where she spent most of her day with only the bench style and location changing. Being five months pregnant is limiting when you are in a theme park, however she didn't seem to mind. She could watch people – her favorite, relaxing past-time. For the first time since our plane adventure through Beirut, I actually had some quality time with Madawi without the kids or Francis. After a bit, I even mustered the courage to ask if I could take her picture, which is seen by some Arabs as taking their soul and I most certainly didn't want to offend her. Expecting a more conservative response, I was shocked when she happily agreed and posed for several.

By the end of the day, we were completely exhausted. Walking arm in arm, we strolled down "Main Street USA" and found a superb spot to watch the closing fireworks, which couldn't have been a more fantastic conclusion to a most memorable day.

All of the children were sleeping, snuggled with their latest stuffed toy from the park completely exhausted and probably dreaming of the fun day they had had. When we reached the 5th floor, each nanny with a little one in arms or tow disappeared to the bedrooms while Madawi and I stepped into the salon for a few minutes and a recap of the day. Kicking off our shoes, I fell onto the sofa and Madawi her chair.

We couldn't help but laugh about various events of the day. Then unexpectedly Madawi blurted out, "would you like to go out with me tomorrow?"

Surprised and excited, I replied without hesitation. "Sure! That would be great."

"Good" she smiled as she sipped her tea, becoming quiet from exhaustion. "I will tell the girls. Now, sleep," she encouraged. "I see it in your eyes. You need to sleep." I agreed and we said our goodnights. Once again on the 4th floor, I tiptoed past Mama Amal. Being as quiet as I could so as not to disturb her prayers, I dressed for bed believing that sleep would come quickly. However, even after I snuggled deep under the covers, I couldn't sleep a wink for remembering the day and thinking of tomorrow.

The next day was a whirlwind as well, but one of a different sort. Rather than walking, we were in a stretch BMW. Instead of shopping for the latest western music CDs and videos, we were shopping on one of the most famous designer drives in the world, *Victor Hugo*. After visiting what seemed like every shop, Madawi suggested that I indulge in a special treat and have my hair done at this really famous salon she knew.

After a wonderful lunch, fortunately not at *Pizza Pinos*, we shopped some more before the beamer pulled in front of a ritzy salon to drop me for my appointment, which Madawi had made in Arabic on her cell phone at lunch for me. Her signature smile flashed as she motioned for me to get out. She seemed to enjoy my surprise as I landed on the curb. "I will go rest now and the driver will return for you," she instructed. "Enjoy!" she exclaimed just as the driver closed the door.

Two hours passed in a blink. I so enjoyed the pampering that accompanies a style in a French salon. The stylist was funny and he kept me laughing the entire time he cut, combed, and styled. When he finally turned me to face the mirror, I was pleased and thanked him for a fun afternoon. I then gathered my things and went to the counter to pay when I was quickly told that my services had been covered. Returning my wallet to my handbag, my look of surprise must have been obvious because the gentleman smiled and then nodded, "Your driver is waiting outside, *Madame*." Feeling like a princess myself, I slipped into the backseat of the beamer for my return to *Avenue Foch*.

Excited, I literally ran out of the elevator onto the 5th floor. I was already talking and asking for opinions before I entered the salon where Madawi sat with Mama Soha and Francis. "Oooh, la la" they began, each making a different gesture to reflect their approval. I spun in a circle to further reveal the new style. All I could do was thank Madawi for the wonderful surprise. "You are most welcome, Mrs. Teresa," she replied. "And the style really suits you." She flashed her special smile. The one she possesses that passes warmth without a word and convinces the senses that all is good.

After slipping into lounging clothes and fluffy slippers, we sat, talked, and enjoyed an evening in for a change. We talked about the little things, nothing of real substance, just great "girl talk." After a bit, Madawi and Francis conversed in Arabic, glancing at me and then back. I continued to munch from the little silver tray as they continued their observation and Arabic commentary.

Becoming a bit uncomfortable and sensing that I was most definitely the topic of their conversation, I gave them a look of exaggerated question, raising a brow for emphasis. "What?" they laughed in unison.

"You tell me," I asked, starting to giggle simply because they were. The way a person does when they are a bit uncomfortable and wanting to appear collected. They continued in Arabic, glanced at me, and then began talking again as if they were debating something about me.

"Okay, enough!" I exclaimed with a giggle. "What is it?"

"Oh, Mrs. Teresa," Madawi sputtered out. "It's your eyebrows."

"What?" I exclaimed personally feeling quite comfortable with my eyebrows.
"What's wrong with my eyebrows?"

"It's nothing." Madawi muttered nonchalantly between nibbles of her sandwich.

Unwilling to let this one lie, I probed. "It is something or you two wouldn't be giggling like schoolgirls, so spill it!" I laughed. Turning on her accomplice, Madawi told me that Francis felt my eyebrows were too thin. "Thin? You have got to be kidding?" I started. "I've always thought they were too thick."

"Not at all." They replied in harmony, gesturing in agreement, and we continued to discuss my eyebrows for the next ten minutes. How we got off on them, I'll never know. But with the hair issue on the table, our conversation turned to leg hair. Becoming serious almost instantaneously, they both began to inform me that the simply did not understand American women.

"How in the world do you American women shave your legs like a man shaves his beard?" Madawi announced rhetorically, waving her arm for emphasis and slapping her knee for finality. Never having thought about it before, I told them I did because that is just what you do – at least from an American's point of view.

"Oh no!" They chimed together in response, smiled at each other for affirmation, and exclaimed. "*Halawah*!"

"*Halawah*? What in heavens name is *halawah*?" I questioned with exaggeration. Helping each other with an English description, they proceeded to tell me about *halawah.* Claiming it to be the method used by Cleopatra and smiling with pride to its longevity, they told me that *Halawah* is the way women have removed body hair for thousands of years. It is a mixture of honey and lemon that is cooked in a saucepan to a certain temperature until it turns a golden brown. It is then cooled and used to remove hair, much like a wax but with no paper strips.

Oh, the things women talk about and the crazier things they try! Before I knew it, Madawi had one of the servants whip up a batch of *halawah*. Madawi and Francis had me stretched across the bed trying to decide if this was something that I really wanted to experience or not. Yes, I had wanted a "girls' night out," an "adult girls' night," but was this what I had had in mind?

With Salwa, an African servant that had been with the family for years, kneeling beside the bed, rolling the *halawah* in here hands to keep its consistency; I mentally questioned my participation again. Did I really want to go to this extent to bond with my new found friends?

"Wait!" I said breathlessly as I sat straight up, circled by a curious audience surrounding the bed. "Does this hurt bad?"

"It's hot, Mrs. Teresa." Salwa replied in her melodious, broken English, smiling wide with her really white teeth shinning bright against her very dark complexion. My eyes widen and darted at Madawi. Hands to face, she reflected mixed emotions. She giggled yet seemed concerned and ran into the hall while Francis, chuckling, sat down on the other side of the bed and readied herself to hold my arms, if necessary. I took a deep breath and paused before declaring my decision.

"Okay." I declared breathlessly. "Let's just do it." I added with sheer determination. I lay back again and looked around. Madawi peeked through the door from the hallway with curiosity and concern, while Francis encouraged me with her smiles. Salwa then proceeded to spread a long, warm strip of **halawah** down my shin.

"No problem" I convinced myself quietly. Then as she ripped it off, "Big problem" blurted from my mouth as I jumped straight off the bed, laughing and crying at the same time. My female audience could not help but roar with laughter because they too had felt the burn before. To relieve it, I hopped around the bed for a moment and then decided that I would prefer to sit rather than lay so it would be easier for me to hop around between pulls. We continued with Salwa pulling and ripping, me hopping, Francis laughing, and Madawi worrying. About half way through my right leg, Madawi came charging in the room from the hallway, obviously unable to take my pain any longer and pronounced, "***Kolasse!***" Everyone stopped laughing, with me being the last, and when the silence became awkward we all looked to her for the conclusion.

"Mrs. Teresa, your skin is too fragile for this....too fair," she stated in a matter of fact tone. "We will finish this at the salon tomorrow where they can be more gentle with you." She concluded, turned and left the room while silence remained. It was her obvious concern that really touched me. Later, I learned that she felt like because my skin was paler, it was more sensitive and the pulling of the **halawah** would hurt me worst than her. The next morning, the driver took me to yet another posh salon where they were expecting me as a result of another appointment made and prepared to complete my waxing. Again, all expenses paid.

Since that first experience with *halawah*, I have read other accounts of it by American authors claiming to understand its ritual and purpose for Saudi women. Through their rhetoric, I found these accounts give the impression that *halawah* is some sort of torture for the Saudi women, and a custom that is forced upon them by the men of the culture to remove their body hair. However, I found nothing further from the truth. Not only is it good for the skin, but the women feel a sense of pride to the heritage behind the sweet mixture. Young Saudi women actually anticipate their first time, seeing it as a celebratory right of passage, if you will. I, too, saw its benefit and still use *halawah* today.

Much to my delight, Madawi began to include me in more adult evenings out with her and Francis. The majority of my time, however, was still devoted to the girls, but the dinners with Madawi became a welcomed distraction. Following each scrumptious dinner at a different elegant restaurant, Madawi liked to top off the night with an evening stroll. To compliment our walk, we would find a sidewalk café somewhere along the way to enjoy a sweet and more people watching.

From the moment we met, Madawi seemed to love being out-of-doors and watching people above all other activities. I, too, enjoy watching people, yet

Madawi seemed to cherish it more than most. Perhaps it was because she could sit under the starlit sky and feel the breeze on her face, or perhaps it was the fact that she could watch people without a layer of black gauze fabric covering her face. But whatever the reason, Madawi simply loved to frequent sidewalk cafés that are so typically Parisian and watch the masses going to and fro.

Just as I was beginning to adapt to their nocturnal, Arab schedule and acquaint myself with the ins and outs of Paris, it was time to move along to our next destination. As the drivers collected my bags and I surveyed my room for a final time that first summer, I felt a hand upon my shoulder from behind. Startled, I turned quickly to find Mama Soha smiling and beckoning me to follow with her hands. As instructed, I walked into the smaller TV salon on the 4th floor. There I found Mama Amal sitting with a small package in her lap. When I entered, she smiled. Genially, she stood and placed the package in my hands. Surprised, I questioned why I would be getting a gift. Mama Soha, smiling and nodding to boot, conveyed to me that Mama Amal wanted to give me some perfume. Honored, I accepted graciously.

In the reverse of our arrival, the motorcade departed following moments of precision chaos. As the girls romped and giggled jutting around randomly in the parking garage, the nannies earnestly attempted to scoot them toward their assigned car while the drivers stood at attention or exchanged last minute route plans. In a whirl, we were off just as before and streaming down the freeway toward the airport and the south of France. Madawi looked exceptionally pretty that morning to fly to Cannes. She smiled when I remarked. Yet, I'm not sure if it was my compliment or the fact that she would see the Colonel, her husband, in only a few short hours that forced the smile.

Chapter 4
The South of France
Summer 1992

I was mesmerized as the motorcade curved its way up the winding cliff. I never dreamed the French Rivera could be so breathtaking. As we neared the top of the seaside mountain, our line of cars filed onto the brick circular drive nestled behind an ornate privacy wall, which attractively marked the estate. Almost simultaneously, the numerous doors swung open and people piled out from every car, covering the drive with curious travelers.

The sea-weathered stucco villa hung majestically from the hillside with crimson oleander draping from the balconies. Surrounded by natural landscaping lofting in the summer breeze, the villa epitomized the classic Mediterranean architectural style. Majestically, our home for the next three weeks beckoned our exploration. Three floors, if you include the underground level, offered plenty of sleeping quarters for the females of our entourage and the Colonel. Fahad had his place and the drivers theirs. I never saw either. With a 240 degree view of the Mediterranean Sea, the swimming pool was the first feature to catch our attention. Nora, Fatma, and I agreed that this would most definitely be the first thing we would experience once our tour was complete.

The common areas were located on the ground floor with Madawi and the Colonel's quarters consuming the entire second floor. Although the salon offered a spacious, beautifully decorated area, a big screen TV, and the same magnificent view as the pool, most of my time with Madawi was spent on her veranda looking into the western sky over the famous sea. Ironically, it was nearing sunset when we arrived and one of the first sites we saw after climbing to tour the second floor was the most magnificent sunset between the two jagged mountain peaks directly across the sea. Perhaps it was this sunset that set our path and called us to return each afternoon to this balcony for the rest of our stay.

  The next morning, I went with Sabre down the mountain into Cannes to pick up my rental car. It seemed as if Madawi decided I should have one. I wasn't involved in its selection but pleased. Sabre pulled up beside a navy blue Mercedes 300 and handed me the keys. It was a peppy little five speed complete with sunroof and, when I could get the gears correct, fun to drive. I was thrilled to have a car at my disposal and feel a sense of freedom I had not felt since I was in the states almost a year prior, yet I was nervous. This was only the third time in my life to drive a stick shift and even the smaller hills posed challenges for me.

  It did not take Maha and Bandari, the "little girls" as Madawi called them, long to find the local junior hot spot – the *malahee*. It was an instant hit and word traveled quickly. Before I knew it, Nora was at my door asking if we could meet the little girls there that evening before our dinner and next American flick. I couldn't help but agree. After all, everyone loves an amusement park.

The **malahee** was exhilarating with lights and whistles exploding from every direction. Both big and little girls talked at once, each making sure her favorite ride was listed in the group's to do list chatter.

They simply could not get enough of the carnival games that bombarded us as we made our way along in the salty evening breeze. The portable store fronts lining the park path cackled with callers enticing the girls to give their game a try. Out of all of the girls, Nora was the most athletic with a quiet, competitive personality to complement her physical talents. She could not resist shooting the balloons with the bee-bee gun. She laid down her Francs and the young man, flirting to some extent, handed her the roped off weapon. She hoisted the butt to her shoulder as if she did this daily, cocked her head to sight-in the red balloon and – POW. The crack of the bee-bee resonated and the carnival worker grabbed his side. He was bleeding! Unbeknownst to him, he had just been shot by a princess dressed in western jeans, behaving as any western sophomore would behave. I was startled and immediately began to ask about his condition. He laughed, applying an old rag to his wound, that he was fine. Still unsure of what to do as I watched the blood ooze through his fingers, I turned to Susan and announced I was getting one of the bodyguards assigned to the girls the day we arrived.

Knowing they would not be conspicuously near but close, I looked left and then right along the crowded footpath, but I didn't recognize a soul. Becoming a bit more anxious, I looked again when the hedge across the way attracted my attention. Perhaps one of them was there. Trying not to appear alarmed to the Carney, I casually made my way across the path to the bench in front of the hedge and whispered to the bush, "Abdullah…Abdullah." Feeling somewhat like an anxious Nancy Drew and silly that I was talking to a bush, I whispered again. Just then, he stepped from behind the shrub just as a loaded hot dog headed towards his mouth. Excited, a synopsis of events flooded out of my mouth but only consisted of two sentences. "Nora shot the carnie! What do we do?"

Immediately, his demeanor changed and the hotdog clamored into the trash can to his side. "Leave," he answered and started towards the girls. I told Susan and we all began to move along at a quickened pace without alarming the girls. Simultaneously, I concluded with the carnie by asking one last time if he were truly okay. He never knew how easily he could have owned the carnival.

In my first month of tutoring the family, "Mrs. Teresa's story time" became popular and within months, infamous. I originally used my "story time" as a way to let my new family get to know me, my culture, and my religion. It just seemed more effective, more personable, and definitely more entertaining to share a story rather than simply agree or disagree with the topic at hand. In the beginning when an appropriate experience would pop into my thoughts, I would announce to the girls, "story time!" and they would immediately circle up to hear. Soon Madawi and the Colonel joined in as the girls began to ask for story times rather than waiting for one to simply strike Mrs. Teresa.

For one reason or another, our veranda chat turned to the topics of snow and skiing that evening. Fondly remembering a funny story that was shared with me, I announced a story-time. Happily, the girls cheered and everyone snuggled a bit deeper in the fluffy cushions of the rattan furniture to listen. Moving to the end of my chase lounge, I paused to enhance the mood and smiled to heighten curiosity before my story-time began.

There was this delightful lady in my hometown that I remembered being as sweet as the day is long. It seemed as if life always gave Mrs. Anna Gayle fun experiences and God blessed her with the personality to take them in stride and share them with others.

The story was that Mrs. Anna Gayle had decided to accompany her son and his family on a snow skiing trip to Colorado. In spite of being rather heavy set, she decided to give snow skiing a try. Dressed in the latest skiing fashion, she followed her son to the top of the mountain for her very first lesson. Rather shaken by the lift, Mrs. Anna Gayle announced that she had to use the ladies room before attempting to ski. Unfortunately, there were no restrooms available. Unwilling or unable to accept this fact, she decided to use nature's restroom behind a large tree off to the side. Feeling as if she were comfortably out of sight, Mrs. Anna Gayle proceeded to do what people do. Just as her knees bent, the downwardly pointed skis began to slide, yet she was anything but ready to ski! Bare to the world, she crashed directly into a tree!

Now Mrs. Anna Gayle is not the type of person to let a "little 'ole broken leg," as she would say, spoil her fun or the fun of others. So the next morning, she happily requested to have her wheel chair parked by the fire in the lodge so she could read and socialize while the rest of the family continued the skiing part of the trip. Snuggled with her afghan and book, she readily noticed the young man on crutches that approached the lounge area with the same affliction as she. Wanting to share skiing "war stories," she simply couldn't resist asking about his broken leg. Closing her book, she leaned forward with a smile and began, "so is this your first time to ski, also?" Shaking his head with a chuckle, the young man replied, "No Mame! I've been skiing ALL MY LIFE, but if you had seen what I saw on the slope yesterday, you would have hit that tree, too!" Surprised, she listened to him tell about the lady, intimately revealed, sliding down the hill and into the tree. Inwardly, she thanked the good Lord that he didn't recognize her better side!

Mrs. Anna Gayle's skiing adventure was an instant hit and became a long standing story-time favorite among the family. I honestly can't recall how many times I told that story to the family and their friends. Even the Colonel would chuckle way down deep each time the skiing adventure was retold.

It was that lazy time of day when every one would disappear for a nap or a good, quiet read. The

Saudis, like many nationalities, enjoy the afternoon siesta as they are nocturnal for the most part. I, on the other hand, had only been in the Middle East a short while and still found myself operating on American time. Hence, I simply could not lie down during the middle of the day. From the veranda off my sleeping quarters, I could see the water of the private pool glimmer in the mid-day sun. It was inviting and I wanted to accept the invitation. Not wanting to swim alone, I decided to wander around the villa to see if I could find a willing volunteer to join me.

An eerie silence fell over the villa every day during the lazy time, which made me self conscience as I moved through it. Trying to be quiet as possible so as not to wake anyone, I moved slowly through the foyer looking for anyone that would want to join me for a dip. As I silently peered around each doorway, I was startled when Madawi broke the silence in her normal speaking voice.

"Mrs. Teresa, do you feel good?" she questioned with a huge smile on her face. Puzzled, I replied, "Well, as a matter of fact, I do." Yet, she quickly picked up on my confusion and curiosity.

It was no wonder my face revealed my emotions with Fahad close behind Madawi seemingly about to bust at the seams. With his smile stretching from ear to ear, he obviously wanted to say something, yet yielded the floor to his mom.

Madawi's eyes widened at my response and another pause ensued to heighten the anticipation.

"Oh no," she laughed while she moved her hand to indicate that we were way off topic and she continued.

"No, do you know 'I feel good' by James Brown?"

"Oh yes" I answered somewhat shocked that James Brown would be a topic of conversation for us. "I do love his music."

Her smiled widened when she announced, "then we see him tomorrow night. In Monte Carlo!"

"Monte Carlo? James Brown?" I questioned as my voice revealed my shock.

"Yes! Awad got us tickets. It will be me and Awad, you, Fahad and Nora." Before I had time to reply, she continued. "We will meet Mohammed, Awad's brother, Wafa, his wife, and their daughter, Safa."

"Oh…okay," I said simply to offer a reply, yet I was clueless who these people were and what was to come. Even so, it was exciting all the same. Monte Carlo, Monaco, I could hardly believe what was happening to me.

I simmered down just a bit to focus on her words. I wanted to get the details straight. Already I knew that Madawi typically did not repeat herself so it was best to get it correct the first time. She began.

"You can take your car to Monte Carlo and you can leave when you want in the morning. The dinner and show doesn't begin until 7:00 so we can meet at the Lowe's Hotel at 6:00 p.m."

My face must have revealed my concern and she picked up on it immediately.

"I thought you may want to sight see a little along the way." She said with a smile.

"Oh yes," I answered. "I've never been to Monaco!" I smiled and then paused as my next question popped up. "But what about you guys? Don't you want to see some sights also?"

Responding as politely as she could, overlooking my ignorance of her world travels, she replied. "Oh it's okay," as a big smile broke across her face, "Awad and I have seen all of Monaco we want to see."

The idea of touring Monte Carlo the following day was so exciting, yet my face revealed my concern of driving alone in a foreign country to yet another foreign country. It was something I had not experienced. Madawi was the world traveler in the group, not me. I was simply a very lucky lady from Georgia faced with an opportunity to experience "lifestyles of the rich and famous." Sensing my concern, she added more details.

"Danny will go with you," she stated. Now whether or not that meant Danny was going by choice, I was not sure, yet she continued. "You two will have fun together, and she can show you the way." Feeling a little more comfortable with the idea, I decided at that moment to leave early the next day so we could take advantage of maximum our sight-seeing time. Madawi agreed and invited me for some tea on the veranda where we chattered for the next couple of hours about what to wear and pack, what to be sure and see along the way, and a little bit of dancing around the veranda to our off key, poorly sung, yet fun rendition of "I feel good."

It was misty the next morning as the sun had yet to burn the daybreak fog hovering along the edge of the Mediterranean. Even so, I was up and moving, incredibly excited about the day that lay before me. Perhaps the slowness of her packing was a sign of things to come, but I failed to pick up on it. Happy and feeling like nothing could change that, I paced the entry of the villa while Danny finished putting the last of her items into the little Mercedes. Just when she slammed the trunk closed, I felt a hand on my shoulder. I turned to find Madawi in her sleeping caftan, her pjs so to speak, standing with a smile on her face having come out to wish us safe journey.

"You two will have so much fun," she announced with a smile and a hug. "Be sure to see the palace and get a good lunch." She remarked as she handed me a folded bill. Feeling it in my hand, my face revealed my question before I had time to verbalize it. "For your expenses," she replied with that soft side smile she flashes when genuinely happy. Just then, Danny stepped up from the car to receive a hug and a bill in the hand as well.

"Just don't forget," she continued with last minute "reminder" comments as people do when those they care about are about to travel. "Be at the Lowe's Hotel, ready for dinner at 6:00 p.m. in the lobby" she confirmed. We assured her we would be there, too, and waved like crazy as we skipped to the car and buckled up for a day of adventure. It did not take long for me to see that a challenging trip would soon follow. I drove as far as I knew down the side of the mountain from our villa into Cannes. I headed straight to the downtown market area in order to find a major road going east. I wanted to buy a map, yet Danny assured me that finding Monaco and, subsequently, Monte Carlo would be no problem at all. And honestly, I am sure that it was no trouble for her. Yet for me, it was the most frustrating afternoon's drive of my life. We did not even get out of Cannes before we were lost and wasting time. Being that Danny was the only one of us who spoke fluent French, I became so frustrated at each road crossing when I could not read the signage. Danny, on the other hand, was completely comfortable with having her window down, foot on the dash, radio cranked to the max with American tunes while starring off at the beauty surrounding us.

Perhaps she did not understand her role as navigator on our little journey, but she got the point after I began to pull off the road at each stop until she would confirm for me that she had in fact read the direction sign and we were on the correct path. Finally, after many sighs on my part and several hours, we made our way east far enough to find the major seaside highway to Monte Carlo.

As I rolled down the two lane highway, seemingly hanging onto the ledges of the massive cliffs lining the French Rivera, I could not help but take in the breath-taking view. The warm breeze streaming in the sunroof while I wound my way around the edge of the *Cote d'Azure* enhanced the magical sensation and forced me to enjoy every sense that was bombarding me as new. With the hairpin curves, hundreds of feet above the jagged water's edge below, I thought of Princess Grace of Monaco and the fact that she had died on these winding curves many years before.

    Curve after winding curve we continued eastward enjoying the sparkle of the Mediterranean water as it flickered from the bright summer sun. Suddenly when we rounded yet another curve, my breath was taken away. The city of the world's rich and famous, nestled among the mountains and snuggled around the protecting cove that is so associated with Monte Carlo, lay before me hundreds of feet below. On the Western hillside of the cove was the palace of the Monaco royal family. Overflowing with tourists snags, the little sub-village by the palace was bustling with activity. Cars jammed into the narrow cobblestone streets, with shop doors only a foot or two from the road and tourists all in between and oblivious to the cars. Finally, we found a legal place to leave the car and off we went to see what we could find. We enjoyed a delightful lunch of cheese sandwiches, fruit, and wine at an open air street café. We meandered through the shops and made our way to the palace. While waiting in line for the tour, we decided to see if these guards were as good as the ones at Buckingham Palace in London, and we did our best to make them move, smile, grin, or smirk while we took pictures of our play. Much to our dismay, we could not make them flinch and we gave them a big thumb's up when it was our time leave and join the palace tour.

After a long tour of ornate rooms and treasures abound, we knew it was time to find the hotel and start getting ready for the evening. Again, Danny did not seem to feel the need to guide me, only answer should I specifically asked if I should turn left or right. Finally, we pulled into the valet drive at the Lowe's Hotel in the heart of the Rivera after another excruciating hour with Danny's tour guide service.

The little Mercedes Madawi had rented for me was a fun car to drive and sharp looking to the eye. Yet, it simply could not hold a candle to the other cars that roared into the circular drive. Everywhere I looked there were Ferrari, Lamborghini, and Rolls Royce. At that moment, there was no doubt for me that I had simply fallen into a dream.

I approached reception a little nervous. I had never checked into a hotel before, much less an international one. My dad or husband had always done this for me. But here I was in this very posh international setting, with experienced global travelers all around, and I did not want to make a blunder. I was not exactly sure what to do, but I felt confident that the $1,000 Madawi had placed in my hand that morning would cover any unexpected expenses.

When I stepped to the counter, the gentleman and I exchanged greetings. I began to fumble through my handbag for my wallet when we got to the part where he asked my name. Immediately he stopped my registration and threw on a larger smile than before when I replied, "Teresa McCown."

"Ah, Madame McCown, we have been expecting you. Your suite is ready." He paused to complete some paperwork. "You are down the hall from the princess," he explained as he gave me my keycards and paperwork. "Pierre will take your bags and show you to the room."

Surprised at the ease of my first hotel check-in, I flashed a smile and thanked the gentleman for his help. I then turned on my heels with an extra kick in my step to follow "Pierre" to our suite at the Lowe's. Naturally, we found all of the little amenities and services befitting a five-star hotel in the heart of Monte Carlo. Yet, we did not expect to find the breath taking view from our veranda that Pierre revealed in his in-room "welcome to the Lowe's (and I deserve a good tip)" speech. Never could I have dreamt that this would happen to me and I took a moment to be grateful.

Parched from our sight-seeing, we ordered some tea and snacks from room service to enjoy while we dressed. We cranked up the music on the television and enjoyed ourselves in the lap of luxury. Before we knew it, we were refreshed, dressed to kill, and ready to head to the lobby to find Madawi and the Colonel.

Walking through the massive marble reception, we looked in each direction for Madawi, only to find Fahad and his cousin, Abdullah, looking very dapper in their western style clothing for a black tie evening. After a bit of cutting up and picture taking with the guys, the Colonel and his brother, Mohammed, approached with Khalid and Sabre close behind and also dressed for the evening.

While we waited for Madawi, Wafa and Safa to join us, the Colonel asked me what I knew about casinos and I quickly explained that I knew relatively nothing, only once had I even walked through a casino and had never gambled in one. Being the fun, jovial person he is, the Colonel could not let that one lie and felt compelled to show me inside. Hence, he replied, "come" with a huge smile of wanting to share a secret. Mohammed, Fahad, Abdullah, Danny, and I followed as the Colonel showed us the different tables and games being played. Everywhere there were dings, whistles, flashing lights, and conversations in many languages.

When we approached the black jack area, the Colonel reached into his pocket. He stepped up to the table, threw down a thousand dollar bill, and played it on a hand. With nervous laughter mingled with silence and anticipation swirling among our group, the dealer dealt. Although I had never gambled in a casino, I had grown up in a home that loved to play black jack for pinto beans, so I had a clear understanding of the game.

The Colonel casually reached for the cards, looking slowly at each of us with a daring grin to heighten our excitement. The corner of the cards revealed a queen and a five, probably the worst hand in black jack. I sighed as I could not bear the thought of loosing that much money on one hand. My heart seemed to pause and my breathing stopped as I waited to see how this would play out. After what seemed like forever, the Colonel indicated for the dealer to give him another card. I took in yet another deep breath and held it as I prayed for a low card. The cheers went up when we all saw the four of spades flop onto the table. He was sitting on 19 and things were definitely looking up. All eyes then turned to the dealer as we waited for the outcome.

Seeing our excitement, the dealer earned his pay by adding a little theatrics to the game. First he revealed the jack of clubs and the gasps followed. Then after a few comments and chuckles, he revealed his second card, a ten of hearts. Loud sighs followed on the heels of the gasps, and I felt as if I would go through the floor at the idea of loosing that kind of money that quickly. Turning to the Colonel to some way offer condolences, I quickly saw that it was nothing to him. He acted as if he had just lost $20, not $1,000.

Still laughing and replaying "the hand" with our conversation, we returned to the lobby to find Madawi, Wafa and Safa elegantly dressed in the latest Parisian styles waiting for us by one of the enormous, ornate marble columns that lined the Lowe's main thoroughfare. After our hellos, the girls began to talk and fell in behind the men heading toward the hotel exit. As we walked, Madawi slowed up a bit indicating she wanted to say something to me and

Danny away from the others. We continued to move forward, only slowed our pace, as she approached the subject.

"Tonight," she paused. "We need to stay calm." A bit confused, I continued to listen with heightened interest.

"Wafa," she continued, "is not as…" she paused searching for the words, "as active as we are." Madawi paused again realizing that her message was confusing, yet she was unsure how to say what was on her mind and not offend.

"She is very… conservative." Madawi continued appearing a little uncomfortable. "She would not understand dancing and having a party."

That was the sentence that made it all click for me. Apparently, Wafa was more conservative and Madawi did not want Danny and me to get carried away with our western ways at the James Brown concert. I could not help but smile while I reassured her I would be on my best behavior. After we exchanged understanding looks, Danny chimed in with her compliance as well.

It was a short walk along the sea and such a beautiful evening to do so. In a matter of minutes, we arrived at the *Monte Carlo Sporting Club* for dinner and a show. Situated on the shore of the Mediterranean, the club was phenomenal. I almost tripped looking at its unique features and décor as the host showed us to our stage-side seating for the evening. The room was huge. It was shaped in a semi-circle with the stage as central focus on one side and a wall of glass on the other, positioned to offer the best view of the cove and the magnificent yachts moored there. The roof was rolled back, literally, to reveal a gorgeous, starlit, cloudless evening sky.

We were taken to a long banquet style table where our party of twelve rapidly became a party of twenty when security guards that I had not even known where following took their seats at our table. On my side of the table and nearest the stage was the Colonel, across from Mohammed, and Madawi to his right, across from Wafa. Then I was seated next to Madawi facing Safa with Fahad to my right with Abdullah across the table and Nora after Fahad across from Danny. Then the stream of security filled the remaining eight chairs.

The evening began with pictures and fun conversation while the orchestra played dinner music in the background. We were delighted by course after course of wonderful French cuisine and spoiled by the lavish service.

On several occasions, my Southern accent was a conversation point in the early years, and this night was no different. They all knew I was originally from the state of Georgia and they all knew that I would be leaving the group in a few weeks to go stateside when they continued on to London. Hence, when James Brown started into "Georgia on My Mind," all heads turned to me. Honestly, I was a bit teary eyed because I had not been back to the states since I had left eight months prior. Yet, I could not help but blush and laugh when they all looked so obviously to see my reaction.

    The evening was going along beautifully and everyone was having fun. I felt moved to wiggle a wee bit in my chair as James Brown belted out his hits. Although, I remained calm and refined as Madawi had requested. Near the end of the performance, the stage suddenly went dark while James Brown took a moment for a sip of water on stage and the audience looked on with great anticipation. At that very moment, out he broke with "I feel good," and the crowd went wild! Even though it was absolutely killing me, I remained as controlled as humanly possible for someone with my spirit. Madawi and I exchanged looks and a smile, both understanding the other. Then to my amazement, I looked back across the table to see Safa dancing in her chair! With that shock, my head immediately snapped back in Madawi's direction to find her noticing the same turn of events. With a gulp and a smile, she motioned for me to join in on the fun and up I went in the little black dress and heels onto the cushion of the dinning chair at the *Monte Carlo Sporting Club.*

    As I wiggled and shimmied as much as possible without moving my feet, I felt a presence behind me. In the excitement of the music and conspicuously moving to the beat, I wiggled so that I could look behind me where I found one of the eight security guards poised and ready to break my fall if necessary. After an awkward hello, I looked back to find that Safa, Nora, Danny, Fahad, and Abdullah all had security men behind them as well. Heaven forbid that any of us would be hurt while partying in Monte Carlo! Who would have believed it?

Even following formal evenings out, Madawi liked to end with a stroll if the weather permitted, and this evening was no exception. Thinking of the evening and Wafa's face during the concert we roared with laughter, but our laughter was broken when we rounded the curve of the sidewalk along the Mediterranean. It was the Colonel a few feet behind us speaking with Khalid that drew our attention. Although I couldn't hear well, he was upset with Khalid who had obviously drunk too much alcohol at dinner. Through the commotion, I could discern that Khalid had to be ready to leave when we were ready the following morning or he could make his own way back to Cannes. The Colonel was angry and it was understandable. Madawi whispered that Khalid had been doing this often lately and the Colonel had had enough.

After a lazy start the next morning, we assembled in the lobby as the concierge took care of our baggage and the valet our vehicles, but no Khalid. We continued to chat as the Colonel completed checkout. When the conversation turned to my sightseeing adventure, Madawi was shocked to hear how long it took us to get to Monte Carlo the day before.

"But Mrs. Teresa, we took less than two hours here. What happened to you?" she questioned with amazement and laughter. My eyes darted in Francis's direction and Madawi chuckled even deeper. As kind as Francis was, she and I were on opposite ends of the spectrum with personality characteristics and Madawi knew it. I am more meticulous, opinionated, and conservative. Where as Francis is more lackadaisical, laid back, and liberal. The differences in our personalities were not insurmountable, just problematic from the beginning. She was the "oil" in the pair and I was the "vinegar," and the two simply were not mixing comfortably.

Madawi could not help but continue to laugh as I am sure she could picture the events of our wayward travel the day before. "Do not worry, Mrs. Teresa," she continued, still laughing. "You can follow Awad back and we will be there soon," she winked and smiled as she turned to follow the Colonel out of the hotel. We gathered again just outside at valet to load up and still no Khalid. He had missed the boat.

Nora, Fahad, and Abdullah joined Francis and I in the Mercedes for the return trip to Cannes. They wanted to crank up the music and sing in my car, which gave the Colonel and Madawi a bit of private time as well. With our route set, I followed the Colonel out of the hotel drive and to a more modern, four-lane highway which would take us to our destination without the hairpin curves of the older, seashore drive. The Colonel enjoyed pushing the engine of his special edition convertible Mustang shipped to France from the United States. It was equipped with every feature available and handled the curves along the Rivera with ease. I, having a tendency to be a little heavy footed myself and having grown up with sports cars, enjoyed the drive as well. Although the Mercedes could not overtake the Mustang, I had fun keeping up.

As the sun melted behind the trees and the warm breeze flowed into the car, I took the opportunity to pass the Colonel when we came upon what I assume was a suburb of Cannes. Nearing the central area of the village, we came to a roundabout and the Colonel was right behind me. At this point, I assumed the Colonel would once again take the lead and guide us to our villa. The Colonel, on the other hand, thought I knew my way so he continued to follow rather than pass. After three complete revolutions around the roundabout, I heard a faint cry over the kids' blaring music. Not sure what I heard, I strained to listen as I continued to drive in circles. Frustrated because I could not discern what I had heard, I made the kids turn down the radio. Just then all three in the backseat began to roll with laughter and yelled. "It's Baba Mrs. Teresa! It's Baba!" Low and behold it was the Colonel and Madawi yelling from their convertible, "Mrs. Teresa!"

Everyone was stricken with laughter and we began our 35 mile per hour circular conversation. From the "Mrs. Teresa" I heard, they had obviously been yelling my name for quite a while. I responded out of my window to let them know I had heard them finally. Then the Colonel shouted through his laughter, "Where are you going, Mrs. Teresa?"

Flustered, nervous, and chuckling mostly from embarrassment, I replied. "I don't know!" His laughter could be heard as we continued to make the circle. Fortunately there was no other traffic to avoid as we chatted. Knowing it was my only choice I fell in behind the mustang and began to follow. Shortly, I realized that I did know where we were and that I could find the villa from our location. Seizing a traffic light opportunity, I pulled up beside the Mustang and spoke to the Colonel through Francis's window.

"I DO know where we are!" I shouted over the rumble of the Mustang's powerful engine.

The Colonel replied, "You do?" flashing the same smile I had seen at the casino the evening before, "Then we race."

Unable to walk away from such a challenge and assuming it was okay since he was the one that had suggested it, I replied with confidence, "You're on!" and I punched the gas as the light turned green.

The kids went wild with excitement as the race began. We headed down the road, more in jest of racing than racing, never doing anything that would put anyone in danger. Yet, with each traffic light, we joked as to each car's performance, operator competence, and revved our engines a bit to accentuate the fun. Rather comical, I believe, as I truly could not have held a candle to him, a jet fighter pilot and seasoned driver, but he was kind enough to let me pretend. A few miles later, we reached our villa and laughed about our race as we made our way inside. Tired, but not sleepy, Madawi and I met on the veranda in our pjs and fluffy slippers where we remained for a few more hours, sipping *ghawa*, and reminiscing of Monte Carlo.

Chapter 6
Weaving the Friendship
Summer 1992

It was two days before I saw Khalid again. Madawi told me on the veranda the next morning that he had overslept with very little cash on him. The Colonel had refused to pay for a rental car for him the first day and made him sweat it out until the second. At which time, the Colonel did cover the cost for Khalid to rejoin the group.

Lazy days and adventure filled nights best describe my summer of '92 along the *Cote d'Azure*. Almost every evening brought an outing that proved to be unique and memorable or one of those special times when we decided to hang out at the villa and play spoons until the wee hours of the morning. On Bastille Day, I found myself with the entire entourage celebrating French Independence from a yacht under the stars and musically accompanied fireworks. On another, I graciously enjoyed a formal dinner with only the Colonel and Madawi, partaking of my first glass of wine in front of my new Saudi family. The Colonel offered, Madawi nodded, and I accepted. Being five months pregnant, Madawi naturally passed. Yet at this point in time for her, I don't believe she would have accepted even if she could.

With Madawi's encouragement, blessing, and money, Francis and I headed out one evening to experience a French discothèque. Madawi did not seem willing to come along, plus she had to accompany the Colonel for dinner. Waving goodbye from the door, she reminded us with a mischievous smile that she wanted a full report the next afternoon on the veranda.

Juan le Pain, just east of Cannes, was the hot spot. Café after café lined the streets with the most posh of French discos sprinkled throughout. Unfortunately, my head was pounding after only an hour of being smashed between people, choked by smoke, and deafened by music in the overcrowded bar. Finally after much encouragement from me, Francis agreed to leave. Ironically, we found ourselves following true to Madawi's summer training and ended up in a sidewalk café for a cappuccino night cap. Unknowingly, the café was full of Saudi women.

The next afternoon when I stepped casually and somewhat sleepily onto the veranda cuddling my oversized cup of coffee, Madawi stood immediately. She was obviously upset, almost frantically so. Honestly, I thought something had happened to one or more of the children from her behavior. After our kisses, she encouraged me to sit with her because she wanted my opinion.

While the series of events flowed from her lips, I sat quietly. Sarah, who was another princess and Madawi's cousin also vacationing in Cannes, had just called. She told Madawi that she had seen Francis and me in the café the evening before and recognized Francis as a woman that "goes with Saudi men."

Her hands flew as she spoke, returning to her feet from sheer emotion.

"I can't let a woman like this be near my husband!" she exclaimed catching a breath in between. "She can't be near my family," she declared definitively.

Although I totally agreed with Madawi that I would not want a woman like that near my husband either, I still could not help but feel numb and a touch frightened at that very moment. Albeit Francis was not one of my favorite people and she had driven me crazy for most of our trip, but I felt she was being treated unfairly. From everything that was said, this woman was being tried and convicted on a single rumor. Twice I started to defend Francis by offering alternative explanations, but Madawi's verbal and nonverbal reactions were such that I backed down quickly. She was not open to opposing views. As Madawi continued, her oral thought processing posed numerous questions to me as if she were seeking my opinion. Yet, in reality, she was simply seeking validation of the decision she didn't know she had already made. Seeing as I could not save Francis's job, I could at least question what would happen to her. I was quickly told she would be paid her wages and flown back to Paris immediately. Unfortunately, I never saw Francis again to even offer condolences or a goodbye.

Out of the blue, it had happened. It had happened just as quickly as Dick had said it could just a few short months before. The day I started working for the family is the day I learned that the lady I had interviewed with and been hired by the night before to teach her five children to read, write, and speak English was actually a member of the House of Al-Saud and thus, royalty. That memorable morning, I telephoned David more often than normal because of my excitement. During one of our conversations, he told me a story that Dick, a company coworker, had shared with him.

Before Dick worked at the airbase for an American company contracted to the Royal Saudi Air Force (RSAF), he had been the private security lead man for a powerful prince. Somewhere along the way, the relationship went bad and Dick was removed from the prestigious life of traveling the world with a Saudi prince and reassigned to an office cubical on the base where he handled mundane housing assignments for the RSAF. The details of the story are foggy, but I vividly remember David telling me that Dick cautioned me to "watch my step with the princess as things can end as quickly as they start when it comes to the Royal family. One minute you can be in their favor, their golden child, and the next, you can be out of the country bearing an exit only visa," which means that you cannot return. I took this advice with a grain of salt that particular morning, but I thought of it again on that breezy afternoon in Cannes.

Without hesitation, I welcomed Madawi's dinner invitation. After the day we had had with Francis's termination, a relaxing evening would serve us both well. Strangely, it was years before I understood the significance of the night.

There was this quaint little restaurant that Madawi had heard about and wanted us to try. Naturally, it was in Juan le Pain. With Sabre driving, just the two of us headed out and we were not disappointed with what we found. Unlike all of the other restaurants we had tried, this one was down to earth and unpretentious. Nestled off the beaten path, the cozy mom and pop place simply offered delicious food and we ate until I thought I would pop.

Naturally, our evening walk followed. It was dark and the breeze was warm. There was not a cloud in the sky and the stars twinkled as far as the eye could see. It was delightful. Arm in arm we strolled chatting about this and that. Sharing – teaching – she would tell me the Arabic words for things we saw and I would repeat the English term. Then I would point to something, enunciate the English word, and she would echo the Arabic. She laughed deeply at my attempts to utter the sounds of her language with my Southern drawl, yet it didn't offend me. She was correct. The sounds that came out of my mouth sounded nothing like the ones out of hers, so I couldn't help but chuckle as well. Unexpectedly, I saw an umbrella near the seashore, half propped in the sand obviously left open from earlier in the day.

"Umbrella," I stated as I pointed.

"Shamsiyah" she replied with an idyllic smile. Pausing, she added, "but it goes much deeper."

I knew why she said that the way she did, but I did not grasp her meaning at first. In the few short months I had been in Kingdom, I already knew many

Arabic words had multiple meanings, depending on the situation. I also had a clear understanding of the significance of shelter from the sun in an arid climate where literally life and death could depend on that shelter. Thus, I could surmise the importance of something which protects from the sun would have in their culture. Yet, I still did not understand her meaning.

Arm in arm, we continued and so did Madawi. "So how did this happen?" Still confused and a bit unsure if or how to reply, I simply looked up at her as our paced slowed even more. "Us." She stated emphatically, stopping to make her point and looking me straight in the eye. "How did WE happen?" her hands flew through the air to emphasize.

Although she asked the questions, I don't believe she was looking for answers from me, perhaps from a higher being, but not from me and she continued. "How did we happen? You from America and me from Saudi." She paused while looking away, possibly searching for the right words to share the feelings she felt. Compelled to interject and clarify what I thought she was implying, I broke the silence.

"Yeah, it is pretty amazing. I mean, we have me...a regular American woman that grew up in a small, regular American town in Georgia, and then we have you..." I stopped talking when my reality hit. "...a princess." I could not help but go silent when I heard that word come out of my mouth. I looked deeply into Madawi's eyes, perhaps looking for the same divine answers as she.

A long, comforting silence ensued. "It was meant to be," she said definitively as her signature smile broke and she grabbed my arm to continue our walk. Smiling, I stepped into stride. It was then that I understood and felt exactly the same.

It seemed as if the adventures were never ending that summer on the *Cote d'Azure*. Much to my surprise, the next morning Madawi suggested a different thought for our evening out. Instead of being chauffeured and guarded by security, she wanted us to head off alone with only Nora and Fahad. I would be the driver in my little Mercedes. Excited about the idea of our independent outing, we all dressed quickly that afternoon and headed for Juan le Pain.

Happy as larks, we drove into the posh French village only to find a major problem we had yet to face. There was no parking. It was actually kind of funny that we were all surprised by this normal fact. But considering the drivers usually handled parking, we had never had to give it a second thought and I can see why we were surprised. Only a touch bummed that we had to waste fun time to locate a place to leave the car, we began to circle the blocks. Unfortunately, with each turn we found another narrow street lined with parked cars and no open spaces. After almost an hour of weaving the city streets to no avail, we were all becoming irritated and the happiness had left our group. Within two more streets, Madawi began to express her frustrations.

"THIS" her hands flew as she spoke. "THIS is why I have a driver!" Her exasperated sigh said it all when her hand hit her knee, and so must have my look when my eyes became wide and mouth gaped open at her proclamation. Just then, we all broke into uncontrollable laughter. Even with humor in the mix, I became even more anxious to find a place to stop. For about the hundredth time, we were excited at the glimpse of a potential space only to be disappointed when we saw the same little sign indicating that we could not block the private drive. For the next two streets, we debated. There was simply not a legal parking spot. We actually considered driving back to Cannes and having a driver bring us back to Juan le Pain, but we all agreed that wasn't the best solution. Obviously having had enough of this part of the adventure, Madawi declared. "Just park!" Her hands began again. "Just park in a space and I'll pay the ticket."

Open to the idea but wanting to clarify, I pointedly questioned "are you sure?"

"Yes!" Again, the hands soared.

Taking a deep breath and releasing with a smile, "Okay, if you say so." Nora and Fahad had long since unfastened their safety belts and were now both leaning into the front seat helping us look for the next available "do not park here" sign.

"There!" Fahad pointed quickly and overly proud to be the one to see the space first. "There is one, Mrs. Teresa!"

Seeing it on the left-hand side of the road, I pulled forward a bit and turned on my signal to indicate my intentions. As I looked into my rearview mirror to begin my parking attempt, I was blinded by the headlights behind me. I put my hand in front of the mirror hoping the driver behind me would see it and know that I was blinded, but the car did not budge. Exasperated, I began after getting the gear-shift into reverse. I cut my wheels to the left only to become somewhat jammed into the tight space available. Consequently, the bright headlights were so close to my bumper that they could have easily occupied my trunk.

Irritated at the other driver, believing he or she should have respected my signal and held back for me to park, I commanded Fahad. "Hop out and tell them to move back."

Willingly he opened his car door and stepped out to shout at the car behind us when he then casually and smoothly made a complete turn and sat back in the car without saying a word, gently closing the door.

"Why didn't you tell him?" I questioned looking back through the split in the seats. Fahad, whose face looked like he had seen a ghost, quietly added, "It's the police, Mrs. Teresa."

"Ooooh!" was all Madawi could utter with her eyes becoming as big as saucers and her hands subconsciously grasping her pregnant womb. Nora clapped her hands, followed by a finger snap and a grin to indicate she was up for the excitement, and Fahad broke into tear-filled laughter. I, on the other hand, remained outwardly calm and simply replied "oh…I think we'll find another spot" and I put the car in drive. But inside, I was dying. Headlines flashed before my eyes. *"American Arrested with Pregnant Saudi Princess in France,"* or *"International Incident...Princess Arrested Because of Deviant American Driver."* It was not a pretty thought.

Just then, things went from bad to worst. I was stuck! I had wedged the car into the space and simply could not get it back into the tight, single lane of traffic I was blocking! The headlines reappeared, *"American Causes Traffic Pileup Trying to Park in Illegal Space while Chauffeuring Saudi Royalty!"*

Madawi's "ooohs" increased and the kids were rocking the car with their laughter from the backseat when the French officer kindly stepped up to direct me out of the space. Incredibly embarrassed, all I could do was wave and call "merci" from the open window as we rolled forward to continue on our way. Inwardly, I was thanking God that he had not given me a ticket or hauled me to jail!

Often I felt as if I were a true to life "Lucille Ball" on this particular trip. Things just seemed to happen. At lunch the next day, well breakfast for us, Madawi told me we were going to a ladies' party that evening and she suggested what I should wear.

"A ladies party?" I muttered while stuffing a piece of French bread with cream cheese into my mouth.

"Yes!" a big smile broke as she passed me the tea. "There are many Saudis here and we are having a party at Wafa's tonight." She smiled yet again, obviously loving the thought of a Saudi ladies' party.

Then she proudly added, "The first wife of the King will be there."

Being new to this royalty business, I was unclear what that meant and asked, "You mean the queen?"

Laughing Madawi explained. "No, we don't have a queen. But the first wife is very special." Her hands began to move to explain and her face added cues. "She is respected by ALL others."

When the time came to leave that evening, Madawi suggested that I drive us and the girls would come later. Surprised that she still wanted to ride with me after the parking incident, I happily ran and got my keys.

As we made our way through Cannes and started up the hills to Wafa's villa Madawi talked about the party and what we would do. Listening, yet concentrating on my driving, I began the incline to Wafa's, located unfortunately on the top of the mountain. Probably nervous from the last time I drove her and desperately needing more lessons from Sabre, I made the hairpin curve and gave it gas to push into the next gear. Suddenly, the car died and started rolling backwards. Madawi got quiet and grabbed her seat. When I realized what was happening, I slammed on the brake and we looked at each other. Her looked questioned what was going on and mine revealed an apology. Embarrassed, I gave it another go. Now unable to get the car into first gear, I had to brake again to keep from hitting the car behind us.

"I thought you knew how to drive!" Madawi exclaimed.

"I do!" I blurted without thinking. "It's the gears, Madawi. It is very hard on this steep hill!" Both sighing, I gave it another try. Nothing was said when I had to brake yet again. I looked at her and she at me. I knew this was the last try. Shaken, I cranked the car again and looked at my friend for luck. The split second it took for the car to shutdown seemed like an eternity. When I hit the brakes the final time, her arms flew up and back down with exasperation and she whispered, "Oh, let's just get the driver." Just then, Sabre was standing in the street outside my window! It was he that I almost rolled into several times. Embarrassed and frustrated, I stepped from the car and he opened the back door for me. As I bent to sit, he smiled offering me encouragement without saying a word. It was a good five minutes before anyone said a word. The resonating sounds of Sabre changing the gears was all that could be heard as we wound our way up to Wafa's.

I was in complete awe of the beautiful villa we entered. Madawi explained that this was Wafa's villa and not a summer rental. I have no idea how large it was because I did not see most of it, but I do know the room where we had the party was huge on American standards. Immaculately decorated in the latest styles sprinkled with Arab touches and Persian carpets, the room comfortably accommodated five setting areas with sofas and chairs, plus all of the extra seating brought in for the party. One entire wall was glass doors which opened onto the pool deck and offered a 180 degree view of the Mediterranean. Built to look as if the pool poured into the sea, it was breathtaking.

    Because I had only been with the family a few months, I was still not comfortable with their customs. With no other westerner there to ask about etiquette, I decided to hang close to Madawi so I would know what to do. During my first week at the palace, I learned you stand when royalty enters the room. But, I had no idea what to do if everyone in the room was royal. After our initial hellos to the ladies already there, Madawi made her way to the sitting area in the middle of the room. We found a good spot on one of the sofas and the servants brought tea. Arab music played in the background while the sounds of individual conversations came from every direction in the room. As new ladies would enter the party, some people would stand for them and some would not. Curious, I began watching and could not determine a reason for this, so I asked Madawi about my observations. In essence, she explained that there is a hierarchy within the royal family, describing herself as a "medium princess." A bit tickled by the idea of being a low, medium or high princess, I was clueless to the differences, but nodded understanding. Still observing and not knowing who was low or high, I decided to simply stand when Madawi stood.

    You could feel the excitement in the air as everyone anticipated the first wife of the King. With each announcement of arrival, Madawi either stood momentarily and then sat again or seemed as if she didn't notice, but each time I would pop right up beside her. One time in particular, she stood and so did I. Suddenly, the noisy room became quiet and I immediately felt as if all eyes were on us. Without moving my head, I surveyed the room with my eyes. We were the only two standing out of the 100 plus ladies there. It was an awkward moment when Madawi smiled for the onlookers and asked in a whisper from the corner of her mouth, "Why are you standing, Mrs. Teresa?"

"Because you did," I replied in the same spy like manner, smiling at the ladies checking out the American.

"But I am only straightening my blouse," the pregnant princess replied.

"Oops" I uttered with a humiliated laugh and dropped to my seat as quickly as possible. After the car incident, this was more than I could bear and I decided to find the ladies room for a brief reprieve from my embarrassment. Politely excusing myself, I made my way through what I thought was the hall to the restroom. Rather, I ended up in an intimate salon filled with Saudi men watching a large screen TV. Thankfully, I saw the Colonel straight away and we made eye contact, but I went no further into the room because of the men.

"Ah, Mrs. Teresa" he spoke loudly as he stood. "Are you enjoying your evening?"

From the doorway, I replied sincerely, "Oh yes, Sir," watching my behavior because I didn't know the other Saudi men.

"Can I help you with something?" He politely questioned.

Somewhat embarrassed yet again, I casually stated that I was only looking for the ladies room. Laughing, he agreed the house was confusing and he gave me directions. When I passed the doorway on my way back to the party, I heard the Colonel call my name.

"Yes sir?" I leaned into the door and smiled.

"Come in please," he requested and I entered.

All of the men were dressed in traditional Saudi attire and on the edges of their seats with their elbows to their knees, intently watching CNN. Surprisingly, the Colonel questioned just as I began to excuse myself for intruding earlier.

"Oh no," he laughed. "Forget that," his hand motioned finality. "What do you think of this?" He gestured to the TV.

CNN was hosting a big discussion about the upcoming 1992 U.S. election. I had my opinions, but I thought it was best not to share them because the company had advised that we not talk religion or politics with the Saudis. Plus, I felt awkward in the room with only Saudi men, so I held back towards the door.

Sensing this, the Colonel reassured me. "Yes, please come in. We want to know your opinion." Still skeptical, I relaxed once I saw that the other men concurred with their nods and smiles. Honestly, I don't remember the discussion on CNN nor my response. But what does stand out to me from this event was that these Saudi men wanted my female American viewpoint and validating it once stated. Many information venues report as if all Saudi (Arab) men hate women in general and have no respect for their views. In my time with the Saudis, I found nothing further from the truth. There are good people everywhere.

Over my embarrassment and tickled the gentlemen wanted my opinion, I returned to the party. Our evening was typical of a regular ladies' party in Saudi. The ladies talked and ate until wee hours of the night.

The next morning was lazy because of our late night at Wafa's and neither Madawi nor I stirred before late afternoon. Still in our pjs, we decided to eat and then relax with a good game of cards.

Commandeering the corner of the large dinning room table, which we never ate upon, Madawi and I settled in for a competitive afternoon of Rummy. With snacks delivered regularly and the moist, cool sea breeze flowing in the doors, this was definitely the way to waste away an afternoon. Focused on the hand, we were both startled with Maha's cry "look at me!" Quickly, we both turned to find her covered from head to toe in baby powder. We couldn't help but break into laughter because she was so darn cute spinning around like a model. Then Madawi inquired, "why **habebee**?"

"Because I want to be just like Mrs. Teresa!" she exclaimed.

My heart leapt from the sincere love of a child that I felt at that moment, but then I thought of Madawi. How would she see this? Our eyes met.

"Oh Maha," Madawi began. "We all love Mrs. Teresa, but you must be happy with you. You are a special person." Agreeing this was a wonderful learning moment, I joined in to encourage Maha's self-worth and we all ended in hugs and kisses.

Turning back to our cards, we continued. Madawi and I are both blessed or cursed depending on your perspective with a competitive streak and the score was neck in neck. Our conversation was dominated by "hmmms" and "ahems" as we each studied our cards, planned our game strategies, and peered over our cards at the other with impeccable poker faces. Between hands, we laughed and joked as to whom would be the victor, shuffled, and dealt again.

After a few hands, our silence was broken by the Colonel bellowing "Madawi" from upstairs. It was very loud and our eyes met instinctively. She smiled a forced smile and called something back in Arabic before continuing with her turn. A few minutes later, he shouted again. She replied but seemed more irritated than before. Sighing, she continued her discard. Before long, he hollered more intently. We looked at each other and she smiled humbly. She was obligated to go and I knew it. Yet, it was if a string immediately shot between us and another knot was tied in our carpet of friendship. I felt sad for her at that moment, but I smiled to let her know that I understood.

With mixed emotions, our trip came to a close. I was sad that this special time with my new found Saudi family was over. Yet, on the other hand, I was happy to be on my way to meet David and visit my family in the states, which I had not seen in almost a year. The family, however, would leave that evening for London and we would all meet back in Kingdom in October. While the car sat running, we hugged one last time before I was off to the airport when Madawi reviewed the normal travel checklist like she had done before.

"Passport? Ticket? Money?" She confirmed with a smile holding my hands as if not wanting to let go.

"Yes, yes, and yes," I replied with a huge smile touched by her concern.

"You take care, huh?" She said caringly with her signature smile, nodding to reiterate.

"I will, Madawi." I responded. "Thank you so much for everything."

"Oh Mrs. Teresa," she laughed as if embarrassed at my thankfulness. "We are the thankful ones, but," she hesitated. "*Afwan*, Mrs. Teresa," she concluded with the gentlest of smiles.

Stepping into the open car door, I waved back to my Shamsiyah on the porch, "See you in October!"

"***Insha Allah, yellah***" my friend replied and then blew me a kiss good bye.

Chapter ٦
The Year of the Dance
August 1992 – May 1993

I hated to see the summer pass and the travel end, but nothing lasts forever. David and I had enjoyed several weeks with family and friends in the states and a two-week driving tour through Europe. Even though I had enjoyed all four months of my international travel, I was more than anxious to wave good bye to suitcases and airports and return to daily life in the desert. I was thrilled to death to open the door and see my big, black Kenyan standing on my front porch, grinning, and ready to drive me to the palace to tutor the children once again.

My senses heightened when I entered the palace and smelled my favorite Arab smells. Stopping and speaking to each servant I saw, I made my way to the main salon, which was the most intimate family room. Beautifully yet comfortably decorated, the room felt cozy and personal. On the large wall behind his and her leather recliners were large portraits of Arab men, a pictorial family lineage hung with reverence. Reflecting Madawi's ancestry, the oldest patriarch, Abdulaziz, hung higher that the rest. It seemed as if I had been there only the day before when I stepped over the threshold and back into my daily routine.

Like before, I plopped onto the sofa beside Madawi while she nibbled her lunch from the little silver tray on the small table beside her. Without hesitation, I joined in by selecting the specialty of the palace's Filipino chef, Ben's famous **sambusha** that I had so desperately missed. Just as we had done before the summer, Madawi and I used this time to connect. Some days we would just sit and watch the news, and other days we would talk insatiably. The topics of our conversations ran the gambit from compound gossip and airbase scuttlebutt to parenting issues and private female matters. There were days when we would sit on the floor of the salon and thumb through Western clothing catalogs and magazines like *Cosmopolitan* or *Mademoiselle*, showing each other what we liked and what we did not, critiquing each other's taste as to whether the outfits we saw would really look good or not on each other.

Each afternoon when the children arrived from school, I would leave Madawi in the salon and go upstairs to tutor the girls in the girls' quarters. Each daughter had her own room encircling a communal salon where they would watch television, play games and hang out. Their rooms were decorated with the finest, but sparsely so. Unlike Americans, Saudis do not adorn their surroundings by hanging many pictures and displaying knickknacks around the room. The necessities were there, perhaps even the extravagant in terms of electronics, but there were not many items displayed in the way of decorative touches, as Americans know them.

Our study time always began with a break – an afternoon meal in the girls' kitchen. The daily lunch included delicious dishes and at least three servants to serve it! The meals consumed in their little kitchen sparked my love of Arab food, and the girls would always take the time to tell me the names of the foods, the ingredients, and other interesting facts they could think of that related to a particular food. During this special time each day, I believe they learned more English than they did during their individual study times. It was during this time that we learned each other's likes and dislikes, shared dreams, and became like family to each other. They would tell me events that had happened in school during the day, both the good and the bad. In time as adolescence rolled around, our conversations deepened and they would ask my advice about friends, relationships, and other aspects of their lives.

After stuffing ourselves, I would start with Bandari, the youngest in the beginning. Employing age appropriate and proficiency level materials, Bandari and I learned English and Arabic. We sang English songs and learned English rhymes. When it was "her turn to teach," a daily practice we used, I gathered an innocent vocabulary of Arabic words on the backyard bench we loved to find. Before long, her English had improved tremendously. She loved to study with "Mrs. Teresa" and always yearned for more. After a year with me, Madawi actually pulled me aside and asked that I slow down with Bandari's English lessons as she was becoming better in English than in her native Arabic language.

After Bandari, I would study with Maha. At first she loved to learn, but as time passed, her desire to study English dwindled to only completing the required work from school. Any additional, traditional study attempt was an enormous effort for both of us, but we managed. To this day, I still remember her precious little face our first summer together in Cannes, France when she covered herself in powder exclaiming she wanted to be like "Mrs. Teresa".

Fatma followed and was always my greatest challenge. She had driven the other tutors away, and tried her best to do the same to me, but to no avail. Self-determined and somewhat defiant at first, Fatma hated to study but did so under stern direction from her mother.

In the beginning, she would say to me as we studied, "I hate you Mrs. Teresa," and then follow it with choice words in Arabic. I would always calmly respond by saying, "No, you don't hate me. You hate studying English, but we have to do it anyway." I would then pause, give her my tilted brow look, smile, and say, "By the way, the Arabic doesn't bother me because I don't know what you're saying!" In response, she would dart her huge black eyes at me, sigh loudly, and we would continue the lesson. In time, however, the sigh was followed by a deep run of laughter when this little exchange became almost a daily routine and our private joke.

Fatma hated traditional school and seemed to prefer a more Montessori approach to learning. As I got to know her, I learned that it was her immense creativity and imagination that made her despise the traditional style of studying. Realizing this, I used alternative methods to reach Fatma. Ones I eventually employed with Maha. We would swing on the play set as we practiced her spelling words, or splash in the indoor waterfall of their atrium. We would play various games incorporating her English studies as we played. And when all else failed, I would bribe completion with the promise of a fun day at my house on the compound, with no studying! Little did she realize how much English she practiced as we read English recipes and baked delicious cookies. Covered in flour and the kitchen a mess, we had a ball.

Out of all of the girls, Fatma loved coming to my compound the most. She yearned for western ways and simply couldn't get enough. Once I understood her and she me, we got along beautifully and our friendship deepened as the years passed. Ironically in a few short years, it was this feisty child who hated to study English that stepped up to the plate and made her mother and school proud as she dazzled an auditorium with her eloquent command of the spoken word.

Nora, like Bandari, was easy to teach. She was such a responsible, focused young lady of twelve. Nora was the picture perfect princess child. She was always ready to show me her required work and always ready to learn more. From the first day we studied, she told me she wanted to continue with school, go to the university and then run her father's company one day. Upon graduation, she in fact did go to the university, and she did excel as she said she would.

After studying with the girls, I would return to the downstairs children's salon to study with Fahad.

Essentially a mirror image of the upstairs girls' salon and decorated comparably, this salon was for all to share, even Madawi's only male child.

The pre-teen prince was such a smart young man, but aware of his intelligence and not always outwardly receptive to my instruction. Even so, he seemed to enjoy studying and would never reveal that I had taught him something new. A normal response, I suppose, for a royal teenage boy still trying to find his way in a society dominated by males.

During our only year to study English together, I learned so much about Fahad. Being a young man of fourteen, he naturally loved cars and told me how one day he would buy his own red Ferrari. Which in fact, he did just a year later in spite of his mother's objections. He revealed his love of music and art and his fear that his father would not want him to be anything but a military man. Daily, between our English studies, he would discuss the latest music star, song, or Hollywood movie. Fahad knew all the stars and all the new releases. He would even have the latest videos shipped in to him, a privilege we Westerners did not have, and he would let me borrow movies on the weekend. He had so much pride in his family, his country, and his customs, as he should, and he shared these with me with amazing excitement and vigor.

In retrospect, I believe Fahad had a crush on me in the beginning, which I assume many 14 year old young men have for their teachers at that age. He beamed as I opened the flower-shaped emerald and diamond earrings he presented me for my birthday in late 1992. As if handing his teacher an apple, but in royal style, he smiled from ear to ear as I raved over his gift. I believe Madawi sensed his infatuation as well because I no longer studied with Fahad after December of that year. Rather, a male English tutor was hired for the young prince and lessons given in his personal villa.

As time passed and their culture dictated, we saw less and less of each other. We were in the same location often, but rarely sat and chatted like we did in the beginning. Yet, the bonds of friendship had been laid. When an English application needed review or he had a new car or toy to show, he would appear at my front door. When his high school graduation rolled around, he called me to help decorate the hotel for his celebration. Although I kept up with his progress at the University, I never saw Fahad again once he flew stateside to become a collegiate.

It was from one of my afternoon chats with Madawi that a culturally radical idea sprang in the fall of 1992– dancing instruction. Inspired by my "story-times" during the summer, the idea for *Jadawel Jazz Comprehensive Dance* was born. In France, the girls' eyes widened each time I told a childhood memory about my dancing, which I began at the age of three. Knowing the girls would respond well to this type of reward, I offered to teach them a little ballet, tap, and jazz dancing with Madawi's permission and, of course, if they did well with their studies. Madawi not only gave her blessing, but took the idea a step further by suggesting that I offer a class or two on the compound so the western children could enjoy them as well. By implementing what began as a creative reward for good students and incorporating Madawi's idea, I unknowingly started my first of two businesses in the Kingdom of Saudi Arabia.

With Madawi's support, I began teaching combination classes that included ballet, tap, and jazz dance instruction on the compound in October. Utilizing the long, rectangular recreation room, I held three classes per week for one hour each. Madawi encouraged her daughters to join their age appropriate classes with the western girls, rather than isolate themselves to private instruction. However, she did decide to have a room in the palace converted to a private dancing room so the girls could practice outside of dance class. Converting an existing unused bedroom, Madawi had floor length mirrors mounted on two walls and hard wood flooring installed. To make the room complete for ballet instruction, she ordered wood bars from Europe and had them mounted on the glass walls at varying heights to accommodate the different sizes of the girls.

In the beginning, it was more of a healthy hobby for me and only consumed one day a week of my time. I would choreograph in the morning before tutoring in the afternoon, and then ride back to the compound with the girls to teach the three dance classes from five to eight in the evening. The girls looked forward to Monday nights with great anticipation and always made a night of it with dinner on the compound or a swim in the pool around the class times.

Unfortunately with drivers and nannies in tow, the girls were anything but inconspicuous when they visited, and their presence did not help my compound relations. I believe many saw me as stuck-up simply because of the company I kept, whereas others obviously sucked up for personal gain. But I learned to recognize intentions quickly and I kept my personal distance from them to survive.

Three of the girls simply could not get enough dancing in the beginning and the weekly classes soon extended to daily private instruction in the palace dancing room. Fatma simply loved jazz dancing. She loved to wiggle and shake, mimicking her favorite American top forty idols. Bandari was the ballerina both in spirit and in stature, and Maha the tap dancing queen.

Nora seemed to enjoy dancing, but she was shy and reluctant to take the personal risks needed to make new friends in the class. The Americans girls, on the other hand, knew her position and were afraid to reach out as well. Plus, many of them held the mislaid views of their parents, which hindered attempts at friendship. Sadly, many westerners on the compound vented their frustrations of a radically different culture on the people of that culture and passed this dislike to their children. Many hated the Saudis simply because they were Saudi, without ever giving the person beneath the veil or under the *guthra* a chance. Out of the entire class, Nora had the prettiest figure and natural rhythm of any of the dancers, yet she seemed more uncomfortable because of it. With all these factors rolled together, Nora, unfortunately, decided to quit after only a few months.

Shortly after *Jadawel Jazz* began, a huge blessing came into our lives and further bonded our friendship. Little princess *Farah bint Awad bin Turki bin Abdulla Al-Saud* entered this world on the sixteenth of November in 1992.

Focused on education, business, and the act of being my own person, I was a twenty-nine year old woman who had been married for seven years and appeared to most as a never-to-be mom. Yet, Madawi altered that by asking me to be with her for the birth of her sixth child. This experience changed my life and blessed me with a newfound sense of what it means to be a woman, and I will always be grateful to my friend for sharing this understanding. Only a few months later, I learned that I was expecting.

It was obvious the Colonel was elated with Farah's birth and grinned from ear-to-ear as he welcomed us and other guests who arrived at the hospital to celebrate her birth late into the night. That evening, I watched him talk with their visitors and I thought of how contrary he was to what I had recently read.

Shortly after my arrival in Kingdom, a friend gave me a book, a recent release she had smuggled in from the states, that was about the Kingdom and supposedly true. I remembered the book insinuating that Saudi men do not acknowledge or care for their female offspring, but nothing could have been further from the truth with regard to the Colonel. Perhaps there are some Saudi men that disregard their female children, as there are American men that do, but the Saudi men I knew were not that way. The Colonel adored all five of his girls. He praised their accomplishments and encouraged their further success. His concern for their well-being was obvious with the way he supported their education. Plus, as many fathers do, he gave them almost everything they asked for. I never saw a lack of love from the Colonel or any other Saudi man that I knew when it came to their children, males or females.

    In early spring of 1993, my Mom and Dad decided that they were not ready for retirement and they returned to the Kingdom for a two-year contract. Working for the Department of Defense, my Dad was involved with F-15 jetfighters from their inception in the late 1970s, and he worked stateside on the Saudi F-15 program until I graduated from high school. Once I was out of the nest and attending the university, he and my Mom decided to take the next step and mobilize to the Kingdom where he supported "program depot maintenance" (PDM) of the Saudi's F-15s. My parents lived in **Riyadh** from 1985 to 1990.

    David and I were inspired by their stories and adventures in this distant world and they were the reason we decided to experience the Kingdom. Having loved their time in Saudi and my being there pregnant with my first child was enough of a reason to pull my Dad from the lush, green golf courses of the states to return and tee-off in the sand once again. I could not have been happier when they not only returned to Kingdom but were assigned to *Dhahran* and my compound. My parents have always been incredibly special to me and I was thankful my Mom would be near when I stepped over the threshold to motherhood. From the moment they stepped off the plane, they supported every endeavor I undertook with zest and vigor.

Unexpectedly, nineteen ninety-three became the year of dance and I found myself dressed in dance attire more than anything thing else. To encourage the *Jadawel Jazz* dancers and give them the opportunity to show what they had learned and develop stage presence, I decided to have a small dance recital near the end of May. I had 26 eager students, a compound theater facility that simply yearned for a performance, and four months to prepare.

Unable to locate any dancing costumes in Kingdom because dancing is actually illegal and not enough time to have purchased ones shipped in from the states, I turned to the parents of the dancers to have them made locally. Out of all that stepped forward to help, there was one lady in particular that shown above the rest and jumped into help with extra vigor. As the mother of two, she was more than willing to work hard to make the show special for them and, more importantly, relieve her boredom. After our first recital experience, Molly not only became my dear friend but was the one that altered the path of *Jadawel Jazz* in the years to come.

Because Fatma's enjoyment of dancing was insatiable, Madawi decided she wanted to include a few dances that I could choreograph to western music in her school's graduation party in May.

With her request, I fondly remembered the first graduation party I attended almost a year prior when I had been employed by the family for a week and in Kingdom for only a few months. I was excited to attend as Madawi's guest and shocked to find a school for girls behind the towering, plain walls that encircled *Al-Hamdi Girls' School*. Cloaked in mystery with graduations held in secret, Madawi's school offered the best instruction available to young women in the Eastern province, and their graduation parties were no different.

Under the starlit sky and within the confines of the school's privacy wall, I unexpectedly found a most elaborate, temporary stage in the school courtyard, complete with fantastically painted backdrops. In front of the stage were rows and rows of chairs, placed impeccably by unseen servants. Normally, it would not be unusual to see rows of chairs in front of a stage. However, in this culture, it was definitely different and held an underlying meaning. The various types of chairs marked each lady's place in the societal hierarchy. The first row consisted of huge, overstuffed, fabric chairs that you would find in a living room, complete with Persian carpets and coffee tables elaborately decorated with flowers, expensive chocolates, and tissues. These chairs were reserved for Madawi, other royal attendees, and honored guests.

Behind the first row were four rows of nice, upholstered chairs much like dining room chairs. These rows were reserved for women of second tier importance, honored non-royal guests. Behind these rows were numerous rows of metal folding chairs reserved for the regular moms of the students. Being that the Saudi society is segregated in all aspects of life, the fathers were not allowed to see their daughters' graduation from high school, only the moms. That first year, my first of nine *Al-Hamdi Girls' School* graduation parties, I was seated in an overstuffed chair next to Madawi.

The ceremonial performance began with lengthy introductions to reflect the names of the royal attendees. Special words of thanks were given to the headmistress and other honored female guests from the Ministry of Education who were there to observe, critique, and report any deviance from what is considered acceptable by the Ministry. A respectful, solemn reading from the ***Quran*** followed. Then we all stood as the Saudi Arabian National Anthem was played.

With the formalities complete, the party began. It was not like what Americans would call a graduation. I equate it more to a play or dance recital. Each class/grade level performed a play, a dance, or a reading depending on what they had learned that year. Throughout the evening, I was impressed with the level of performance by the girls, the style of the costumes, and the complexity of the sets. It was truly a first rate school program, notably marked with a strong American influence, and I was honored to attend.

Because of the fond memories I had of my first *Al-Hamdi* graduation, I was excited and honored to help with the second. At Fatma's request, I choreographed a cute dance to *"Rockin' Robin"* for her class. Beginning one month prior to the graduation party, the driver took me to practice with the girls every afternoon for an hour or more to teach and rehearse their dances. We practiced on the basketball court under the sun shelter while the girls endured the heat from beneath their calf-length school uniform skirts covering their western trousers. I believe the students enjoyed our time together, and I know that I did. They were very attentive and anxious to learn. Before long, all the girls at the school knew me, perhaps because they enjoyed our dancing so much or perhaps because I was the only American woman there. As I walked in the courtyard or through the halls, the girls would call out "Ello, Mrs. Teresa" as I made my way through their private, secluded world.

Mama and Madawi hit it off when they met, just as Madawi and I had the night I interviewed. Immediately Madawi revered Mom simply because she was older, as is her culture, yet over the years to come, they, too, developed a unique and special relationship. Consequently, Madawi asked Mom to attend the graduation, where she got an overstuffed chair.

The night began as the year before with lengthy introductions, thank yous, respectful readings from the

Quran, and the Saudi National Anthem. However, this year as the lights rose for the performance to begin, I did not get an overstuffed chair on the front row; rather, I was in the second, dining room chair row. Mama Ann, however, got an overstuffed chair and I presume it was because she had only recently met Madawi.

At first thought, this chair change could be seen as a demotion, when in reality, it was a promotion. After a year with Madawi and the girls, I was seen as part of the family, and they felt no need to impress me. The front row, on the other hand, was needed for attending royals and honored guests, not family. As everyone settled in for the four-hour performance, the food was delivered in the caring hands of a dozen servants, and the party began.

This graduation party was just as beautiful and well coordinated as the previous year. I beamed with pride as the girls performed *"Rockin' Robin."* They did a terrific job! They wore Capri pants made from a wild floral print and coordinating pastel tee shirts of four alternating colors, black sunglasses, and tennis shoes. The girls brought down the house. The mothers went wild with their performance, and the auditorium shook for at least five minutes afterwards from the cheers and traditional shrieks.

Zipping out of the graduation through the back door and into a waiting car, I then flew to the compound and the dress rehearsal for *Jadawel Jazz's* first dance recital, *"An Evening with the Stars."* Saleem laughed down deep when I jumped from the backseat, already in jazz boots but still in my evening dress, and dropping high heels and other items as I ran up the compound theater steps. Inside, David had done everything short of the hokie-pokie to keep the dancers busy until I arrived almost an hour late. The parents were irritated, and rightly so, but didn't verbalize it. Fortunately, the rehearsal went well and the dancers were as ready as they could be for the upcoming performance.

    The following evening, I aggravated the parents and audience alike when I delayed the start time to wait for Madawi to arrive for our first recital. I was still in shock that she had not only agreed to let her daughters participate in a public dance performance wearing ballet costumes, but that she had agreed to come and watch as well. In such, I did not want to begin without her. After forty-five minutes and just as I was about to run out of excuses for the delay, I saw her car through the glass wall at the front of the theater. Smiling with relief, I stepped onto the stage and began to welcome the audience and praise the dancers until I saw her seated in the front row.

    Probably feeling as if I didn't know how to put on a show because the audience wasn't served any refreshments during the performance, Madawi sent word to the restaurant via Alma, her lady in waiting, that she wanted a cup of tea. Returning with Alma to claim that they weren't allowed to serve in the theater, the TCN stopped near the door and asked my father who ordered the tea. Babba John explained that it was the princess on the front row, but the TCN was still unsure and unwilling to comply. Because my dad cared about all of the workers on the compound and did not want to see him lose his job, he encouraged the waiter to not only serve the tea, but to do it quickly by reminding him that it was the princess' husband who owned the compound.

With glittered, Styrofoam stars hanging by wire from the ceiling and three complete costume changes for each dancer to perform their three numbers, *"An Evening with the Stars"* was a huge success. The recital exceeded everyone's expectations and the girls danced their hearts out. I truly could not have been more proud of my dancers than I was that night. In spite of my pleasure with our efforts, I felt that one critical component was lacking – a spotlight to compliment the theater's existing lights.

Chapter V
Second Time Around
June 1993 – August 1994

After the two performances back to back, I felt as if I could sleep for a week, but there was no time. I had to pack. It was never asked nor accepted, just a given that Mrs. Teresa would travel with the family for summer holiday. Happily, I climbed the steps to the Boeing 747 from the desert tarmac after slipping on my sunglasses and mentally into travel mode yet again. In many aspects the summer of 1993 mirrored the summer of 1992. Yet, there were a few things that uniquely distinguished the two.

Mirroring my first summer with the family, we started our holiday in Paris, and I in my familiar room in Mama Amal's flat on Avenue **Foch.** However, unlike before, I rarely saw the girls and spent most of my time with Madawi. Instead of movies and *Pizza Pinos*, it was art galleries and five-star restaurants. It only took a week for the disgruntled mumbles of the girls to draw our attention and I was in the middle of the dispute.

The girls wanted me to walk the *Champs d'Elysee* with them and see things through my eyes, while Madawi wanted me as her companion. Appealing to their sense of family and compassion for my pregnant condition, Madawi convinced the girls that it was better if I attended things with her this trip. Begrudgingly and loudly, the girls acquiesced. And to be honest, even though I adored the girls I was happy that Madawi won the toss. Being five months pregnant with my first child, I truly needed my Shamsiyah.

Sabre traveled with us as he had the year before, but an American man, the Colonel's right-hand man, Jackson Westmoreland, took Khalid's place. Although I never saw Khalid again after my first French summer, Nora and Fatma told me what had become of him. Crouching beside the beamer in the garage, they whispered as they told me their "scoop," like little roving reporters with a massive secret to share. Apparently, Khalid believed the error of his wild, partying ways caught up to him and he blamed himself for the illness his new baby suffered. They said he believed that he had been possessed by the devil and he became a **Muthawen** to repent. Although a little shocking, it was believable once I remembered his behavior the year prior.

Instead of the blue waters of the Mediterranean, the next leg of our journey took us to McLean, Virginia where the Colonel had business and they had purchased a home. Because the house was not ready for occupancy when we arrived, the Colonel had made arrangements for us to move into the *Ritz Carlton* hotel for the interim. Consuming an entire floor, the presence of our entourage did not go unnoticed. In no time, the concierge and almost every other employee there knew of the Saudis on the sixth floor.

After finding the room marked "the teacher" on the list I was given at reception, I was curious to discover a set of car keys on my suite's desk when I arrived. Without hesitation, I called the concierge to report the lost keys. Much to my dismay, he informed me that they had not been left, but in fact they were mine and that my Mercedes was waiting at my disposal in valet. Excited, I ran down the hall and found Fatma to go with me to check out my new wheels. Never saying no to an adventure, she took off with me in a flutter of laughter. Since we were not allowed into valet to simply see the car, we decided to zip out for an ice cream instead. Fatma clapped with laughter as the candy apple red Mercedes whirled into the hotel drive. I, on the other hand, privately chuckled when I saw that this summer, my car was an automatic. Obviously, Madawi had remembered the hill incident in Cannes as well.

From the moment our feet hit Virginian soil, it was go, go, go. Madawi had an entire house to equip, furnish, and decorate and she wanted me to help. However, we had to keep the kids occupied, so my initial task was defined. Never having been to the D.C. area as an adult, I was clueless where to begin. I knew I had to find a camp or activities that would be fun and educational. Yet, the organization would have to be sensitive to the privacy needs of royal children, understand their diplomatic status, and offer the security that the children required. I most certainly did not want them to feel awkward with a bodyguard shadowing them as they tried to make friends with the American kids. Wisely I called my Mom for her advice. But she didn't see this as a big problem and immediately offered the solution. I should contact my hometown U.S. Senator's wife, Mrs. Cathy, who happened to be in Washington at the time.

Naturally, Mrs. Cathy was more than gracious and offered the information I needed. She then went the extra mile by having her staff assist me with the recommended camp, and she gained access to the Merchandizing Mart for Madawi and me to shop for items for the house. One thing led to another and before I knew it, we had set a lunch date for her and the princess to meet. As suspected, the two hit it off immediately and I was happy that I had brought them together. Thanks to Mrs. Cathy, all four girls were enrolled in a prestigious camp for diplomatic children that including everything from zip-line and swimming to arts & crafts and undercover security. Unwilling to go at first, the girls soon realized how much fun camp could be and they didn't argue again about their lack of Mrs. Teresa.

Fahad, on the other hand, was a different story. Although he didn't complain, it was obvious he wasn't having much fun solely hanging out with his bodyguard. What fifteen year old young man would? Unexpectedly, the answer to his woes came to me in the form of a surprise from Madawi.

With the baby due in November, I knew I would not get back to the United States before the baby's birth. Consequently when we booked our flights, Madawi had given me permission to scoot away for a long weekend while we were in McLean so I could visit my older sister in South Carolina. A few days before my flight, Madawi asked about my nephew,

Chip, who had been a central character in several of my "story-times" and who just happened to be fifteen. She believed Fahad would enjoy having an American male buddy to hang out with for the remainder of our stay, and she was curious if I thought Chip would be interested.

    Nepotism, I must clarify, is not a negative term or practice for the Saudis. After all, it is a family owned country. In such, it would stand to reason that since Madawi saw me as a "good" person and she loved me, surely she would love my good nephew as well. Consequently, she graciously asked for Chip to join us in McLean. All expenses paid, of course, and he would go back to South Carolina when I left for Kingdom four weeks later. Thrilled, we made the arrangements and I returned on Sunday with Chip in tow. He and Fahad hit it off immediately and we rarely saw them after their initial introduction for more than a fly-by through where we were and off to their next outing.

    With the girls attending camp and the boys doing their thing, I was finally free to spend all of my time with Madawi. We had only a two short weeks to get her new home ready before the Colonel's mother, Mama Sita, would arrive for a visit. There was no time to waste. Comically, I actually thought I had an understanding of what it meant to "power shop" before I outfitted and decorated with a princess. To equip a home that would accommodate a family of seven and eleven servants with simply the basic necessities was no easy task. But to select and purchase everything was a formidable quest. I couldn't help but grin to myself when we would enter a shop, and I would hope for the salesperson's sake that they worked on commission. It wasn't two sets of sheets, but rather thirty-four, seventy-two bath towels, 36 hand towels, and you can imagine what was left to buy.

Every morning after breakfast with the girls, Madawi and I were off in my little Mercedes where we were free to simply be two girlfriends on a mission. Without a man behind the wheel or a bodyguard riding shotgun, we were free to chit-chat openly between our destinations and simply be friends. After all, it is sharing those little experiences – the ordinary, mundane things we all face daily – that build a friendship. Bar none, the best cup of cappuccino is the one enjoyed with a friend after a long day of shopping when you both complain about your feet hurting, recap the bargains of the day, and bitch about the snappy salesclerks.

As soon as we had the basics purchased such as beds and chairs, the family and servants moved into the house. The girls were incredibly anxious to sleep in their new rooms and enjoy their new swimming pool. For the sake of privacy, Madawi decided that Fahad, Chip and I should remain at the *Ritz* for the remainder of our stay where we could have our own rooms and baths. A bit bummed at first, I found it to be no inconvenience thanks to my little Mercedes and their home less than a five-minute drive from the hotel. A typical day became waking to breakfast via room service, off with Madawi only to return and collapse from exhaustion in the wee hours of the night.

Understanding the physical challenges of pregnancy, Madawi always encouraged me to go and take it easy when our schedule permitted. Consequently, it was unusual for her to call me at the hotel after she had sent me there to rest. Yet, she called one afternoon to ask me to come and get the boys because they needed a ride to the movie. Somewhat confused because that was Sabre's job, I told her I would come straight away.

Alma stopped me in the drive before I could enter the house. "Sabre has left, Mrs. Teresa."

"Left? Where did he go, Alma?"

"He has runaway," she answered somberly. Just as she spoke, the boys emerged from the house and were ready to leave. Glancing once again at Alma, I got back in the car to drive. Honestly, I was shocked. Sabre had always had a smile and seemed so happy. He made a good wage with every benefit imaginable plus regular, all-expense paid international travel to boot. Obviously he believed that whatever pulled him – freedom perhaps – was worth more. Oddly, no one ever mentioned his name again.

Although I usually drove us shopping, our trip to the Furniture Merchandise Mart seemed like a great time to utilize the privileged luxury of a driver. Yet, because of Sabre's unexpected departure, a stateside hired driver was behind the wheel. Unfortunately for him, he was new and obviously unaware of the position he was entrusted. Because the Colonel and

Madawi were so laid back and westernized, it was easy to forget who they were and the positions they held. It was easy to forget that they were royalty because they were so genuine and down-to-earth. However, this particular afternoon, I saw Madawi wield the power she held for a second time.

We had just pulled in front of the Merchandise Mart and the driver had opened our doors. Nora had decided to tag along that day and ran ahead as teenagers will do. Madawi, on the other hand, was still by the car with me when she noticed something she wanted to give to Nora.

"Oh Nora," she uttered softly, but then became quiet and began walking towards her daughter before continuing her comment. The driver, trying to be helpful but stupid in his efforts yelled to get Nora's attention fifty feet away, "Princess!"

Madawi immediately stopped on a dime and her glare darted to the man. Straightening her back, which only enhanced her naturally towering stature, she stepped over beside the man. In a soft but commanding voice she asked, "What do you want to do?" Her hands began to emphasize her point. "Get my daughter killed or kidnapped?" He began to stutter and her hand went up to demand his silence. "You are fired." She turned and nothing more was said as we entered the mart. It was shocking because it was so sudden. When we left the mart, however, there was another driver waiting and I never saw him again.

We spent the entire day at the Mart where Madawi and I found scrumptious pieces for her home.

Reflecting her personality, we employed a modern, eclectic style, mixing leather and hardwoods coupled with wrought iron accents. Carrying the décor throughout, we dotted each room with unique pieces and whatnots that reflected rustic, tribal origin. It was so much fun to spy an unusual piece and hold it up for the other's opinion. Amazingly, we gravitated to and liked the same kinds of things. We saw the same vision for the home and its décor, and we were aware of the intuitiveness after the first few shops we visited. It truly is amazing how much you learn about a person by simply shopping with them.

Two particular chairs in the corner of one of the showrooms got Madawi's attention, and mine after she excitedly pointed them out. Much like café chairs with wood seats and wrought iron legs and backs, Madawi loved those two little chairs from the moment she laid eyes on them. To express why she liked them, she paused looking for just the right English words, and then nonchalantly said, "they are...funky bunky." Astonishingly, I knew exactly what she meant even though she had just coined the term and I was the first human to hear it. From that moment forward, the term "funky bunky" came to mean the coolest of pieces that we simply couldn't live without and a term that only she and I truly understood.

Gravitating to earth-tones, Madawi selected gorgeous leather sofas, chairs, and ottomans for the family salon and an ultra suede ensemble for the more formal, guest salon. After most of the larger pieces were purchased, Madawi had Persian carpets sent from

Kingdom for each room in the colors we were accenting.

Throughout the summer, Madawi's self-confidence seemed to blossom. She was more independent than from I had observed the summer before, yet she still readily acquiesced to the Colonel and his wishes. At his request, we kept a detail record of our expenditures on the house, which would be beneficial upon resale, yet Madawi never asked the Colonel's permission to buy anything, except for one.

Winding through the crowded streets in Georgetown, we found the exquisite little posh gallery hidden at the end of an alley as Mrs. Cathy said it would be. The moment we heard the little bells on the door handle ring, we saw it and knew. There before us was the most fabulous glass dinning room table with twelve chairs that would be perfect for her formal dinning room. The cut glass table alone was $14,000.00 and the chairs were one thousand each. It was the only purchase that Madawi felt we should seek the Colonel's approval. After agreeing to hold the set for 48 hours, the clerk explained that Madawi could pay by check or credit. Nodding in understanding, Madawi explained that I would be in touch with her either way regarding the hold status.

Excited about finding the perfect piece for the last room to decorate, Madawi decided it would be best for us to meet with the Colonel about the purchase over dinner that evening. He listened attentively while she described the dinning room set and her reasons for why she believed they should purchase it. I simply sat, smiling, and nodding in agreement from time to time. Madawi had not wanted her Shamsiyah there to present her ideas, rather simply there for support and I complied. To be honest, I think the Colonel was going to say yes to her before she opened her mouth to ask, but even if not, she presented so well, he simply could not have said no.

The following morning Madawi entrusted me with a bank bag filled with payment in full for me to return to the shop alone and purchase on her behalf. She remained at the house to pray and dress before our lunch later in the day. I was a nervous wreck the entire trip because I didn't have an extra twenty-six thousand lying around to replace it. I prayed that no one would rob me while I searched for the Georgetown alley we had visited the day before. Thankfully, I handed the clerk the bag.

Now that I've mentioned this seemingly extravagant purchase, I must point out that for a princess – someone with her social status and economic backing – Madawi was frugal with her purchases to fill such a large home. From the day I met her, she was never a spend-thrift nor flamboyant. It wasn't her style. By far, she was the most unpretentious, down-to-earth princess I met during my years in the Kingdom.

As planned, I met Madawi at the selected restaurant. It was a special lunch because I was meeting her youngest brother, Khalid, and his girlfriend for the first time. Polite and dashing, Khalid lived in the states and only flew to McLean to visit his sister. Incredibly westernized, he delighted us with his antics for the afternoon. In the short span of a few hours, it was obvious that Madawi and Khalid had a special relationship and that they cared for each other deeply. Perhaps that is why when the day came that she needed a male family members support, she turned to him.

Once Mama Sita arrived and the decorating deadline was met, our vacation in the states fell into a similar path as our lazy days in Cannes. The personal afternoon chats with Madawi and the fun excursions with the kids returned. Like before, one of us was with child for the trip, but this time it wasn't Madawi. As a result, it was I that got the privilege of holding down the benches at the amusement park in July of 1993. It was driving me crazy to see Madawi run from ride to ride with the girls and me not be able to participate, left holding the cotton candies. Watching, I suddenly had a real appreciation of how Madawi had felt at *EuroDisney* the summer prior. Even so, I had a ball at *Busch Gardens*.

Chip, taking star spot for the day, dazzled us all with his golfing expertise by winning each of the girls an enormous stuffed dog. He was doing really well and our cheers were so loud, we drew a crowd to see if he could sink another hole in one. The excitement was intense, but after five wins of their largest prize, the park worker wouldn't allow Chip another swing. Disappointed we all gave him a little bit of a hard time, but realized his situation and went along our way.

With August came Nora's birthday and a secret mission request from my friend. At the time, Saudis typically did not celebrate birthdays, and I was aware that the Colonel was adamantly against it. Madawi, on the other hand, wanted Nora to have fun on her special day, and she was willing to take the risk to make it happen. At brunch, she nonchalantly asked if I would take the girls out for the evening since she had to attend a business dinner with the Colonel. Knowing full well it was Nora's birthday I looked directly into her eyes, "do you have any suggestions?"

"Awad thinks a movie would be nice for you all, but I know Nora prefers roller skating" she replied to my gaze. "But it's not a party, huh." Immediately her familiar mischievous face appeared as she raised one brow and smiled.

"Oh, of course not," I replied with a smile as well, fully understanding her unspoken request. She then passed an envelope to me across the table. "For your expenses" her smiled continued. "I really want the girls to have fun tonight." Rising to leave, she added "I have so much to do for the dinner and I think you have some things you want to do, too, huh?" her smile broadened and she winked. "Let's plan to meet back here tonight, huh."

"You got it."

"*Insha Allah*."

After quickly finishing my food, I ran upstairs to drag Fatma out of bed. Announcing we had a mission, she moved faster than she normally did for 10:00 o'clock in the morning. While she dressed, I called

Fahad and Chip to tell them our plans. Word spread quickly and in a matter of no time, everyone was involved with the event. Poor Nora spent much of her birthday alone as each sibling with nanny in tow snuck away to purchase birthday surprises. We were fortunate that the nearby skating rink had a party room available, so we booked it. We purchased a cake, candles, table decorations, and helium balloons.

Fahad, Chip, the girls, their nannies, the drivers, and me coupled with a few Saudi relatives, their nannies, and drivers who were also in the area comprised our group and made for a nice size party that evening. Doing exactly what people do at a roller skating rink, we skated, attempted new tricks, laughed, fell, and ate until the establishment closed.

On the way home, my car was busting with people, more than the car accommodated, but since it was very near to the house, I let it slide. Just as we topped the hill before the residence, it hit me and I pulled to the side of the road, causing everyone in the car to go silent with anticipation as to why I stopped.

"The movie!" I exclaimed and everyone stared at the others. Unsure of the latest releases I clarified, "which movie did we see?"

"Oh," Fahad's eyes became as wide as saucers "uh."

"What about 'Free Willy'" Fatma suggested.

"'Tom and Jerry'!" Bandari shrilled with delight, obviously believing we were discussing where to go next, not where we had supposedly been.

"Oh, 'Weekend at Bernie's'" Fahad added. "I just love that movie when they drag that dead guy around with them in the golf cart." His hands flew to emphasis his point which was so like his mom.

Fatma jumped in her seat repeating, "'Hocus Pocus'"

"'Sleepless in Seattle!'" Nora exclaimed as she snapped her fingers in agreement.

"What about 'The Fugitive?" Chip added. "But the little girls could not have seen that," Fahad added with a shake of the head and flip of the wrist.

"Guys!" the level of my voice immediately got everyone's attention. "We are NOT picking a movie to go see. We just need to all know the same movie we didn't see if *Babba* asked." A long, awkward silence loomed before laughter rocked the car. "We most certainly can't all say a different movie if your father asks." I took a deep breath and pronounced through my chuckles, "'Free Willy,' we saw 'Free Willy'"

"'Free Willy' it is," Fahad agreed loudly and nodding heads concurred. Fortunately, the Colonel was not at home when we arrived.

As if I had not had enough shopping for the year, I had one more purchase to make before my flight home. The compound theater was perfect for performances, but it lacked one crucial piece of equipment to stage a top notch show – a single spotlight that could follow solo performers or simply enhance the overall lighting. Because of the success of *Jadawel Jazz*, I wanted to buy a 2000watt spotlight and ship it to the Kingdom where spotlights were unavailable no matter how much money you had to spend. Surprisingly, finding the one I wanted proved as challenging as shopping in Saudi. After numerous calls around the country, I was thankful to locate a vendor in the state of Washington that had what I wanted and could accommodate my unusual shipping requests. Mentally, I could check the box that this task was done.

As teenagers will do, Chip and Fahad quickly developed nocturnal habits to enjoy their summer holiday and I rarely ever saw them. They were typically sleeping when I left the hotel and out when I returned.

Initially, four weeks seemed like a long time for Chip to be with us, but in reality, the time passed quickly. Only a few days before our departure, it hit me how close we were to Washington, D.C. Yet, we had not had the opportunity to even drive by the White House for him to see, which just wouldn't do. Confirming with Madawi that the following day would work with her schedule for Chip and I to scoot off and see a few memorials, I asked if she or the girls would like to come along, too. Just as it was the summer before, the reply was no. This was not the first time they had been to the states and they had already toured D.C. several times. Encouraging us to go ahead, she did, however, ask for us to meet her and the Colonel for lunch at the Ritz before she and I did what we had to do that afternoon.

Excited, I hung up the phone and went to look for the boys. When I didn't find Fahad and Chip in one of their suites, I decided to leave a message at the front desk. In my scurry, I ran into the concierge in the lobby and he asked my rush. Long story short, I asked if he had seen the boys. With a slight smirk on his face, he simply pointed across the lobby. Looking in the direction of his gesture, I saw nothing and he clarified, "lower Madame" he laughed. "Look lower."

Low and behold, I saw a tennis shoe disappear behind the sofa situated on the Persian carpet in the center of the lobby. Stepping quickly to get a better view, I saw Fahad and Chip crawling across the floor! With my verbal surprise they both jumped to their feet, laughing, and explaining their dare to crawl all the way to their suites!

Chip and I woke early the next morning so that we could see as much as possible before 1:00 o'clock. It was a wonderful morning with my oldest nephew and I was so glad we had the opportunity. After a fun-filled, exhausting excursion, we dashed back to the Ritz for our lunch date.

Naturally running late, I was anxious. Typically, it never bothered Madawi if I was a bit late, but I was unsure of the Colonel's response and truly didn't want to find out. I had seen him shout at Jackson for being late and I did not want to be on the receiving end. We whirled the Mercedes into valet and screeched to a halt. Jumping out with the engine running, I shouted and waved back to the valet guys "Running late, fellas, thank you!"

Dashing inside, we made our way to the informal restaurant and I saw the couple near the back.

Slowing to a fast walk, we made our way to their table. Exhausted and out of breath, I fell into the chair by Madawi and Chip by the Colonel. I could see in Chip's eyes that he felt the same unsure tension, and we were surprised with what followed as I began our apologies.

"I am so sorry…"

"Why are you out of breath, Mrs. Teresa?" the Colonel interrupted in his deep, military tone voice.

"Oh, I just didn't want to be late, Colonel" I replied with a nervous smile. "We had such a hard time with parking today and I feel as if I have walked my feet off."

Madawi smiled mischievously while the Colonel continued. "Where were you two?" Dragging out the word "two," he raised an exaggerated brow.

"Oh Colonel, we have been sight-seeing since 8:00 a.m. to see some of the sites of Washington."

"Sight-seeing…" He leaned back in his chair and raised his hands in question. "What did you see?"

Chip chimed in "we saw the White House, Washington Memorial, and a quick tour in the Smithsonian, Sir."

"8:00 a.m.?" His brow furrowed.

"Ah, yes sir." I agreed with Chip while sporting an uncertain smile.

Leaning forward and placing his elbows on the table, he made eye contact with each of us, and then questioned sternly, "Why in the world would you want to go site-seeing at 8:00 a.m.?"

A bit shaken and unsure how to reply I was saved by his punch line.

"Why so early?" His hands went into the air and his face into an exaggerated questioning look with his eyes wide. "The moments have been there a long time and they aren't going anywhere!" He roared with laughter. "You should have slept in first!" He added as our laughter followed his lead.

I found the Colonel to have a wonderful sense of humor even in the earlier days when he seemed more rigid and military. He always had a kind or encouraging word for me and was there when I needed help on many occasions, help that only a prince or Colonel could provide. Yet, he was undergoing personal change as well brought on by, I believe, his participation in the first Gulf War. After all, facing death head on and ejecting from a fighter plane has to have an effect on a person. As the years passed, however, he seemed to mellow but his delightful humor remained.

The evening before our departure, we all ate together for a kind of "good bye" dinner. The girls giggled with glee as they told their Babba about Chip winning the stuffed dogs at Busch Gardens. Fahad and Chip enthralled us with comical events that had happened with them, including the lobby crawl. We all laughed and enjoyed the delicious Arab meal the palace cook had prepared and we discussed the future. The Colonel and Madawi had become extremely fond of Chip during his stay in McLean. In such, they invited him to visit Kingdom the following summer. Elated he agreed.

Both Chip and I were sad to leave because we were having so much fun. But Chip had to return to school the following week, and I had no choice but to return to Kingdom because of my pregnancy. At the time, the airlines would not allow a pregnant woman to fly internationally if she were in her seventh month or later. The day was gloomy and thunderstorms ravaged the area. As a result, *Dulles International* experienced many delays leaving numerous airplanes on the tarmac fully loaded for hours.

Fortunately, Chip's plane made it in the air before the strongest storms struck. However, I was one of those on the tarmac with lighting popping all around and wind rocking the airliner. After two hours and several chapters of my book, I started to become concerned about my connection in Amsterdam. I asked the flight attendant whether she thought I would make my connection and she rudely replied that over three-hundred people were asking her the same question. Frustrated, I didn't ask again.

The storms finally subsided and we made it to Amsterdam, but only a half an hour before my connecting flight to *Dhahran* in another terminal. Things looked grim but I thought I could make it if the airline would provide me a ride to the other terminal. Believing they were helping me and ten others in similar situations, I stepped to the side when asked to wait for the airline representative. After ten minutes, two employees arrived. When it was my turn, the lady asked where I would like to stay for the evening, compliments of the airline, and that they would put me on the next available flight. Knowing the next flight to *Dhahran* was two days away and unwilling to camp out in Amsterdam, I told her I had to make the plane. She insisted I could not, but still I persisted and asked in a polite but agitated tone, "Are the wheels of the plane still on the ground?" When she replied yes, I was off like a shot, running down the moving sidewalks. Out of breath and aching all over, I made it just as they were closing the plane door. The attendants literally scooted me to my seat and made me buckle. I had already missed the demonstration and the plane was rolling.

In spite of only arriving with the clothes on my back, it felt good to be home. From the time my feet hit the Kingdom, I was on the ready for motherhood. While Madawi and the girls remained stateside, I was busy getting the nursery decorated, the nanny trained, and reading everything I could get my hands on regarding the big event—Mason's birth.

Simultaneously, I restarted *Jadawel Jazz* and began preparations for tutoring once the children returned and started the new school year. Fortunately, *Jadawel Jazz* was still small, with only 45 students, and fairly easy to handle but exhausting in my last trimester. The Colonel disagreed with my continuing because of my condition. Every time he saw me that fall he would asked if I had stopped teaching dance, and each time I would assure him I would if I felt the least inkling that it was hurting the baby or me.

The autumn passed quickly with all I had on my plate. The children returned in October and I resumed my daily tutoring at the palace. Between lessons, the nannies pampered me to no end, offering anything I wanted to eat whenever I wanted to eat it. *Jadawel Jazz* classes were weekly and starting to become more difficult for me physically by the middle of October. The last two weeks of classes, I "danced" from a chair, calling out the steps and simply showing with my feet, if necessary. Fortunately, our push to learn at the beginning of September was paying off.

Mason was born by caesarean on the first of November, 1993. He immediately became the love of my life, but my recovery time was an unexpected snag in the wheel. I had planned to be up and dancing again two weeks after birth, but the c-section challenged me more. Perhaps I am a wimp, but it took me a week to even stand up straight!

With the unexpected surgery to bring my Mason into the world, I was more thankful than ever to have my Mom in the Kingdom. Honestly, Madawi and I never discussed when I would return to work after birth, but I think we both assumed around two weeks. However, eight weeks was half of a semester of English study for the girls and they needed a tutor. As so many times in my life, it was Mom to the rescue. She and Madawi had hit it off the few times they had met, so Madawi readily agreed to the substitute idea.

Fortunately, the dancers knew their routines and could continue to practice with Molly coaching. Yet, we had no costumes or set. Joan, our compound recreation director who was a motivating British gal, rallied all the crafty compound ladies to help the dancers put on our holiday show in December. They met in the theater to sew costumes and make sets for our holiday production, and she had refreshments served to make it a party. Because of those ladies and all of their hard work, the new spotlight, and the countless hours the dancers practiced, our desert version of "The Nutcracker," complete with camels and date palm fairies, was a first-rate show that put the entire compound into the holiday spirit.

The first of the year brought much needed rest and an intense desire for life to return to normal. Madawi was gracious enough to allow me time to adjust to motherhood and recuperate before returning to work, while Mama Ann, as she was soon lovingly called, kept the girls up with their English Studies.

Even so, I was happy to finally get back to my routine. My days were filled with tutoring at the palace and learning to be a mom. My reliance on my Shamsiyah was incredibly strong in my initial months of motherhood. It became quite comical after a while because she came to expect and anticipate a daily mother question during our afternoon time. I relied on Madawi heavily while I experienced my personal maternal growth, and she relied on my encouragement as she began to open herself to new ideas and ways of thinking.

Shortly after I returned to work, Madawi decided to spread her wings and take an introductory art class at *King Faisal University* in *Dammam*. Classes were offered to women at the university, but their curriculum was under intense scrutiny by the

Department of Education and thus limited. Nonetheless, Madawi's face glowed when she told me what they would study, her books, and her class color wheel with me. She was absorbed and her desire to learn, insatiable.

The days passed as time will do and I did not travel with my Saudi family in 1994. My time completely evolved around motherhood, tutoring, and dancing. The summer brought a special surprise when my nephew, Chip, who had been in McLean with us was able to visit in Kingdom. By design, he arrived several weeks before Madawi and the family left for holiday so that Fahad could show Chip his world. For kicks, I helped Chip, Fahad, Nora, and Fatma organize several fun events for the teenagers on the compound. We coordinated a sock hop complete with advertising posters, DJ, and refreshments in the large compound theater. Everyone had a blast as they danced the night away. We organized a *"How to Host Your Own Murder"* dinner party in the theater as well. We painted plywood sets in a 1940s theme, organized for the waiters from the dinning hall to serve the dinner, and the kids dressed in time period costume for the meal and role playing. We took Chip camel riding, for a picnic in the desert, and to the limited "hangouts" before the family flew out for the summer.

With the family gone, I occupied the rest of my summer with *Jadawel Jazz*. I was so happy to be able to choreograph again and dance my heart out. I met with Molly three mornings a week and choreographed three afternoons a week. Weekly, we held a business meeting at my kitchen bar over a cup of cap and then Molly, my "right arm," would meet with our newly enlisted costume coordinator, Lisa. By summer's end, everything was organized and completely ready for the entire dance school year. Because of Molly's involvement and our summer preparations, *Jadawel Jazz* was primed for the unexpected.

Chapter 八
The Vision
September 1994 – December 1995

The humid autumn brought my Shamsiyah back with my pupils in tow, my son's first birthday, and an unexpected surprise. I was pregnant with my daughter. My heart clung to my Shamsiyah yet again. I truly needed Madawi's guidance as my family grew. Life was hectic but simultaneously simple then.

Madawi clapped the loudest when we cheered Mason's first birth and his blowing the single candle. She, the Colonel, and family joined us to celebrate our Thanksgiving feast, complete with turkey and all the trimmings, and our Christmas celebrations, acknowledging that "Jesus was a good profit and they could observe His birth." One of the things that always kept our friendship thriving was our mutual respect for the other's beliefs. We celebrated with each other and for each other, but this didn't mean we had to accept the other's beliefs in doing so—simply respect.

As the calendar turned to 1995, we learned that the company was moving us to a newly built *Jadawel* compound (DM22) designed to provide more amenities with larger more westernized homes and heightened security. The Colonel, part owner of our *Jadawel* compounds, beamed with pride when he took Madawi and I for a private tour before the compound was ready for occupancy.

In all sincerity, I think it tickled him to see me so excited when he showed me the new "aerobics room," which he said was added for me. Special flooring conducive to dance and two walls of full length mirrors adorned the new room. I was thrilled and continued to tell him so. Yet, I couldn't resist teasing him about it being labeled an "aerobics" room rather than a "dance" room. I then learned something new about my Kingdom world. Dancing is illegal, but exercise is not. Hence, the Colonel explained that it had to be labeled "aerobics" just in case the **Muthawen** gained access to the facility.

His pride continued as he showed us the new compound theater. Much like the theater on DM18, DM22's theater had a stage and plenty of floor space for compound dances or audience chairs. Unlike DM18, the new theater had curtains, wings and a true "backstage." The Colonel had spared no expense by having the theater walls covered in acoustic board and he had had a special balcony added specifically for a spotlight, or "lamp" as Madawi liked to call it. I was ecstatic and could already envision our upcoming *"Dancing with Disney"* recital in such a first class facility. Fortunately, the compound was ready for occupancy only two weeks before our performance and the dancers were able to enjoy the new stage.

The plans made and work completed the summer before saved me with *Jadawel Jazz* when the pace of life began to quicken in the spring of 1995. Unexpectedly, my healthy hobby had blossomed into a full-fledged, profitable business. It was Molly's idea to offer classes to the children of the American school, *Dhahran Academy*, which was the reason our enrollment topped 100 students in the 1994-95 dance school year and even more in the years to come. I had the creative talent, she had the business insight, and *Dhahran Academy* had over 1,000 western students yearning for a taste of home. From the beginning, Molly understood my commitment to Madawi and my royal pupils. She knew my dedication to the princess would take precedence, even over a lucrative dance business opportunity. Yet, she willingly stepped forward to manage the dance when I could not.

In late May and four weeks before my due date, our talented young ladies, and a few young boys, dazzled an audience of over 600 people with our recital, "*Dancing with Disney.*" It was a phenomenal production with each class performing three routines to favorite Disney tunes.

A very talented, Filipino worker on the compound, the same man that painted murals on the walls of my children's bedrooms, drew and painted a Disney castle for our backdrop and seven eight foot plywood Disney characters to position throughout the theater. I had a Mickey Costume and Disney Mylar balloons flown in from the states to enhance the event. A teenager on the compound played "Mickey" and danced through the entire evening, making the children in the audience believe Mickey Mouse had flown all the way from *Disneyworld* to perform for them. The Mylar balloons were designed to add another element to the recital, but we had one heck of a time acquiring helium. When we did find, it was incredibly expensive and "diluted." It could not even float a 9" balloon.

Sadly, most of them ended up on the floor and the others floated out the front door when guests assumed they were a free souvenir.

Just as it had been the May before and was as long as I ran the *Jadawel Jazz*, *Al-Hamdi's* graduation fell within a day of my recital. This particular year, the recital came first. Not only did Madawi attend, but the Colonel as well. Once again, the start time was delayed for our special guest. But this time, the audience enjoyed impromptu jokes from our master of ceremonies and door prize drawings while they waited.

I am sure the Colonel felt pride in his daughters and the compound theater that his company had provided the residents. However, after this particular show, Madawi pulled the older girls from dancing. And even though it was never discussed, I feel sure the Colonel did not like his developing daughters being in such revealing, American style dance costumes, on a stage in front of an audience of men and women.

The new balcony holding my spotlight enhanced the performance more than I could have imagined. Located approximately 15 feet above the audience and half way between the stage and the back of the theater, the spotlight was the finishing touch that made a terrific performance simply phenomenal. Madawi liked the effect of the "lamp" so much that she asked to use it at *Al-Hamdi* the following evening and, of course, I made it happen.

Being mom, tutor, dance teacher, and a "mom-to-be" again was my world during this time and it was enough for me. My life had purpose, but I had no idea my purpose in Kingdom would have more meaning than I could ever imagine and the opportunity was about to knock.

While working on some lesson plans one May afternoon, Madawi joined me at the table in the family salon. Exchanging kisses and hellos while she pulled out her chair, I pushed my papers aside and waited for the regular chit-chat to begin. Uncharacteristically, Madawi was quiet and I watched while she silently poured herself a cup of tea from the tea tray provided by an unseen nanny. After stirring in her sugar, she leaned back and looked to me.

Obviously, something had been on her mind for quite awhile because she jumped straight into the conversation, causing me to go to peak attention to catch the jest of what was happening.

"I don't want to give a mosque," she stated conclusively.

Completely confused, I replied, "Then don't," and chuckled.

She responded firmly, but caringly, "No. I want to give, Mrs. Teresa, and I am happy to give." She paused and blew her steaming tea. "It is my belief and I want to give back. Most give a mosque, but I don't want to give a mosque." Slowly she blew her tea again and sighed before a long, meaningful sip.

It is Madawi's nature to draw out the surprise and raise suspense, but this time, she was not playing. The suspense was real because she contemplated her every word, as if she were finding the strength.

Quietly returning her cup to the table, she began explaining that many of the moms from **Al-Hamdi** had asked her repeatedly over the years when she was going to open a school for them as well. They had been so pleased with what she had provided for their girls. However, she had been unable to do anything for the mothers because she did not have the right person to take on such a challenge. She topped off her tea and took another long, meaningful sip. She then looked straight into my eyes. "And that is where I believe you fit in, Mrs. Teresa."

Words were not necessary because she knew me well. My face spoke for me and my friend knew she had my attention. My thoughts raced as I tried to anticipate what was next. But even I could not have dreamed the words she uttered at that moment.

"It is important to me," she continued while she slowly sipped, looking off thoughtfully as she formulated her words. "It is important to me." She paused yet again and looked straight into my soul. "If I know that one lady is sitting in a classroom somewhere, learning something—I can sleep at night...*Insha Allah*."

Her sincerity and passion powered through her word as she paused and returned her empty cup to the tray. I could literally feel her passion at that moment in time as sure as I can feel the wind on a breezy spring afternoon. It was empowering and my involvement unavoidable.

"I want you to make the business," she stated as she seemed to morph into business mode from her previous tone. "Do the numbers," her long, slender hands flew around as ideas occurred to her. "Put the details on paper, and we will meet again next week."

I was astounded that Madawi, a royal princess, wanted me to start a business for her – that she wanted me to organize a center for women in Saudi Arabia of all places. Truly her father's daughter, Madawi was stepping over destiny's threshold. I thought of what it would mean to the women and how it would change life as they knew it. I thought of how it would change my life. Madawi dreamt of an educational learning center for ladies within the borders of her country, and I knew I had to make it a reality for her. A tremendous mission lay before me.

From the day we met, I always knew Madawi had an uncanny understanding of the value of knowledge and the benefits a good education would provide. She had been able to implement this understanding for the girls through ***Al-Hamdi***; yet, she had not taken the next logical step to offer educational opportunities for the women in her community—until now.

The following morning, I starred at the computer monitor in front of me. All of the ideas I had noted mentally with Madawi the day before deserted me and an overwhelming feeling flooded my senses. Where to start? This was an incredible endeavor to undertake. A blank slate was in front of me and what it would become was based on what I would develop. After roaming around the villa and the garden for inspiration, I decided a mission statement would be the best place to start. The wording of this guiding document was critical. It would have to express the purpose of the center, yet not offend members of the society. It had to express our academic goals and incorporate an aspect of socialization for the women.

During our initial meeting, Madawi had explained to me that women in her society did not know how to interact with women from different families. She explained that up until recently, women were always with members of their family, their tribe, and did not mingle with those that were from other families.

With that said, it is important to note that the term "family" carries different connotations in Saudi than it does in America. In America, the average "family" usually consists of the parent(s), children, and some extended family members. Yet in Saudi, a family, a tribe, can comprise several thousand people that interact on a regular basis. Madawi had explained that their society was changing and the women were not ready for this change because they were unsure how to interact with unrelated women. Hence, I determined at least fifty percent of the mission had to include basic socialization. The mission statement began to emerge:

> *A unique new place where women can learn skills that are not readily available in the area, meet other ladies, and generally enhance their well-being and*

self esteem through the exchange of skills and ideas.

As promised, I presented my proposal to Madawi the following Tuesday. We reviewed it line by line. The mission statement was the first order of business, as I wanted to be sure that my vision and hers were the same. They were—they always were. We were intuitive that way from the start.

Secondly, I had to run my idea of a name past her. Because the basic goal of the center was to offer ladies the opportunity to learn I suggested: *The Learning Center: A Ladies Place for Personal Development.* In the years to come, the acronym TLC became well known throughout the Kingdom, which always seemed clever to me because of the Western connotation to the same letters, *Tender Loving Care.*

Initially, the center would be a place for women to gain knowledge and skill in the fields of English and French Languages, basic Human Communication, Computers, and various workshops for personal development such as CPR and introduction to business. To locate instructors for these classes, I looked to the local market for qualified Western ladies already in the Kingdom with their husbands.

Interestingly, the instructors I eventually discovered in the quagmire of coffee mornings, craft bazaars, and via word of mouth were women who I found to be much like myself before I was blessed with my Saudi family. They were highly educated women who had left a career in their home country to join their husbands and were unknowingly looking for a purpose for their time in Kingdom as well.

Operating on four terms per year, the center was organized to offer four-week workshops and eight-week courses, depending on the topic and amount of information presented. Each class would be held two days a week for two hours per day, allowing time for tea and socialization at the one-hour break between each class.

After approving the mission statement, the name, and reviewing the proposed logistics of the center's operation, I questioned Madawi as to a physical location.

"Where will it be, Madawi?" I inquired. "I didn't include this in the proposal because I don't know how it works here. Do we rent? Do we buy?" I paused momentarily. "It will have to be a place with enough space to offer classes simultaneously, yet have a large space for the women to gather and visit."

She hesitated thoughtfully at my questions and then reached over the table to touch my hand. "Don't worry about the place," she smiled reassuringly. "Awad will help us." I would have never guessed that she meant we would use one of the facilities governed by the airbase, a facility that would cost us nothing to use and offer us protection and seclusion. With the structure and cost analysis of start-up determined, the issue of funding arose. Madawi explained that she had the capital; however, she preferred to obtain funding from a local bank. She made it clear that she would provide the start up capital via the loan—the means by which to get TLC started—but the center would have to operate as a non-profit organization, responsible for generating its own operating capital, and repayment of the loan. Naturally, she did not want financial gain from the center.

"I really like it, Mrs. Teresa," she said as she closed her copy of the proposal. "Sila will call you tomorrow with the name of a bank and a man to see about the money," she continued. "Have David go with you and present this to the man," she instructed referring to the proposal.

It seemed as if a blink of time passed between our initial meetings about *The Learning Center* and the birth of my daughter, named after my princess, on the 2nd of June in 1995. Michelle Madawi's birth coupled with a royal wedding, **Al-Hamdi's** end of the year exams and graduation party, our move to MD22, the new compound surrounded by the sea, *Jadawel Jazz's* recital, and other daily life drew our attention from the center's development for several weeks. But given little Michelle Madawi joined us the natural way and I didn't have to contend with a c-section recovery, I was back on my feet in no time and anxious to begin.

Before I knew it, Madawi and I were meeting regularly again on Tuesday evenings and the center was our focus. As planned, Madawi and I met to view three locations that the Colonel had offered for possible use. As we went through the first one, we discussed the pros and cons. It was a single-family villa formerly used by David's company to house the in country program director and his family. It had nine rooms on two floors, a large, elegant living area that would work nicely for socializing, a large kitchen for refreshment preparation and a private swimming pool. All of these were good points, yet it had a major disadvantage. As Madawi quickly noted, it was in a local neighborhood and only protected by its own privacy wall. Too many people would question the number of people and cars coming and going every two hours. The location of the villa would draw attention to us, leaving us open for ridicule and possible closure. Because of security, we ruled it out immediately.

The second location was also not located on a protected compound, but it was not in a neighborhood either. Rather, it was on a major street in open sight. Currently it was empty, but it had previously been the medical clinic for our company. The few neighbors that were around the facility were accustomed to people coming and going. Hence, it was a possibility, so we continued to investigate. It was four apartments within the same structure, divided inside by a central stairway housing two apartments on each floor. It had plenty of rooms for classes, plenty of bathrooms, and nice areas for our proposed teatimes. Still, we did not feel it was the perfect choice, until later – just over a year later.

The third potential location seemed perfect almost from the start. It was located on the compound from which my company just moved, surrounded by a fifteen-foot privacy wall with a gated entrance. In addition, the gate had a security bar that could be lowered to block entry and a huge iron gate to close if more security was required. Inside, we were offered two of the villas near the gate, leaving the other seventy-three villas vacant. Because we were on a compound, we would eventually have, with permission, access to all the facilities the compound had to offer: swimming pool, dinning hall, theater, tennis courts and the like. It took six months for us to realize the potential of these additional amenities. Our focus in the beginning was strictly ladies' classroom learning, but in time that focus expanded to include children, sports, and numerous other areas of learning. With the safety concern solved, the choice of location became a mute point.

We took possession of two adjacent villas on DM 18 a week later. We utilized the villa closest to the guard gate as the administrative villa, with the downstairs accommodating reception and plenty of room for socializing. My office and two classrooms were housed upstairs in the same villa. The second villa was used strictly for classes, with the first floor completely consumed by the computer lab and three classrooms upstairs that were suitable for language classes.

In spite of the fact that it had been over two months since Mr. Abdul was instructed to set up our meeting with the banker, we still had not met the man. Nothing, and I mean nothing, ever happens quickly in Kingdom, that is a given. But Mr. Abdul had the habit of making even the slowest look speedy. Finally, on July 26, 1995, David and I presented the business plan to Madawi's banker. After our presentation, the banker stated that he felt the idea was good and that he would speak with Mr. Abdul as our funding was made available.

We were granted a loan of four hundred and fifty thousand Saudi *riyal* ($120,000) to start the center. Unlike stateside banks, however, we would be required to pay the loan back in three large payments of one hundred and fifty thousand *riyal* each within a nine-month period. The first payment was due only one month after the center was scheduled to open. Hearing these terms made my heart sink. How in the world could we outfit the center, cover operating costs, and make this kind of payment in only one month? We were starting a new, illegal business in the eyes of the Saudi government, which meant advertising would only be by word of mouth, and we had to generate 150,000 *riyal* ($40,000) in our initial month of operation. I knew that this would be problematic, but I took the step as Madawi instructed.

Although illegal with respect to governmental agencies, there was a point to which the things we were doing in the center would be tolerated. After all, education of females is allowed, and having a princess behind the endeavor afforded us a further point of tolerance than would be allowed for a non-royal. From the beginning, I knew that if we ever crossed that unspecified line of tolerance, I would be the one to endure the consequences. After that, however, I could only rely on Madawi to protect me. We had an understanding, although never specifically stated, that

I would be the face of the center, and Madawi would remain backstage to free me if necessary.

Albeit I knew that what we were doing was an underground operation, counter culture so to speak, but I was willing to take the chance because I wholeheartedly believed in the center. I knew what we were doing was fundamentally correct. Consequently, I naively fluttered through our weakest time, the first years of the center, without fully understanding the ramifications of my actions. Many times now, I stop to consider if Madawi did. Did she know or stop to think of the jeopardy in which she was placing the two of us?

Once the capital was received and the kids were out for summer vacation, Madawi left the Kingdom, leaving me behind to have her dream ready by the time she would return in October.

With her notice to proceed, the physical, exhausting work began. It was non-stop days of shopping and nights of assembly and organization. I began selecting, refurbishing, purchasing, and decorating. I returned to the coffee mornings and wives group meetings in search of instructors and interviewed between shopping runs. At night, when I wasn't at the center, I would hibernate in the computer room and develop policy sheets, registration forms, and all other paperwork required for the center. Because the majority of textbooks that the instructors wanted to use could not be found in the Kingdom, my nightly computer time eventually included typing and binding them.

Although four hundred thousand *riyal* sounded like a lot of seed money, in actuality it was not. By the time we bought the computers and appropriate computer desks, televisions for the computer room, five whiteboards, twenty classroom desks, and a few artificial plants, much of our money was exhausted. Hence, we had to be resourceful. David was able to obtain unwanted desks from the base for my office and the reception area. Fortunately, we were able to utilize the sofas, chairs, and coffee tables that came with each villa, which worked nicely for our social area. With funds running low for additional desks, it worked nicely to use the two dinning room tables provided with the villas as classroom seating for our discussion style classes.

Over the years that the center was under my direction, instructors and staff came and went for one reason or another. However, there were a few that became the pillars of TLC and their tenure within our walls reflected their commitment to the Saudi women. Of all of the teachers that crossed our threshold, only one started with me during the summer of 1995 and continued non-stop until she kissed me goodbye almost seven years later.

Mona, an intelligent, caring Lebanese lady, came on board as TLC's first instructor, hired to teach French language. Fate brought us together via our husbands, but commitment to the shared vision kept us together. Yacoub, Mona's husband, worked at the airbase with David and expressed that his wife would be interested when he learned about the new center. In order for us to meet, we invited Yacoub and Mona for dinner one evening. From the moment we met, I knew Mona possessed all of the intangible attributes that I required for an instructor in our center in addition to the essential education needed.

Quite frankly, I initially thought all Western or non-Saudi women in the Kingdom held the same attitudes I held with regard to Saudi women. Yet as I interviewed numerous women from various countries, I quickly realized this was not the case. Typically, potential instructors fell into one of two categories. On the one hand, there were the women that did hold my values. They were respectful of the Saudis and genuinely interested in helping advance the plight of the women. The other, however, outwardly claimed these values, but in actuality held the opposite.

From experience, I soon learned how to distinguish between the two. I would listen intently during the interview and guide the conversation to see what their heart truly felt. I was amazed at times to hear a potential instructor express how much she wanted to help and be apart of this ground breaking endeavor, but then later in the interview make a "Saudi ninja" joke, which was rampant among some westerners, or reference the Saudi women in a negative way. I would literally seethe when I would hear someone jest about "Saudi ninjas," referencing their wearing of the traditional *abaya* and veil. How utterly disrespectful this was. Obviously, I most certainly did not want these women in our center no matter how formally educated they were.

Originally expecting my Mom to help me with reception and teach English language, I was thrown off course emotionally and professionally with her unexpected heart attack, surgery, and subsequent recovery. Fortunately, she and my Dad were in the states when the heart attack happened and she was able to get the best care available. However, Madawi, the ladies, and I would simply have to make do until her return.

Luckily, one of her dear friends on the compound stepped up to help. Margaret, a delightful older Scottish lady, joined our team. She held the values I wanted plus she had experience that only my Mom could rival. When Margaret joined TLC, she had already been in various regions of the Kingdom for over eleven years. She had the intangible I sought – a true understanding and respect of their culture coupled with an intense desire to help the women succeed. I was so thankful to have her, particularly when the religious police came knocking at our door.

Blessed yet again, I found a lady on our compound that I had known for years, but didn't know she held a master's degree in English until I was fretting over coffee at the recreation center one morning. Becky also held respect for the Saudis and was eager to help, yet she was shy, which would lead to a short tenure with TLC. The idea of learning in this way was completely foreign to the adult ladies in the region. Hence my teachers not only need the intangible values and a good education, but they needed energy and enthusiasm as well in order to encourage the Saudi ladies. They needed to be extroverted and optimistic so that they could jump in and show the way, not simply teach it.

Although English language was vital to the students, our computer class offerings are what truly placed TLC on the cutting edge. The majority of our startup funds had been spent to establish a state-of-the-art computer lab because we felt this knowledge was essential to pave the path for the future. Because the field was relatively new, even in the states, finding an instructor became an ongoing quest for me. Initially, I hired a lady named Barbara. She was well qualified and held the necessary cultural values, yet she was a pessimist and unable to bend, which was an incredibly important character trait when working in an illegal school in the heart of the Muslim world. The word "no" simply could not exist in our vocabularies, rather a "what next" attitude had to prevail. In such, Barbara only taught for two terms.

In addition to what could be deemed "basic" coursework such as English, French, and computers, I wanted to offer additional new, exciting, and foreign information as well. I was fortunate to find a lady, Sharon, who was certified in CPR and more than willing to pass this knowledge along. As luck would have it, our compound clinic owned "Annie," a CPR training doll and graciously let the center borrow her.

Surprising to most Westerners, Saudi women have money in their own right, independent of their husbands'. In such, I wanted to offer a workshop that would help them put their money to work for them.

ॐCreating Shamsiyah ॐ

Lauren, a good friend from my compound, had all the attributes I sought in an instructor and immense marketing experience. At first she was a bit apprehensive because she had never taught before. Yet with encouragement and teaching guidance from me, she developed a workshop entitled, "Starting Your Own Business." It was this workshop that changed the course of many of our initial "pace-setting" students' lives, and partially responsible for the fact of over 4,000 Saudi women owning businesses when I left the Kingdom in 2001.

The shakiest branch we stepped upon our first term was a workshop addressing basic human communication. With my masters in the field, I taught concepts that were completely foreign to the Saudi ladies. Realizing this, Madawi worked with me to fill my first class with forward thinking, pace-setting women that would be receptive to such new ideas. My first interactive workshop looked at the fundamentals of communication such as the essentials of listening and non-verbal communication. The ladies were enthralled with these ideas and absorbed them with unexplainable vigor. As time passed, this vein of instruction expanded to include culturally radical concepts such as conflict resolution, negotiation, and even assertive behavior. Directed by destiny, Madawi provided the umbrella – the shamsiyah – for the women of the Eastern Province and placed it in the desert sand. It was then up to the women to take advantage of the learning shelter she envisioned and I implemented. As ready as we could be, the doors to *The Learning Center* opened on November 2, 1995.

The ladies loved the center from the beginning. In spite of our scavenging for furniture, it all fell together and looked elegant. It was a warm, inviting place were ladies liked to be even if they were not in a class. As the ladies entered the administrative villa, they were greeted by soft background music, a reception area to the right of the marble foyer with white upholstered sofas, and chairs positioned throughout in a way to encourage open conversation and mingling during teatime.

On opening day the center was a buzz with women selecting courses and seeing who was there. Although I am sure some of the women came to learn, I feel that there was a large portion that came just to say they were rubbing elbows, so to speak, with royalty. Real excitement filled the air.

In the middle of all of the commotion of registration, Madawi pulled me to the side.

"I have a special project, Mrs. Teresa," she began with that look of hers that always indicated planning and possibly mischievousness. "Her name is El-Bandari, and we have to encourage her," she whispered, smiling so no one else would know the topic of our conversation. "She needs the center to fill her mind. She has had such misery. Many bad things have happened in her life," Madawi added with true concern for her friend as she shook her head in grief and disbelief. "She will be here today, and I will point her out to you."

"I'll be on the lookout," I answered. "Don't worry. We'll get her involved."

Before long the nod came from Madawi as she stood near the doorway. I moved from the social area and made my way to the reception desk targeting the woman dressed completely in black. Stepping up at the opportune time, Madawi introduced me to El-Bandari who was completely veiled, wearing black gloves and socks as many of the more fundamental women do. As Madawi spoke, El-Bandari raised the black fabric from her face, revealing a tired looking woman with no make-up and no joy. Madawi patiently presented the class offerings to her, and she eventually agreed to take the *"Starting Your Own Business"* course that debuted at the center the following day.

The dawn of the next day saw the memorable beginning of classes at *The Learning Center*. We had 29 ladies enrolled, five teachers, a hostess, and me, the director. To fulfill the socialization aspect of our mission, all classes would break for fifteen minutes so the ladies could visit and have refreshments in the main villa. I made it a point to appear at every tea-time, mainly to make the ladies feel welcome, listen, and learn. On that special day, I greeted every student personally to welcome them to the center and inquire as to how they liked things so far. As expected, I saw El-Bandari. She was despondently dressed with no make-up and had obviously made no effort with her hair. I spent additional time with her to make sure she felt an extra sense of belonging and encouragement.

With classes just beginning and me learning as I went, many details had to be tended to in those first few days. Feeling somewhat nervous with this ambitious, illegal endeavor, Madawi felt it was important that we maintain a list of each student's car, including make, model, color, and license plate number so the men manning the security gate could make sure that we knew who was in the center and for what purpose. Hence, I developed a car registration form and proceeded to speak with each student to gain the necessary information for our files.

While I made my way around the room during break time, the ladies soon knew my purpose, even those that did not speak English very well. It became somewhat of a bragging opportunity, when each woman would tell me in a rather loud voice the make and color of her vehicle. I still chuckle to this day with one particular student's response.

"I need to know what kind of car you have," I questioned, speaking slower than normal in the hope that I would be better understood. Johara, who was a student in our beginner's English class, proudly began her response.

"I have Mer—ce—dees," she stated, wanting so badly to respond correctly.

"Okay," I replied as I jotted down the make of the car. "And the color?"

"Maroony," she replied.

"Maroony?" I questioned, not really understanding what she said.

"Blue," she then stated as if clarifying.

"Oh, a blue Mercedes," I replied encouragingly.

"Yes," she responded smiling, "Maroony, blue."

"I'm sorry," I said. "I think I've got it now. You have a maroon Mercedes."

She looked at me, obviously becoming as confused as I.

"Gold and black," she replied.

"Okay," I answered yet again somewhat discouraged by my lack of understanding and fearing that I was making her feel uncomfortable. "You have a gold and black Mercedes," I said still smiling. But she shook her head no.

Overhearing the conversation and knowing that we were both becoming frustrated, Nadia, who was much more fluent in English, intervened to help.
She stepped in between us and turned to Johara to clarify in Arabic as I waited patiently and relieved. Then Nadia turned to me.

"She has a maroon, a blue, a gold," she began looking to Johara as she spoke and counted the colors on her fingers, "and a black Mercedes," she concluded as Johara nodded in agreement to Nadia's English response.

"Oh," I stammered almost stunned, "so she has a car of many colors?"

"No," Nadia laughed, "she has many cars of different colors."

Smiling wide, and completely embarrassed, I answered as I wrote down the various colors. "Oh!" drug out of my southern tongue. "I get it now!" And we all smiled and nodded to pass the awkward moment. How silly of me not to know that everyone has many cars of different colors! At that moment, it became crystal clear that I had a lot to learn about the ladies I was now associated with. They had money and lots of it. In spite of this, they did not have something I took for granted. As women, they did not have freedom, and they did not easily have the opportunity to gain knowledge, an oversight that the center was determined to rectify.

Just in time for the second half of our first term, Mom returned to Kingdom and was eager to jump in with both feet. In spite of still recovering from her surgery, she is simply not the type to sit idly by and watch. Intuitive to the Saudi ladies on a level that most can not comprehend, Ruth wanted to offer a special workshop to them. She entitled it, "Frugal Elegance," and its premise was to offer ideas about how to decorate on a budget and redecorate a room in one of the student's homes as a class project. Nadia graciously offered her family salon for the assignment.

Now obviously, decorating on a budget was not an issue for any of the TLC students. They had money. Yet they needed something deeper and Ruth recognized and fulfilled this need. Within a week, the workshop was all the rage and essentially turned into a bi-weekly shopping trip. The class would gather at TLC before heading out in the center's van for their next shopping adventure, which always concluded with lunch or tea at a local establishment. Even though our classes were scheduled to run for two hours each, the Frugal Elegance class always consumed the entire

ॐCreating Shamsiyahॐ

afternoon. She showed them places they had never seen although they had grown up in the area. Ruth took them out into the desert to shop at a relatively unknown nursery, to fabric shops, and the mall to name a few. The entire center was curious each Tuesday and Thursday to learn where the gals were heading next.

Although many comical events transpired from this workshop, one in particular stands out in my mind and probably always will. Of the nine ladies in the class, one, Nadia, was a princess but neither Mom nor I knew she was at this point. Treating each lady as she would me or a close friend, Ruth had no trouble telling them to arrive in blue jeans and be ready to work.

On this particular afternoon, Ruth had planned for them to visit Nadia's house to brainstorm for ideas and determine what they would need to achieve their decorating design. When they arrived, it was obvious that the furniture needed moving because the designer Nadia had probably paid a fortune had not placed the furniture in the best places to compliment the space. After a discussion of flow and room composition, Ruth reached to move the sofa, yet no one else budged. Looking up, she saw Nadia standing there watching her. Ruth then, in her special but direct way, told her to grab the other end of the sofa. Astonished Nadia replied, "but, but I'm a princess, too, Mama Ruth." Without breaking stride, Ruth replied, "Congratulations, now grab that end chick." The other eight ladies probably almost fell over with Mom's response to a royal, yet Nadia grabbed the sofa and began to push without daring to question Mama Ruth!

The bonds of friendship developed in that particular workshop continued long after the four-week class was over. For years to come, many of the ladies continued to get together weekly for an afternoon outing to shop and snack.

Unfortunately, the center could not give the ladies official certification or diplomas for the classes they completed, in spite of the fact that all of our instructors were degreed in their fields and many held masters' degrees. We were only able to offer them our certificates to indicate that they had in fact taken the class and been exposed to the material. This was a shame because as the years passed our offerings were to the same standards of many stateside colleges.

Supposedly our existence was a secret, and I soon learned just how secret. Transportation is an understood necessity that is always provided for women because they can't drive themselves. For this reason, Madawi purchased a minivan for the center's use, complete with curtains to hide our femininity. One morning, we needed supplies but Saleem was busy with the van running teachers to and from work. Hence, I had to take a taxi to run the center's errands. Upon my return to the compound, I could not help but chuckle at the Indian taxi driver as he unloaded my packages.

"This is a new place," he began, smiling and swaying his head back and forth as Indian nationals do. "A place for ladies," he remarked proudly showing that he was in the know.

"I know," I replied, not daring to tell him that I was the director. Then holding my finger to my mouth, I said, "Shhh, it's a secret."

"Yes, Madame, yes," he answered quickly and smiled broadly. "It is a secret!"

In most countries around the world, the level of international terrorism in 1995 continued a downward trend similar to recent years. However, this was not the case within the Kingdom as terrorism drew closer to our door. On November 13, 1995 a car bomb exploded outside the **Riyadh** headquarters of the Office of the Program Manager/Saudi Arabian National Guard (OPM/SANG). The safety of our existence in Kingdom suddenly came into question. Eventually, in the not so distant future, this event would directly affect *The Learning Center*. OPM/SANG, the central **Riyadh** office building housing U.S. military and civilian personnel, was bombed. Five of the six people killed were Americans, and 30 Americans were among the more than 60 injured. The explosion was deemed to "demand the withdrawal of all foreigners and foreign forces from Saudi territory," as reported by the U. S. Embassy in **Riyadh** on the fourteenth of November (Appendix). The report further stated that future "isolated bombings are possible," with attacks most likely at housing installations…foreign military or security personnel." Basically, our company fell into the listing and our security began to heighten—but only a little. None of us ever considered that any group, not even radical Islamic extremists, would attack women and children. Casually concerned, we did take a few measures with regard to the center: we closed the curtains lining the windows of our minivan and closed the huge iron-gate at the entrance when it was convenient.

  Our first term proceeded beautifully. All of the students enjoyed their classes, coming to the center just to visit, and many brought a friend along as well to see the new place. Each day I visited with them and learned their interests so that I would know what classes to offer in the future. I was fortunate to see El-Bandari every Tuesday and Thursday. At first, she continued to look as she had the first time I saw her, somewhat unhappy and plain looking in dull colored dresses. Then after about four weeks, I was amazed one Tuesday when I was helping set out the coffee and tea for the morning break time. In front of me was a lovely lady. Her hair was curled, she had nicely done make-up, she wore a bright, stylish dress, and she was sporting a proud smile.

  "El-Bandari?" I questioned in amazement at her transformation. I stopped dead in my tracks still holding the teapot.

  "It's me," she replied, beaming as she held her arms out for approval.

  "You look fantastic!" I exclaimed.

  "And it's all thanks to you, Mrs. Teresa," she remarked. "Can we sit for a moment?" she questioned. "I want to tell you something."

"Sure," I replied anxiously as I put down the teapot and moved into the sitting area.

"I want to share a story with you," she began, as we got comfortable next to each other on the sofa. "I want to thank you," she said earnestly as she reached for my hands. "Amity Madawi, you, and *The Learning Center* saved my life," she stated as tears of joy began to fill her eyes. I sat and listened, deeply touched, as she explained.

At the first of the year, she had lost her brother in a horrible car accident. Then in the summer her father had died either from old age or a broken heart. I could not distinguish which from her broken English. As if this was not enough, El-Bandari's daughter was in a comma and the doctors had no idea if she would regain consciousness or not.

"Oh, El-Bandari," I exclaimed as my heart deeply ached for this lady, "I am so sorry."

"Thank you," she answered and continued. "I was truly; truly drowning in my home…I was dying." El-Bandari paused to wipe a tear. "But, I then found you, **bisme Allah**. Because of Madawi, I came even though I didn't want to at first," she explained. "And you made me feel welcome. You made me feel like I was alive again. It is because of you and the center that I am alive again!" She exclaimed, "**Shukran**, Mrs. Teresa, **shukran** from the bottom of my heart!"

It took everything I had not to break down and cry with her. I was so touched by this story and so overwhelmed with a sense of purpose. I knew then that the center was good, really good, no matter how hard I had to work to make it so. Even if I never heard another story like El-Bandari's, it would have been enough to know that we had helped one lady. But I did hear more stories. I heard many stories over the course of the next six years. I heard so many stories of women and their plight and how the center was instrumental in bringing positive changes to their lives. It was truly inspiring.

As our first term drew to a close, I knew we had to do something extra special for the ladies that had taken the initiative to support our new venture. I needed to think of a way to commend them on their achievements and to entice new students: we would have an end of the term party.

We were able to use the dining facility of the compound to hold an elegant dinner party, an elegant dinner party that I had to pull off on an extremely tight budget. To offset cost, we sold tickets to cover the price of the catered dinner and we encouraged each student to bring a friend as well. Decorating, however, had to be squeezed from the center's budget above and beyond our loan payment. However, I pulled if off in spite of the financial concerns. Remembering the idiom, KISS, "keep it simple stupid," I decorated with burgundy candles of different heights, greenery from the floral shop and burgundy ribbon. Simple and inexpensive but beautiful, and the ladies had a ball.

During the course of the evening, we honored the ladies who had completed their coursework and focused on the center's achievements as a whole. All night, TLC was the rave. Current students discussed what classes they would take next, and the visitors talked about what classes they hoped to take. From the evening's feedback, I knew we would have a tremendous winter term to follow. Seventy-two ladies dressed in their best attire attended our end of the term party, and it was the social event of the month. Again, I knew many ladies simply wanted to rub elbows with royalty. But, I did not care about the motive for their attendance. I was just happy they were there, laughing, socializing, and broadening their horizons.

Before *The Learning Center*, most Saudi women filled their days with sleeping, eating, and beauty enhancement. Their nights were occupied with parties and visiting friends. The idea of attending classes and learning was almost non-existent; although I am sure some had dreamed of the opportunity like Madawi. Consequently, to convince these ladies to be more productive with their time and to motivate them to enhance their minds was not an easy task. This is where the party idea came into play. Through the parties the center sponsored, we brought the ladies to our door, and the exposure to the possibilities of learning made them stay.

In spite of the success TLC was riding, Madawi faced a personal challenge that reaches the pinnacle for a married woman—the colonel had demanded a divorce, checking the worst choice he could check on the divorce decree—no reconciliation. I knew she had been down for quite a while, yet she had never uttered a word that things had deteriorated so between them. The news came as a shock to me and the details of which I will not share. It is enough to say that it happened. But from this cloud came a silver lining. Madawi stepped up to the plate as a woman. She reached deep within herself and began her journey to empowerment. She began to take control of her own destiny.

Chapter 9
Redefining
January-June 1996

After our first party, Madawi, the staff, and I were elated with what had been accomplished in our first term. We were pleased with its initial success and confident for the future. Consequently, we were completely unprepared for what took place.

The following Saturday, the entire staff showed up for work to greet and register the new students we were expecting for our winter term. We waited and waited, but the door rarely opened. When registration was complete, we only had twelve ladies enrolled. We could not imagine what had happened. Where was everyone? At the party, they had all said that they wanted to enroll, but where were they? I became very concerned, to the point of physical sickness, as I knew we had that huge loan payment looming. What could I do? How could I keep Madawi's dream alive? Days passed and I could not help but worry.

The center was like a newborn, barely hanging onto life. Unlike starting a business in the U.S., everything I did posed challenges. Things I never dreamed of became issues when starting an underground educational center in the Kingdom of Saudi Arabia. Simply buying five identical televisions brought questions as to my intent for their use. We were not sanctioned by the Kingdom's Department of Education because not all of our teachers were Muslim and we did not want our curriculum "edited" by the government. We were "gathering," which is illegal to do if more than six people are not members of the same family or tribe and the list goes on. Yet, the ladies had come before so why not now?

A week passed and I heard nothing from Madawi, yet I entered the center as I did everyday in the hopes that more students would show. The center was quiet and things were starting to look really bad. Our first payment to the bank was due in less than three weeks. As I sat at my desk, trying to accomplish something, I finally broke, put my head in my hands and let out a deep sigh of frustration. Suddenly, the telephone rang. It was Layla.

"Ello, Mrs. Teresa," she began, "it is Layla."

"Oh hello Layla," I responded. "*Kayf Haalik?*"

"*Tieeb, al Hamdulila. Kayf Haalik?*" she questioned.

"Well honestly, Layla," I started, "I'm not so good."

"Why, Mrs. Teresa?"

"No one is coming to the center," I declared, verbalizing my frustration. "We only have twelve ladies enrolled!"

"That is why I call you," she remarked in broken English. "I want to ask you something for the children," she explained. "The children are home for the winter break and this is why no ladies. Can you do something for the children to keep them busy, huh?"

My mind was clicking as she spoke. That was it!

"Of course we can!" I exclaimed with excitement and relief. "I'll call you as soon as we have the program organized."

"Very good, Mrs. Teresa," she remarked, seemingly happy with my agreement to her suggestion. "*Insha Allah*, they will come, *Insha Allah*."

"*Shukran*, Layla," I answered. "Oh thank you for the idea! This is the answer to our problem."

"*Tieeb*, Mrs. Teresa, *ma'assalaamah*," she replied.

"*Shukran* Layla, *ma'assalaamah*." I answered and I heard a click as she hung up the phone. A new phase to the center began as Layla, whom I referred to as my *Saudi guardian angel* from that day forward, had given me the answer to our survival. From then on, *The Learning Center* was structured to offer classes for ladies in the fall and spring terms and for their children in the winter and summer.

I immediately called an emergency meeting of the staff for the next morning to determine what we could offer the children. We also had to discuss whom we could recruit to teach children from the compound. Our meeting was very productive and our first children's program, *Winter Jamboree '96*, was born. For a one-month period while the children were on school break, we offered English, arts and crafts, music, computers, cooking, painting, and exercise. Our first *Winter Jamboree* had over one hundred and fifty children enroll, and my prayers were answered thanks to my Saudi guardian angel.

Not only did the first of the year bring challenges to TLC, it brought serious personal challenges for Madawi, and she entrusted me to keep her dream alive while she weathered the inevitable – the mourning of her marriage. She was self-absorbed and only stopped by my office occasionally to touch base between her classes. Coping with her recent divorce and intense heartache, she was soul searching. She had to determine where life would take her. This emotionally wrenching time in her life marked a turning point for Madawi. She was intensely focused on education, personal growth and empowerment. Basically, she was redefining Madawi and faced two options: roll over and die or rise to the challenge. Madawi chose to rise.

Two weeks into the program, all was going well with our *Winter Jamboree* when a knock came at the door. Shortly after the children had changed classes that morning, MaryAnn heard a knock on the villa door, which was highly unusual as most just entered without knocking. Not sure at first if she had actually heard a knock, she turned down the music and listened intently. Yes, it was definitely a knock. Curious, she went to the door and opened it slightly.

There were two Arab men standing there with long red-tinted beards sporting Western suits that did not fit them properly. Knowing our illegal status and extremely familiar with Saudi customs, MaryAnn stepped outside the door and handled the situation beautifully.

"May I help you?" she innocently queried in her Scottish accent, knowing full well that something fishy was going on.

"We want to come inside," one of the men replied in broken English, as he fidgeted in the suit that did not fit him.

"Oh," MaryAnn began in a charming way as her mind raced with what to do. "I would love to invite you in from the heat," she remarked theatrically, "but I can not."

"Is this a school?" the man asked.

"No," MaryAnn answered, thinking quickly and smiling the entire time.

"We have children inside," she paused, "Western children." This was not a lie as we did have a few American kids in attendance. "For fun activities," she stammered a bit. Without allowing the men to respond, she continued, "Would you like to speak to our director?"

"Yes."

"I will go and get her. But you must remain outside because there are women and children here," she said as she turned to slide back through the door. Wanting to kill them with kindness, she hospitably asked before she disappeared, "May I get you some lemonade to quench your thirst from the heat?"

"No," they answered coldly while simultaneously wiggling in their inappropriate attire. With that, MaryAnn returned inside and locked the door before coming to me. She came running, literally, into my office, breathless from her trip up the stairs.

Adrenaline pumping from her encounter with the men at our door, she explained what had happened.

I took a deep breath as I stood, adjusted my dress, and assessed the situation. We were not doing anything visibly wrong. All of the ladies there were dressed appropriately, and I would just stall them until I could somehow get help. From the day the center opened, I always knew that I, personally, was on the line. I always knew that if a problem arose, it would be me that would go to jail. Hopefully, Madawi could get me out. Above all, I would not let them in or allow them to harass any of my teachers or staff. Taking yet another deep breath for confidence, I prepared myself mentally as I headed down the stairs to the waiting confrontation.

Pausing with my hand on the lock, making a final attempt to gain inner strength, I released the dead bolt and opened the door. In dismay, I found no one was there. I looked at MaryAnn and she at me. Extremely concerned, we stepped out further to check the sides of the villa. Still no one was in sight. Confused, I ran over to the gate to speak with the guards. They had seen no one, but only the security bar, not the sliding iron-gate, had been used that morning. Even under repeated questioning, the guards swore they had seen no one enter or leave our wall of security. We surmised that they must have snuck under the bar avoiding the attention of the guards. With the guards help, we searched the entire compound. The two suspicious Arab men with beards and suits were nowhere to be found. They had disappeared without a trace. Following the search, I called Madawi, and I explained what had happened.

"Have them close the big gates, *yellah*," she answered. "I'll be there soon." The phone went dead.

As I waited for her, I paced my office wondering exactly what had happened. Who were these men? What did they want? Were they *Muthawen*? Madawi would hopefully have the answers.

Although I had had very little contact with *Muthawen* at this point, I was aware of them and their position in society. The Kingdom has an official committee called the "Committee for Public Morality" – the *Muthawen* as they are known in Arabic. It is the mission of the people associated with this committee to make sure people in the community adhere to the principles of Islam and they dictate the standards of social conduct in Saudi Arabia. The only problem I saw was that they insisted on adherence to their interpretation of Islam rather than the interpretation of mainstream Muslims. At this point, I assumed all *Muthawen* were men and it was several years before I knew differently.

Arriving quicker than usual, Madawi never gets in a hurry, her BMW pulled in front of the center. By this time, I was downstairs, anxiously waiting for her. Once inside, she removed her *abaya*, and we settled down with MaryAnn in the social salon to recount the events. Madawi listened carefully to every detail without saying a word. When MaryAnn finished, Madawi interjected.

"*Hiyah,*" she stated firmly. "It was the *hiyah,*" speaking as if she were trying to convince herself.

"*Hiyah?*" I questioned. "What is the *hiyah?*"

"They are part of the *muthawen,*" she explained. "The ones that work with Westerners."

"How do you know?" I questioned further.

"The way they acted…their beards," she continued seeming somewhat anxious. "They probably wore the suits to trick you into letting them in," she said as she glanced to MaryAnn. "You were right not to." She paused yet again in what seemed like deep thought. "They will come again. Next time…they will come officially."

"What do you mean?" I questioned becoming concerned for my own safety.

"Next time, they will bring the police," she remarked and turned to get her cell phone from her bag. Within an hour, she had extra guards on our gate and instructed them to always use the big, iron gate.

"Do not," she repeated adamantly to the guards, "let anyone in unless you know they are a student." Then she turned to me.

"And Mrs. Teresa," she began, "you make identification cards for all the students, immediately." Seeing the look on my face, she added, "But do not scare them, huh?" And she smiled reassuringly.

"I will have them ready by tomorrow," I answered.

"*Insha Allah,*" she replied as she entered the BMW to leave. "*Ma'assalaamah,*" she called from the back seat.

"*Ma'assalaamah*," I answered. "I'll call you tomorrow."

"*Insha Allah*," she returned, "*yellah*." Abdullah closed the car door.

That afternoon, I held another emergency meeting with my staff. This time, however, I was not meeting to motivate them; rather, I was meeting to warn them. I shared the events of the morning and stressed the severity of the situation. I explained the steps that Madawi and I were taking for security and reassured them that everything would be okay if we all followed a few simple guidelines. Giving them the plan of action, I reinforced the need to wear appropriate clothing to work and even encouraged that they wear their *abayas* in the van on the way to the center. I insisted they go on about their business; yet, if any unusual telephone calls came in or if any suspicious visitors arrived, they should not confront the situation but refer it to me. Madawi called at least once a day, and usually more, to see if "they had come back officially." My answer was always the same. No.

"They will not come," Madawi stated firmly in my office over two weeks later. "If they have not come back by now, they won't. They must have been satisfied by what MaryAnn told them," she concluded, and we never spoke of the incident again.

Following a successful *Winter Jamboree*, we enrolled over 70 ladies in *The Learning Center's* first spring term. The term saw the repeat of our core classes, such as English, French, basic computer skills, and business management, adding the next level to each to accommodate our first term students' needs. Moving forwarded, we added parenting skills to our workshop offerings and basic keyboarding to our computer program. We had not even considered that the ladies may not know how to type when we first offered basic computers, but our first term revealed the need. With these additions, our momentum began to build yet again.

As we grew, our needs did as well and our first spring term saw the addition of a part-time Assistant Director. Sue, a retired Major in the Army, was the perfect choice. She was organized and professional while friendly and open to the ladies. It was a good fit, but sadly Sue left Kingdom with her family a few short months later. Fortunately, Sue had had time to establish office records and our filing system before she departed. In such, another Assistant Director was not hired until much later.

Madawi's divorce was in full swing and she hit the pinnacle of her evolutionary bounce full force. It was her most extreme time and she was taking the future head on with sheer determination. Self-exploration consumed her. She took every single class TLC offered and pointedly paid for those classes in line with every other student at reception. She was intensely curious about anything new and open to the ideas it brought forth, yet a unique interest in art began to emerge from within Madawi. Perhaps as a result of her exposure to art in her introductory class at *King Faisal University* or perhaps because it is art that touches the very soul of humans and brings out our deepest passions, but either way she felt inspired. Consequently, she wanted TLC to offer art classes. Rarely did she suggest ideas for classes, but when she did I naturally did my best to make it available.

Consequently, I began to look for an instructor, determine a physical location, and purchase all of the supplies necessary to open an art classroom. I had four weeks. I knew the addition of these types of classes would further the center's vision, but more importantly, I knew what they would do for Madawi. In such, I felt the instructor for this new branch under our shamsiyah was critically important. In my return to the compounds and coffee mornings, I found the hunt for a local art teacher in general more challenging than expected. I collected business cards, names, and numbers of many potential instructors, but none capable of teaching art.

Exasperated, I began to share my frustration with Betsy as she cut my hair one afternoon. As most women on the compound, Betsy had found her niche and became the compound stylist. Relaxing in the barber's chair she had imported from the states at huge expense and frustration, I admired how she had decorated her new salon, which was her villa's former maid's quarters.

"So you mean you're looking for an art teacher?" she asked returning the conversation back to the school.

"Yes and I'm running out of time."

"You know," she began. "I paint," she blurted out in a matter of fact way. "I could teach them classes," she stated smiling broadly at her idea.

Suddenly my ears perked up and I looked straight at her face smiling at me through the mirror. "You really think you could that?" I questioned in amazement and potential relief.

"Shoot yeah!" her country accent reverberated as she smiled even broader.

"Let me see your work!" I exclaimed as I hopped out of the chair with my haircutting cape still around my neck and clippies in my hair.

Proudly, Betsy showed me a dozen oil paintings that she had done since she had moved to Kingdom. Very realistic, full of color and texture, Betsy's paintings were good. She obviously had a God given talent because I learned she had never had a formal art class in her life. But for what she lacked in formal training, Betsy made up for in personality. She was delightfully refreshing, yet outside the typical. In her country accent, what Betsy thought, Betsy said, and she never made excuses for it. Intensely honest, she just called things the way she saw them. Unpolished, but genuine, Betsy eventually filled a special niche in the center's developing organizational culture. As a self declared "white witch," Betsy was intensely spiritual, but not religious, and in tune with the feelings of others. It was these qualities and others that made Betsy a perfect find for our first art program. After seeing her work and talking with her more about the vision and mission of TLC, I knew I had found the perfect art teacher – the critical link to making this class offering a reality. What remained to be done was simply logistics and creativity on my part.

I made arrangements with the compound manager, Nashad, to use the old general purpose room on the compound as a studio to teach oil and watercolor painting. I finally located eight easels in the market from different merchants and a short barstool for each. Although the eight did not match, I did not care. I was simply happy to find them. There was not a huge demand for art supplies in the Eastern Province so only two stores even stocked them. To offset the cost of establishing the studio, the students paid an art lab fee to cover the cost of basic class room supplies and then were required to supply their own personal paints, brushes, and canvases.

During this time, Madawi toyed with the idea of bringing a children's museum to the Eastern Province. To investigate and analyze the possibility, she sent David for a site visit to one that had recently opened in the country of Oman. Simultaneously, she and I registered to attend a children's museum conference in Minneapolis/St. Paul to learn the vision, mission, and logistics of opening and running a similar museum in Kingdom. Professionally, the trip went no where and neither did the idea of the children's museum. Yet, our trip was tremendously significant with regard to Madawi's personal growth.

This particular trip to the states brought many adventures our way. From watching the actor, Arnold Schwarzenegger, actually film, "*Jingle All the Way*," in Minneapolis to hanging out of the limousine's sunroof in New York's famous Times Square, there was never a dull moment. I was exhausted from my work with the center and motherhood so I graciously welcomed a break from the daily rigors. Madawi also welcomed the trip because she was still defining herself and consequently absorbed every sensation of our trip.

We were ecstatic because this would be our first trip to travel without husbands, kids, security, or nannies. Because I would be returning to Kingdom before Madawi, we ended up on different flights to the states. In such, the plan was for me to rent a car, register us with the conference, and then pick up Madawi at the airport the following morning. Expecting only Madawi, I was surprised to see Elizabeth with her as they approached baggage claim. Yet, I immediately knew why Elizabeth was in tow. Madawi could not fly or travel completely alone and, with me already there, she had to have a companion en route.

Elizabeth was Jackson Westmoreland's wife and only beginning to establish a friendship with his employer's spouse. When I first met Elizabeth, she was quiet, reserved and rarely talked. They were the same age and height, with me being a good eight inches shorter than both of them, but they were opposite in physical coloring. Whereas Madawi had black hair and eyes with an olive complexion, Elizabeth had blonde hair and pale skin. When I first met Elizabeth, I actually saw her as a rather "mousey" woman, yet in time I learned that she was most definitely not. She was opinionated and blessed with a good heart, which made her good for my Shamsiyah.

After navigating our way through the airport and locating our rental car, off we went to the hotel and our latest adventure. Because our rooms were adjacent, it was easy to run back and forth as we prepared to go out the evening. We had decided to make the most of Minneapolis' night life since the conference didn't begin until the following morning. Plus, Madawi had never experienced a "girls' night out," American style, and it was high time that she had. I spoke with the concierge and secured us a taxi for a ride to the restaurant. Before we even left the hotel, I could tell Madawi was a bit nervous about what a "girls' night out" would entail.

They giggled like school girls during dinner when I told them about Arnold Schwarzenegger being in town to film *Jingle All the Way*." I had heard people talking about it around the hotel and I had actually watched a scene being filmed the day before while having lunch. From that point on, I think all three of us were subconsciously on the lookout for Arnold for the remainder of the trip. After stuffing ourselves with a scrumptious meal and desert, we all pushed back to enjoy a cup of cap and decide our next move. Joking soon turned serious and suddenly, Elizabeth and I had Madawi agreeing to go to a local nightclub!

Before I knew it, I was sandwiched in the middle seat of a taxi backseat, asking the man for a fun night club to visit. He indicated he knew just the place and we pulled to a stop about 15 minutes later. From the outside, I immediately knew this was not the place for us and particularly not a good choice as Madawi's first bar experience. The metal railing lining the five concrete chipped steps to the warehouse entrance blended with the graffiti on the outside walls gave me the distinct impression we should leave. Smoke bellowed out of the door as Elizabeth ran ahead and began speaking to the bouncer. I followed with Madawi as close to me as she could get without being on the other side. Suddenly, she was quiet and I knew. She was not ready. I looked into her eyes just as she unknowingly grabbed my hand. With her big black eyes wide, Madawi shook her head "no" but didn't utter a word. There was no need. Without hesitation, I turned to face Elizabeth but didn't make a move closer to the door or the large bouncer. Elizabeth had begun to pay our cover charge and noticed our reluctance to step inside, so she confirmed. "We want to go in, don't we?"

I stammered, "ah...ah…no." I looked straight into Elizabeth's eyes as staunchly as I could, widening my eyes in the hopes she would instinctively know. "Ah, no, it's not….ah," I searched for the words to keep us from going in without shouting over the music that Madawi did not want to enter. "I've got a headache," I finally shouted over the music as the perfect response popped into my thoughts.

"What?" Elizabeth yelled back over the music blaring from the inside.

"I've got a headache!" I yelled even louder so Elizabeth could hear. She nodded that she had heard and made her way down the stairs after thanking the men and making her gracious exit.

By the time we were back on the dimly lit, broken sidewalk, all three of us were talking at once about what had just occurred. After exasperations, giggles, and comments expressed not to try that one again, an eerie silence fell over us as we simultaneously realized our situation. Clueless as to our location, we only knew we were three women alone on the street in downtown Minneapolis at 11:00 on a Friday night. Elizabeth and I looked at each other, both knowing the other factor she and I had to consider – we had a Saudi princess with us to boot! Our shoulders went back as we assumed a defensive posture and we both began to survey our surroundings and look for a solution. A misting rain began and the wind picked up as I walked a few yards in each direction. Fortunately through the foggy mist, I could see a small neon light on the corner several blocks straight up hill. Pulling my coat in closer, I called to the girls that I had found a place and started toward the light, gesturing for them to follow. Being that they are taller and gait longer, they caught up to me in no time. It was becoming uncomfortably cold and wet as we walked, so none of us tried to talk. We simply focused on the light and made our way in our high heels as quickly as possible.

Once inside, we shook our coats as we surveyed our find. It was a quaint Irish pub with a very nice clientele. Feeling relaxed in these surroundings,

Madawi nodded and smiled. We all ordered a nightcap to end our evening on a better note than the first bar experience. Still periodically joking about running into Arnold, we sipped our drinks and talked as women do. As the conversation turned to the latest crazes, Elizabeth piped up with an astonishing trend. "Oh guess what I read?" She paused seeking our nods of encouragement. "Women are now smoking cigars in posh nightclubs in New York!"

Unbelieving, Madawi responded "they do?" And I chimed in "they do not…do they?"

Elizabeth answered moving her hands in motions to indicate quotations with her fingers, "They do, and I've read about it. It is now the 'in' thing for women to smoke cigars."

Considering I had been in Kingdom for five years, this seemed quite new and strange to me as well as to Madawi and we chuckled at the thought. Then suddenly jest turned to challenge.

"You would not smoke that, Elizabeth!" Madawi challenged with a laugh.

"Well," Elizabeth began in her reserved nature. "I would," she smiled in an adventuresome but mischievous manner, seeking affirmation of her decision.

"You would?" Madawi giggled. "Go ahead, *yellah*" she laughed still daring Elizabeth.

Before I knew it, the challenge was in play and we were leaning up over the table looking through the cigar selection the gentleman presented us. As Elizabeth lit and puffed the chosen cigar, Madawi and

I simply watched not saying a word. To accent her proving she would smoke it, Elizabeth kicked her head back with a big puff once she got it going. Laughter broke and we laughed so hard we eventually cried. I couldn't believe she did it and neither could Madawi. As the chuckles died, Elizabeth offered it to me. I gave it a quick ceremonial puff and held it out for Madawi. Her long slender hand rose and she smiled gently, shaking her head no. "Oh, no thank you, Mrs. Teresa, I will pass."

The conference was interesting but did not offer anything special to us. Rather, it was the actual doing it that made the conference meaningful. After two days of workshops, scheduled participant banquets, and tours, we were off to New York to meet Madawi's girls.

Our evening flight arrived and we crossed the Washington Bridge at a steady click in the dark of night. I had never seen the skyline of New York and I found it mesmerizing from the limo window.

"Look!" Madawi repeated as she pointed to well known structures from the edge of her seat. Her excitement was effervescing and she simply could not contain it. The valet attendants snapped to attention when our limo pulled to a stop in front of *Morgans*. I knew the lack of formality, the "just us girls time" was over as Madawi punched the clock as princess again, gracefully exiting the opened door. Jackson had checked the girls, their entourage of nannies, and drivers into the hotel earlier that morning, so Madawi and I simply took the elevator to our suites. Madawi

ॐ Creating Shamsiyah ॐ

almost bounced into the room, her excitement of being in New York still reining. The very first thing she did was fling open the window overlooking the city and take in a huge, cleansing breath.

"I love you New York," she passionately whispered and threw the city a big kiss with both hands and a loud smack. Stepping back she paused to reaffirm the meaning of that gesture, she repeated " I love you," then turned and hugged the children, taking time with each to catch up the past few days.

The next morning was filled with a tour of the financial district, the World Trade Center, and the Empire State Building followed by a delicious, but hurried lunch on the pier. The afternoon offered no rest as we shopped our way through *Barney's*, *Saks*, and *FAO Swartz* topped off with a relaxing afternoon tea. Our whirlwind stopover was highlighted with the Broadway musical, *Greece*, featuring Chubby Checkers that evening. Nora and Fatma giggled in embarrassment and fell together hiding their faces as "Mrs. Teresa" rose to twist in the aisle during the encore. Yet, after accepting the idea that it was okay and simply fun, they joined me with smiles that covered their faces.

On the sidewalk after the musical, Madawi announced that she was tired and preferred to go spend some time with the little girls in the suite. "But you go ahead," she encouraged. "Go, go see New York." She stepped into the limo while she continued to talk. "He will drop me by the hotel and take you all where you want to go." Her focus turned from Nora, Fatma and me toward Jackson. "Make sure they are okay, huh," she smiled stepping out of the car, knowing already that Jackson would. He didn't carry his sidearm for nothing.

I could not process all the sensations I felt when I saw Time Square for the first time while hanging out of the limousine sunroof with the girls. It was exhilarating. All the lights, sounds, and smells bombarded me enhancing my excitement. Smiling at Nora and Fatma, I simply pointed at famous attractions and didn't attempt conversation. After a few minutes, I felt a tug on my trousers when Jackson requested for us to get back in the car.

While we caught our breath and straightened our hair with our fingers, Jackson confirmed with Nora that he had found the place she wanted to see. Like any typical 18 year old, Nora was curious and wanted to see a bar. But not just any bar, she wanted to see a famous, unusual one. Moments later, the car pulled up in front of the *Limelight*. Out of nowhere, four security men I had never seen before each took a corner of the car as their charge while we were escorted inside.

As our lead security guard, Jackson was efficient and discreet as always. He simply made things happen. I have no idea how but we just walked right in past the bouncer and into the first of many little, overcrowded rooms with unusual looking people. Piercings, tattoos, and unusually styled and colored hair were the accepted norm. Nora grabbed my hand. The ceilings were low and the walls black. The floor felt like plywood, but I could never get a look to confirm because it was covered with feet.

We wandered through a series of similar rooms filled with smoke and humans before we entered a large room with high ceilings, overflowing with people, and flooded with pounding music and people screaming. Fortunately, there was a stage looking area that was fairly vacant for some reason and we stepped up to take the spot. After each of us hoisted ourselves up to sit with our legs dangling, a commotion began in the center of the room. The lights brightened and a cage came down from the ceiling with two girls dancing inside. I almost had a heart attack then and there. After my heart settled and my eyes adjusted to the light level, I started looking around. Slowly I followed the high ceiling around to find that we were actually in what appeared to be an old church building. Immediately I got a creepy feeling and became anxious to leave. The girls must have felt the same uneasy feeling because even my wildfire, Fatma, was ready to go. Informing Jackson, he led us to the exit and our waiting limo with the four human corner posts.

  The next morning was rough after our late evening on the town. But we managed thanks to the nannies that had everything ready for us. I was departing for Kingdom to get back to my little ones and TLC. Madawi and the girls, however, were on their way to Italy to shop a little and then on to their London flat before returning to Kingdom.

  Shortly after our return from New York, Madawi called one morning, anxious to meet for coffee at a new café in Al-Rashid Mall, which we had heard had a nice ladies section. She invited me and my Ann to meet her that afternoon. As it was still fairly rare for there to even BE a place in Kingdom where women could meet comfortably in public, to find a clean, new, elegant one was simply icing on the cake.

Surprisingly, Madawi was waiting for us when we arrived, so I knew then she had to have something on her mind to arrive early. The conversation meandered as it typically did for over a half hour with us asking about each other's family and ordering a unique sweet. In such, one thing led to another and the conversation turned to the Colonel and Madawi.

"Last night," she began with a slight smile and a sentimental sigh. "The girls went to visit Awad." She paused, smiling a little more.

"And Fatma gave me this one, small flower from Awad," she said, marking one of her beautifully expressive hands with the finger of the other to show us the flower's size. Her gaze returned to us and her face was simply glowing. It was obvious she still loved him.

Ann and I almost jumped from our chairs with excitement because we both saw it in her face. For the next half hour, we gently questioned Madawi, trying to assess what she really wanted for them as a couple and for herself as a woman before we offered any guidance.

Questioning again for clarification, Ann spoke directly to Madawi, "do you love him?" An awkward silence followed.

"Yes," she paused. "But Mama Ann, you don't understand." Madawi continued, politely pointing out all the reason's why they couldn't or shouldn't be together. Yet she didn't reveal if she wanted the Colonel back or not. Mom and I were simply hanging on the edge of our chairs by this time to hear her response.

"But do you love him, Madawi?" Ann reiterated, more forcefully this time.

"Yes," Madawi replied adamantly.

"Then get him back!" Ann and I answered simultaneously and emphatically while smiling uncontrollably.

"How? What? There is nothing I can do!" Madawi's hands flew while she protested. "The law says we can not see each other or talk on the phone. *How* can I get him back?" She smiled thinking of the possibility of being with the Colonel again, blushing as a young bride would do, but flung her hair from her face in defiance of the impossibility that faced her.

"A note!" Ann blurted as she snapped her fingers. "You can send him a note!"

Silence followed as we looked at each other, considering the feasibility of the idea. We then began to smile because we knew it would work.

"But…what would it say?" Madawi questioned slowly, emphasizing that she was still only considering the idea.

"Oh heavens, Madawi, that's the easy part," I added and Ann concurred. For the next hour we used every napkin on the table to compose the perfect note to Colonel Awad. Satisfied and confident, we kissed Madawi good bye that afternoon knowing that every thing was going to turn out okay for them. We saw it as destiny.

From the moment I entered the compound walls each morning until I left in the afternoon, the center was a constant flow of activity. With our venture so new, I wore many hats in the beginning due to budget constraints. I was the director, an instructor, the hostess at times, and receptionist, when needed. My nights were consumed as well with things I did not have time for during the day. After I performed my duties as Mom and wife, I would go into my home office and work. I produced textbooks with graphics for teachers, completed necessary financial paperwork, organized brochures for the following term, produced newsletters, and much more. Essentially, the center had become my third child.

Because of our *Winter Jamboree* and the ladies spring term success, it became obvious that *The Learning Center* was going to remain alive, even thrive. What we were doing was good, in spite of the fact that we were doing it in a country that frowned on women learning and growing intellectually. Consequently, I didn't dream of the challenge that was rapidly approaching the door of TLC.

It was the end of May in 1996, another pretty day in the desert, and I sat at my desk diligently working on the necessary paperwork of a business. Suddenly, the telephone rang, breaking the silence of my concentration. It was David with startling news.

"Well baby," he began not wanting to alarm me, "it looks like you are going to have to move the center."

"What do you mean move the center? Oh Honey! We've just gotten established…the ladies are coming…people know us here," I protested.

"I just left a meeting with Colonel Awad and several high ranking officers with the U.S. Military, and they are planning to house U.S. troops on DM 18."

"Why here, for heavens sake?" I could not help but question.

"Our security threat level has increased, and they feel that the officers can be better protected there and less conspicuous." He paused as he heard silence on my end of the line. "It's a done deal, honey. There is nothing that can be done about it."

After ingesting the news, I had questions. "When do we have to be out?" I asked very concerned about our upcoming summer program.

"By August first," he answered.

"Well, thank God I can get the children's program done first," I replied. "Where will we move?" Knowing me and how I think, David was ready for the question.

"DM 12."

"DM 12?" I exclaimed not sure of where in the world DM 12 was. "Where is that?"

"Now honey, calm down," he started. "It's the old clinic. You and Madawi looked at it before you choose your current place."

I was embarrassed that I did not know my old clinic was officially known as DM 12. Yet, I remembered it and recalled that it needed a lot of work to be converted to meet our needs. David assured me he could get some of his construction crews to help and make it even better than what we had currently. Feeling relieved, I took him up on his offer to go check it out again after work.

Around four, David picked me up and we headed to DM 12 to make an initial assessment of the facility we had to turn into a school. We entered the facility through a central, common stairwell area where the building split into four identical/mirrored apartments, A through D. Each apartment had a small kitchen and laundry room, a family room, two bedrooms, and two baths. Falling from the walls or cracking from the floor, the tile, paint, and fixtures all reflected a 1970s-style decorated in gold and pea soup green. I walked quietly through the powerless facility, straining to see with very little sunshine peeking through the sand splattered windows. I couldn't even make notes, only walk, look, and try to absorb the amount of work lay ahead. It would be a massive project to change these four dilapidated apartments into a school in only three months on a bare to none shoestring budget. I sighed as we started to leave. David knew what I was thinking. He always did. "*Mofie mushkala*" he said as he opened the door for me. "We will get this place whipped into shape in no time," he remarked to encourage.

The ladies program drew to a close and my focus turned to our next revenue stream – the kids. Keeping pace with previous lessons learned, I developed an extensive summer camp program to follow the ladies' spring term. As the summer break came around, we were able to add swimming and tennis for the children to our repertoire of English, Arts & Crafts, Cooking, and Music. Naturally all of the kids' classes did well, but the swimming class soared. Although I am not certain, I do believe we were the first to offer swimming classes in the province. Tess, a wonderful Australian nurse from my compound, joined our team to teach swimming lessons. Incredibly concerned with safety, I felt relieved once she was on board. It seemed as if she were in the pool non-stop for the entire four weeks. The mothers were ecstatic with the lessons and began to whisper interest in learning to swim as well.

It was a grueling summer and it had only begun. On weekends and when possible during the week, Yacoub would assign some of his construction crews to the DM12's renovation when they weren't busy on base. However, the transformation of the new facility from four old apartments to an educational learning center was slow—extremely slow. It rapidly became clear that if David or I weren't there, the work crews accomplished nothing, which was frustrating beyond expression.

As I went back and forth between the old TLC and the new facility, I watched as cranes hoisted large, concrete Jersey barricades along the road in front of

DM 18, preparing security for the soldiers that would soon live where Madawi's dream began. The sand was shifting beneath us, and I never saw it coming.

In the middle of the center's renovation turmoil, terrorism pounded much closer to home than the **Riyadh** bombing only seven months prior. It was late in the evening on the twenty-fifth of June in 1996. I was exhausted from running back and forth all day, but sleep evaded me.

After getting the children and David to bed, I headed downstairs to my home office to do a little computer work for the center in the hope that sleep would finally come. There was so much that had to be done, and I had no time to waste because David and I were scheduled to go with Madawi the following morning to **Jeddah** for three days to see the work of a local artist that had gained her attention. Madawi's interest in art was growing and moving, beyond her classroom experience. She began to seek out Saudi artists that she perceived as talented. She would buy her favorite works to support their effort. It was not until later did she take her help further.

Oddly just after 1:00 a.m., the telephone rang. It was Madawi.

"Ello, Mrs. Teresa," she began sounding somewhat preoccupied with what was going on in her salon.

"Oh, hello Madawi," I answered, surprised yet happy to hear from her. "I'm almost packed."

"With all that has happened, I don't think it's a good idea that we travel tomorrow," she started.

"We'll reschedule, huh."

"What has happened, Madawi?" I questioned with concern, completely oblivious to the evening's event.

"I don't think it's a good idea to travel with the explosion," she replied.

"What explosion?"

"The government buildings exploded tonight," she answered, as if she were surprised that I did not know. "We felt it here at the house, and the girls are very upset."

"What government buildings?" I questioned with heightened curiosity.

"The ones on the *Corniche*."

"Which ones on the *Corniche*?" I queried, still oblivious to what she was talking about.

"The ones by the water," she persisted.

"Oh," I responded, still unsure but not feeling that I could ask yet again. I knew that the police station and a few other Saudi government buildings were located there, but I was not sure that they were the buildings she was referring to. "Okay," I paused trying not to reveal my disappointment. "It's okay, we can go another time."

"We will," she responded soothingly. "When everything settles down a bit, huh? I'll call you tomorrow. *Yellah*."

"Okay Madawi," I replied in agreement, "I'll talk to you tomorrow."

"*Insha Allah*, Mrs. Teresa. *Ma'assalaamah*," she replied, "*Yellah*."   Anxious to tell David, I ran up the stairs and hopped into the middle of the bed. Shaking him awake with one hand, I grabbed the TV remote control with the other. For some reason, I had an uneasy feeling. For some reason, I did not think the evening's event was as casual as Madawi had made it sound.

"Wake up, David!" I exclaimed. "There's been an explosion."

Half asleep he responded, "Explosion...uh...where?"

Because of my uncertainty, I only restated, "Madawi just called and said the government buildings on the *Corniche* blew up tonight." I bounced a little on my knees to convey my assumed severity of the situation, glancing at CNN to see if they mentioned anything about an explosion in *Al-Khobar*, but nothing was reported. "David, what government buildings are on the *Corniche*?" I pleaded trying to pull him from his sound sleep. "She said there was an explosion!" More awake, he rolled over and we began to talk.

"She's probably talking about the police station," he surmised as he took a drink of water. "You know how these people are. A TCN probably cut a gas line or something," he concluded nonchalantly as crazy things like that always seemed to happen in the Kingdom. "I'm sure it's nothing to worry about. Why don't you get some sleep?"

"No David," I repeated with emphasis. "I think it's something worse than that," I paused unconvinced by his composed manner. "It must have been something worse or she wouldn't have canceled our trip!"

"Really honey," he responded, "I don't think it's anything serious." Rolling back over, he suggested again. "Come on now, sleep. It's late."

Frustrated, I agreed to let him sleep as he obviously wanted to do, but I could not shake the nagging feeling I felt, and sleep was nowhere to be found for me. Getting a snack from the kitchen, I crawled back into bed and lay in darkness watching CNN for the next two hours. Nothing was mentioned, not a word. Over and over I heard the same headline stories but nothing about an explosion. Then around 3:30 a.m., I was half asleep when I suddenly heard that familiar music CNN plays when they run the breaking news graphic across the screen. Immediately, I was fully awake and glued to the TV, straining to listen to the low volume I had set because David was sleeping.

"We have unconfirmed reports that there has been an explosion in *Al-Khobar*, Saudi Arabia," the announcer began as a map of the Eastern Province appeared with a red arrow pointing at where we lived. "Reuters indicates that an explosion occurred approximately four hours ago at the U.S. Military housing complex along the Arabian Gulf. At this time, we have no details as to injuries or fatalities, if any."

Shocked, I came out from under the covers and onto my knees again, shaking David vigorously this time. "David…David!" I exclaimed. "Wake up! Wake up! It was *Khobar* Towers," I shouted. "The explosion was at *Khobar* Towers!"

Startled as well, he sat up still wobbling a bit as

a person does when they quickly wake from a deep sleep. "What?"

Anxiously, I repeated. "CNN...CNN just said that an explosion occurred four hours ago at the U.S. Military housing complex here. Although they didn't call it ***Khobar*** Towers, it must be. I just know they must be talking about ***Khobar*** Towers!" I repeated out of amazement.

More awake, he reached for the remote to turn up the volume, and we watched the TV intently for the rest of the night. Because of shock, sleep did not come for us the rest of that night, and all we could do was wait for details. It all seemed surreal, and our watching was as if we were trying to convince ourselves to believe what we were hearing.

While we listened intently to the sketchy details of each "breaking news flash" deep into the night, all I could do was thank God that I had quit my part-time teaching position at ***Khobar*** Towers in April. Even though I had so much on my plate with the children, *The Learning Center*, and *Jadawel Jazz*, I had decided to teach the military personnel two nights a week for the University of Maryland in January. My class was held in ***Khobar*** Towers.

In spite of my schedule, I had taken on the class because I felt it was important to teach a public speaking class every now and then to stay abreast in my field. Fortunately, I had opted not to teach during the summer term because of the new facility's renovation or I could have been there. After thanking God for my safety, my concern turned to the men and women housed there. I prayed, prayed hard, that no one was injured as the details trickled through on CNN.

Unfortunately, the next pretty day in the Kingdom brought sorrow. CNN reported 19 American soldiers among the dead, and hundreds of people wounded. My heart ached. Because of the events of the night, we did not sleep. We were up very early and David decided to go on into work to see if he could help out and learn any details at the airbase.

Historically, details about events in the private world of the Kingdom do not usually make it to CNN; and if they do, they are usually squelched as soon as possible. The Saudis do not like any attention, particularly negative attention. They have no desire for the outside world to look inside their world. The November bombing of the OPM/SANG building only made the international newscast twice that I heard, essentially one day of coverage in spite of the fact that five Americans were killed. **Khobar** Towers, on the other hand, was different and received tremendous coverage. Sadly, the media didn't often mention the hundreds of Saudis and other nationalities that were either killed or injured because of flying debris with the percussion of the blast. In the weeks that followed, a variety of U.S. facilities throughout the Kingdom received bomb threats. Mine was one of them.

July brought the end of our summer program and the regular summertime exodus of Saudi women and children from the Kingdom to enjoy a holiday and escape the extreme heat and abominable boredom.

Only David, my parents, a few TLC staff, and I remained to weather out the summer, refurbish, move, and be ready to hold classes by October. As we worked long, hard hours on transforming Madawi's dream, I often wondered if we would still be in Kingdom to see it to completion or if the terrorists would drive us away.

Chapter 10
Transforming the Dream
July – October 1996

Before leaving Kingdom for her annual summer exodus, Madawi blessed TLC with a curse. Up until this point, I had had a terrible time securing a reliable female *TCN* in the local market to serve as our hostess. Truly this had been a thorn in my side, and I was clueless where to search next without importing one from another country. In such, Madawi beamed as she told me that she would assign Lulu, a Filipino servant from the palace, to the center.

Initially I was elated. I knew Lulu and I was confident that she would do a terrific job, which she did in the years to come. However, I also knew that she was simply another financial burden to bear. In the beginning, TLC was only responsible for her monthly wages because she lived and ate at the palace. Unfortunately, the day would come when that would change.

Even though I knew I would miss Madawi desperately, I was happy that I had the opportunity to give the new facility my undivided attention now that she was traveling and our summer program over. From the slow progress I had observed to date, I knew the only way the center would be ready in time is if I were to be there daily to oversee and make it happen. So I slipped on the jeans and work shirt and off I went to ensure the transformation would occur. From early morning, past dark, we worked. I became obsessed with getting the facility renovated so I could focus on the actual operation of the center.

TLC's first two terms had taught me well. I knew the work that lay ahead of me after we ripped the place apart, rebuilt, and redecorated. I still had classrooms to set-up, fall term class offerings to determine, teachers to hire, books and brochures to develop and duplicate, coordinate details for an unofficial open house, and more – all before Madawi's return in October only two short months away.

The challenges of refurbishing the new facility came from every direction. Only seven months prior, we had begun to offer programming to children in order to keep ourselves afloat financially and meet the loan repayment obligations with the bank. Madawi, with her recent divorce and summer traveling expenses, was unable or unwilling to add more funds to the center other than the tuition she had paid for her and the girls to take almost every class since our doors had opened. Consequently, TLC had no funds to renovate, decorate and, subsequently, impress.

I was at my wits end and I racked my brain for a solution. For days, my thoughts were consumed with how I could make this work. Finally, after much deliberation and looking at every single avenue imaginable, it hit me. The Colonel – he would help and I was sure of it. After all, he had been the final authority to approve DM12 for TLC's use, even though he and Madawi were divorced. So why in the world wouldn't he help me make it usable? Suddenly, my latest mission was clear. I had to get in touch with Colonel Awad.

I had not seen the Colonel since their divorce, so I was a bit nervous about contacting him. Even though I knew we had always had a good working relationship and that I had always been comfortable speaking with him, I was on unfamiliar ground calling on him now. After all, I was in Saudi Arabia. I was in a monarchy about to call a very busy Prince, military commander, and businessman. I was in a country that is totally segregated based on gender. I was where men and women do not communicate directly with each other, unless they are members of the same family. Even calling him could be a blunder and I not even know it, but I had to try.

I knew the night would be the best time to catch him, so I dialed his cell that evening. I was hopeful that he would have time to meet with me and, more importantly, that he would be receptive to helping. Nervous, I paced as the telephone rang.

In military fashion, he answered sharply, "hello."

Unable to distinguish his voice from such a quick response, I replied, "eh…hello…Colonel?"

"Ah! Hello Mrs. Teresa." I could hear the smile in his voice, which immediately removed all nervousness I had had, so I continued.

"*Kayf Haalak?*" I answered.

"*Tieeb, al Hamdulila. Kayf Haalik?*" he roared his deep, signature laugh with my Arabic attempt. "You are learning! Good job."

As is the Saudi way, he proceeded to take the time to ask about each member of my family by name, and I replied in kind, each time offering well wishes for things to come.

"So what can I do for you, Mrs. Teresa?" He began once the cordialities were complete.

"Well Colonel, I have a wee problem with the center and I was hoping you may have some solutions for me to pursue."

"Problems?" His tone morphed from casual to serious.

"Well, sir" I hesitated. "I don't think it's anything that can't be overcome. I just need your guidance about the renovations of DM12 for *The Learning Center*."

"Ah, the school." I heard his smile return.

"Yes sir." I paused. "I realize you are very busy, but I was hoping you would have a little time to meet with me so that I can explain the situation."

"Have David bring you to my villa tomorrow night" he answered. "Eight o'clock, **Insha Allah**, I have a few minutes then."

"Oh perfect, thank you Colonel." I responded beaming from ear to ear. "We will be there, sir. Thank you again."

"*Mofie mushkala*, Mrs. Teresa" his smile continued. "*Ashufee bukra, Insha Allah*."

"**Nam** and **shukran**, Colonel! *Ma'assalaama*." I answered.

"*Ma'assalaama*." I heard and the phone went dead.

Following his divorce announcement, the Colonel had left the palace for Madawi and the family to live and he took possession of three villas on DM16, one of our company's empty *Jadawel* compounds that happened to be only three blocks from the palace. When Madawi told me where he had moved, she justified it by saying it kept him close to the children. But in retrospect, I don't believe it had anything to do with the children. I believe he wanted to be near her.

When we arrived the following evening, I was shocked to find that he had totally refurbished the already plush villas located there. His villa was stunning with a built in hard wood entertainment center, beautiful leather furnishings, and, of course, the widescreen satellite TV. As I walked around the salon in awe of the beautiful, yet masculine, changes made, the Colonel entered. Sporting his trademark smile while he shook hands with David, he welcomed us to sit. Naturally, the cordial questions began again and the responses the same as the night before. Yet, it is expected. It is the Arab way. Oddly though, he asked me several questions about Madawi, wanting to know how she was, how the kids were doing with their studies, and things of that nature. Well into the second glass of freshly blended fruit juice, served by male servants of course, the conversation turned to the center.

"Well, Mrs. Teresa," he began, sitting forward in his chair with his elbows to his knees, hands clasped. A familiar posture I had seen many times before when the Colonel was turning his attention to more serious matters or to Saudi soccer. "How is the school?" he questioned, raising a brow which was so typically the Colonel.

"So far so good, Colonel," I began. "We started last November with only 29 ladies and we enrolled over 70 in our spring term." I answered, smiling to reflect my pleasure with the center's growth. I continued to list all that had happened since its start, and graciously thanked him for his help with securing the old and new facilities for our use.

"Hmmm," he analyzed, a bit distant in thought. "More than doubling. This is good." His smile returned as he nodded his approval. "And Madawi?" He hesitated, almost blushing. "And is Madawi enjoying the classes?"

"She is doing well, Colonel." I replied. "She's done very well with all of the classes, but I think her passion is the new art class we started this spring."

"Art…" he paused thoughtfully. "She has always loved art." He answered smiling, but I don't think his comment was to me. Then suddenly, at that moment, it took all the constraint I could muster not to smile. I had seen it in his face and I was having a hard time suppressing my excitement. Call it a sixth sense, woman's intuition, or just hopefulness for my friend, but I saw it on his face. I saw it as plain as day. He still loved Madawi.

Breaking from his reflection, the Colonel spoke. "So what is it that you need from me?"

In a rush of emotions, facts, and figures, I started sharing the financial bind I found myself and the expenses that lay before me to keep Madawi's dream alive. He listened intently, not missing a word yet not uttering one either.

"So my dilemma is that I don't know how I am going to get DM12 renovated and ready for October." I paused meaningfully and looked him in the eyes. "...ready for Madawi's return."

In obvious thought, he paused and then turned to David. "David," he said in his military, business tone that he had not used with me. "There are several ways to handle this. We will assign DM12 to you and, naturally, it will need repair." He looked intently at David, "Work with Yacoub and make this happen." Standing, he continued. "I don't mean to be rude, Mrs. Teresa," he said looking at his watch. "But I have others I must meet tonight. I am flying to America tomorrow and my time is not my own now."

"I understand Colonel and I thank you for your time and your support." I answered standing as well.

"Anytime, Mrs. Teresa," he smiled. "Anytime...and let me know if Madawi needs anything, huh?"

"Yes sir, I will." I answered with a huge smile, feeling even more certain that my gut feeling was correct about him.

By saying "make it happen," the Colonel was essentially telling David to utilize all current available contracts to make the facility ready for *The Learning Center* – for his wife. This would not be difficult because DM12 was a government leased building and thus indirectly the Colonel's or his charge. These renovations would only enhance the value of the government's investment so the cost could easily be included in other refurbishment contracts. Although not accepted procedure in the States, it was perfectly acceptable in Kingdom with the Colonel's backing. It is, after all, a family owned country. Even though I knew our "make it happen" would have financial limitations and we could only get the basic, necessary renovations done, I was thrilled to have it and most thankful to the Colonel for offering it.

With that stress eliminated, I headed for the center each morning and stayed until I was either too exhausted to remain or too hungry to continue. For security, we relocated the entrance to the facility to where an apartment porch had been and reception where its small salon once stood. We literally scraped floors of grime with steel wool pads on our hands and knees. We sledge-hammered bathtubs and knocked down walls. We stripped other walls and repainted, ran electricity for computers, and hung white boards for instruction. We cannibalized between apartments just to make it work. In essence, a complete transformation was underway.

Facing the Province Governor's palace across a major street in *Al-Khobar*, DM12 was conspicuously inconspicuous. It always amazed me how an illegal, underground school could be in the middle of all the action on a busy downtown street, yet be relatively unnoticed except by those who were privileged to know. Our plain white wall surrounding our plain white stucco building in an area that was zoned partially residential and partially commercial offered us the camouflage we needed for hundreds of women and children to come and go daily.

Originally, DM12 was four almost identical apartments with a building entry into a central stairwell. The building, naturally surrounded by a wall in Kingdom, was accessed through a double-wide wall door near the building entry. The area between the wall and the building was approximately 15' wide and was covered in terrazzo tile enhanced with built-in concrete flower boxes that were in desperate need of care. The company's clinic once occupied apartment B, but the other three apartments had been virtually closed up for at least five years.

The original wall entry and subsequent building entry into the central stairwell was a security nightmare because we could not monitor it constantly. As a result, Yacoub, the Arab contractor and Mona's husband, suggested we make apartment A (the apartment across the stairwell from the old clinic) the new entrance to TLC. To make this happen, Yacoub had his crew make a new street entry in the wall nearby. This door was a single-wide and we matched the existing wall door as best as we could to keep the new entry from looking like an add-on. The old concrete porch was removed and replaced with beige marble tile leading into the center. Yacoub and David decided to replace the old porch door with a double-wide curved oak door. I was surprised and completely ecstatic about the new door. It was beautiful with its brass handles and a curved design, giving the entrance a touch of class. Yet, for me, it was much more than just a beautiful door. It was symbolic of what we were achieving with the Arab women – opening a door to new horizons and opportunities.

With the Colonel's nod, David was able to secure surplus furniture for our use from another military housing complex that the base had closed. Consequently, we had plenty of identical pastel, floral patterned sofas and chairs, birch coffee and end table sets, birch chest of drawers with removable, matching bookshelf toppers, 12 birch armoires, and 21 birch dinning room tables with 125 matching, upholstered, dinning room chairs at our disposal.

For durability as well as décor, we ripped up the old broken terrazzo flooring in the reception area, bath, and the main hall and laid a taupe designed marble tile in its place. However for a warm, welcoming touch, we replaced the old tile with a short pile, beige carpet in the offices, the classrooms, and social salons of three apartments. In addition, Yacoub was able to obtain new beige mini-blinds for every window in the center and new window air conditioning units which where needed throughout the building.

Because we relocated the main entry to the center to apartment A from the stairwell, it underwent the biggest transformation. The old small salon that connected to the porch became our reception area. It was perfect because it also had doors to the master and second bedrooms. Simply decorated with a soft peach paint accenting the new marble floor, it was welcoming yet businesslike. David was able to get us a used curved desk for the receptionist's use. We then supplemented the room with a flowered chair, an end table to place brochures and center material, and a silk plant.

The old master bedroom became my office by default because of its large window overlooking the porch. I had a window seat to the front door and I was always ready to be the first outside should the police or *hiyah* decide to visit our center for learning. Additionally, from my make-shift dinning room table desk, I could see directly into reception. This was perfect because I was easily accessible to all the students and I was able to keep a pulse on the happenings of the center. The master bedroom also afforded me a large storage area and private bath, which Madawi preferred to use whenever she was in the center. There was no money to renovate my putrid green bath, so I just threw up a shower curtain and said "forget it."

The second bedroom became our business office. It was smaller than the other rooms but served the purpose. I set it up with a birch desk I had brought from home. I added a dinning room table to hold in/out boxes for teachers and staff, a four-drawer filing cabinet, and a plant. A long hall stretched from reception to the original stairwell entry. On one side, there was a large salon with a bath and kitchen on the other.

The reception bath, another major renovation, was completely gutted by sledge-hammer. We removed the wall tile, the tub, and putrid green fixtures, replacing them with new beige ones. Unfortunately, the budget did not allow for the other seven 1970s-style pea green toilets to be replaced. But they had to be functional and the one upstairs had a broken seat. Matching replacements however were not available in the market. So in the 110 plus degree heat and ninety percent humidity, I spent an afternoon in a "toilet graveyard" searching for matching pea green seat to replace the one in the English department bath upstairs. It was actually comical to see me rummaging through a field of sand and broken toilets in my *abaya* and tennis shoes with a Kenyan **Maasai** warrior in tow holding up every non-white seat he found for the Madame's approval.

    The reception kitchen benefited from the best of all four kitchens in the facility. We replaced missing green and gold kitchen tiles with ones pulled from the walls of the other kitchens. We made sure all appliances were working and utilized a washer and dryer set for the laundry from the same compound as the furniture. This kitchen had to be functional and presentable because it would be where Lulu would prepare the daily refreshments, party refreshments, and coordinate service for events and dinner parties to come.

    Foreseeing the main salon would be the heart of the center, I divided it into two conversation furniture couplings to allow for private and small group discussions. Yet, it could easily be opened up to a large circular meeting area by simply moving a few rolling chairs to different locations. Because of our limited resources, versatility and adaptability had to be two of our primary concerns in every facility renovation / adaptation we made, and we had done an excellent job with the center's main salon. I added two long chests of drawers to serve as a buffet for tea, refreshments, and a table top rock fountain I had at home for luck.

Because the salon would coddle the emergence of this awaking for the Saudi women, I felt it needed a special touch and my creative side emerged. There was this pot that I had seen in my numerous clay pot shopping excursions that was unique beyond any other I had seen. The Venetian-style pot stretched almost four feet tall. Its long cone shaped base could not stand without a metal support around its opening. Molded from sand, it absorbed the teal blue paint well and made a beautiful central focus piece in the salon enhanced with silk flowers cascading from its tulip shaped mouth. Uniquely Arab, it was etched with a few lines of Bedouin design encircling the neck of he pot.

To provide space for special what-knots and things to come, I had the workers place one birch armoire and one dresser with shelves in the salon as well. Not only practical, the main salon provided a warm, relaxing place for group bonding to occur. From the moment we opened the doors, everyone felt welcome and comfortable there, even if they were quietly reading alone or meeting a friend to go somewhere else for lunch.

ॐ Creating Shamsiyah ॐ

After simply polishing the existing terrazzo tile and repainting the walls white in the central stairwell, our renovations continued across the hall in apartment B – *The Learning Center's* new art department.

Formerly the company's clinic, I earmarked this apartment for art because of the well-kept terrazzo tile throughout. Unlike the other three apartments, it had undergone modifications that would be beneficial to our needs as well. Years before, the larger, main salon had been divided into two smaller rooms to create a reception area and a waiting room for the patients. Decorating one with our assigned furniture, new carpet, and mini-blinds, I transformed it into a general purpose classroom with dinning room tables, chest of drawers, whiteboard, and a silk plant – our new standard classroom décor.

The other half, which I deemed a "group discussion" classroom, stretched outside the norm for our Saudi students. Yes, they had had formal education in girls' schools within the Kingdom and some educated abroad as well. But for the most part, the idea of a group discussion style classroom setting was new to these ladies. The idea of learning by simply talking was foreign. They associated learning to rowed chairs and notepads to record every word the teacher uttered, not thought provoking conversations and interactive exercises on sofas around a coffee table. In the "group discussion" classroom, I utilized our overstuffed sofas, a coffee table, a whiteboard, and a plant for color to create an environment for open exchange.

The kitchen had been the clinic's lab and converted nicely to a copy / work room. It provided ample space for assembling textbooks and the best copier we could get for 10,000 *riyal* (approximately $2,600 U.S.) a year prior. The centrally located smaller salon, which had served as the clinic's emergency facility, was easily transformed into a salon once again. The two bedrooms of apartment B had previously served as patient examination rooms and had terrazzo flooring for sanitation reasons, which was excellent for our new art studios and the mess they promised.

In each room, I included an armoire to serve as the instructor's workspace. I used the easels and stools purchased to begin the class originally in classroom A to provide an oil painting studio and the dinning room tables in classroom B for future drawing and kids' art classes. The walls were repainted the basic white and the rooms looked rather drab. But that would soon change as the artistic expressions of our ladies began to fill the walls.

Directly above the former clinic, apartment C became the center's new Computer & Languages department. The computer lab was the same size as the main salon and it accommodated the thirteen computer desks, computers, whiteboard, armoire for classroom supplies, and wall mounted instructional televisions beautifully. The computer lab was our pride and joy and the benefactor of most of our original start up funds. There was no other place in the Kingdom where women could walk into such a high-tech room and learn computer skills, particularly one where the instructional material had not undergone the scrutiny of the government's Department of Education.

The apartment's kitchen was adjacent to the new computer lab and initially served as a computer server and storage room. Yet, in time, it would become a control room for another ground-breaking endeavor in the desert sand. Even though it had been the kitchen of the clinic's resident PA, it needed some repair even to use as storage. Numerous tiles had fallen from the walls and the grime on the floor was at least an inch thick. We cannibalized the tile we could from the wall to repair apartment A's kitchen downstairs, creating a large bare cement space on the wall which we simply painted to make it presentable.

One evening as we were reaching the point of exhaustion, but still scraping the grime from the floor on our hands and knees, David reminded us of an event involving the building. An event I had completely forgotten. He could not help but raise the suspense as he reminded us of the suicide. The building had been closed up for over three years since the company had moved all employees and the medical clinic to our new compound by the sea. Before, however, the company housed our medical professionals in apartment C above the clinic. Sadly, one of the company PAs was obviously not well and could not cope with the isolated life of the Kingdom. With access to class III drugs, he had committed suicide one evening in what eventually became TLC's English classroom. Disturbingly, he was found the following morning with the needle still in his arm lying on his bed, naked.

As David retold the events, Lulu and I cringed at the thought of someone dying in the center. I cringed even more when David reminded us of how the Saudi's did not maintain the corpse properly or release the body for weeks because drugs were involved. Spooked by the story and visualizing the event, I typically spent as little time as possible in the bedroom where he died and I avoided it all together when I was in the center alone.

Mirroring the art department below, apartment C's salon was decorated in our floral décor offering a cozy place where students could gather before class or study afterward. The two bedrooms over the art studios became our language classrooms. Utilizing our originally purchased 20 classroom desks, the suicide bedroom became Language A for English instruction. Due to lack of additional desks, I used our standard classroom décor for Language B where we offered French and Spanish. Although not very fancy, the language classrooms were nice and served the purpose.

The old apartment D to the right at the top of the stairs was the least used apartment initially. The kitchen was to the left, which mirrored the hostess kitchen downstairs. This kitchen was old and barely presentable. We had done our best to cannibalize what we could from the art and computer departments' kitchens, yet I wasn't pleased. However, the ladies were since they had no other basis of comparison. TLC was the first and only ladies learning center in the

Kingdom at this point. With no alternative, it was useful as our classroom kitchen in the beginning in spite of its antiquated appliances and lack of teaching counter space.

The large room across the hall from the new class kitchen was identical in size to the main salon just below on the first floor. Because I had experienced Madawi's personal enthusiasm for exercise when she had me help design their personal dance/exercise room at the palace, I felt sure there were other ladies in the area that would be interested in and take advantage of aerobics as well. However, there were no guarantees the Saudi women would be receptive to the idea of wearing exercise clothing in public or even be interested in physical fitness no matter what the attire. Even so, I felt it was worth the risk and the time to spruce up just a bit.

David and Yacoub were wonderful about identifying our needs: the purpose for the renovation, type of classroom, or whatever else we found we needed with regard to the facility. Clearly, the terrazzo tile simply would not work for the floor of an exercise room, but I was clueless as to an alternative. When I presented this to the guys, they came up with a terrific idea. They built a fake wood floor 2 inches above the tile and stained it dark brown. As luck would have it, Yacoub had a few mirrored panels that he had removed from a previous job and used them to cover the entire 15' x 15' wall. I slipped in an armoire for the instructor's use with a boom-box inside and voilá. A fitness room emerged.

With our rush to move facilities as the American military shoved us out of our original villas on DM18, time and resources limited what we could accomplish with this fourth apartment space. Understanding nothing could be done at that point in time I simply cleaned the pea-green bathroom for the exercise ladies' use and utilized the remainder of apartment D for storage. But I saw its potential for the future and put my ideas on the back burner to steep.

It was strange to be the only female working in the facility with authority and only one of two in the building at all. Lulu was with me at all times in the center. She worked just as hard as I did. Elbow to elbow, we scrubbed. Lulu was clever and understood English fairly well. It was so easy to work with her as the language barrier was easily overcome.

Periodically, I would meander through the center to observe the work in progress. Quickly I learned that each worker had their own "area of expertise," and neither God nor high water was going to change it. One afternoon, I walked into the exercise room upstairs to find two workers sleeping on cardboard amongst a stack of old air conditioning units that needed to be taken downstairs and thrown out. When I asked why they were resting and suggested they could be moving the air conditioners instead, one told me "I'm the electrician. No need electrician now." The other muttered, "I do tile. No tile now" and they returned to their napping.

Even though I was fairly new to daily refurbishment supervision, I had already had enough of the "it's not my department" response and I became incredibly frustrated. Exasperated, I sighed loudly to make my point and began to drag an air conditioning unit myself. Surprisingly, my doing so caused an unexpected response. Even though it was not "their specialty," their respect for a woman outweighed their desire to avoid work and the two men hopped to their feet once I started to heave the machine. They refused to let the Madame do anything that physical and they proceeded to remove every unit. At that moment, I felt my halo tarnish a bit when I realized how easy it would be to get things done from this point on. All I needed to do was start doing whatever needed to be done. The men, all from third world countries, would not allow a woman to do such and they would finish the task. To say the least, work progress quickened.

By this time, David started to become comically concerned about my being there while the crews were working. As we were leaving that evening, Riyaz, Yacoub's head foreman, respectfully stepped forward and breathlessly asked David, "Will the Madame be returning to help us again tomorrow, sir?"

We stopped and turned to face Riyaz in response to his question. His face showed intense exasperation when David replied with a chuckle.

"Bright and early, Riyaz," he laughed. "So get a good nights rest." David and Riyaz were great friends so the joke was taken in the best way. "Thank you again for all you are doing," David added, shaking his hand in respect before we made our way to the gate.

Riyaz, on the other hand, shook his head as he headed back inside to collect his crew.

As promised, I arrived at 7:30 a.m. the following morning ready to work. The workers stopped what they were doing and looked at each other when we entered the gate. The glares were so intense that I almost got the woolies and David felt it, too. Once inside my office, he handed me his cell phone and joked. "You might better keep this with you today" he smiled. "In case they lock you in a closet," he added and then roared with laughter.

"What?" my amazement was evident from my tone of voice.

"Just kidding" he chuckled. "Riyaz won't let anything happen to you. But keep the phone with you just in case," he added with a wink and left for work.

After touring the center and greeting every worker with a polite "good morning" and a smile, I began to employ my new tactic of work involvement. Those poor men worked themselves to death, only sitting down to eat with no more naps. After a few days, I became worried that I was driving them too hard and knew I needed to compensate for their extra effort.

Understanding that *TCN*s typically send every bit of their wages to their families in their respective home countries, I knew they had little or no money left for "luxury" items like cigarettes, sodas, and pizzas. To raise moral, the next morning David and I went by the ***souk*** before the center. I arrived around 8:30 a.m. laden with cartons of cigarettes and cases of sodas.

The men were reluctant to accept at first, but when they realized that we had brought these for them at no cost to them, their looks of uncertainty turned to smiles. After that morning, I made it a practice to do something out of the ordinary and special for them each week until the job was done.

It was a steamy hot day in late August as I sat at my desk and tried to concentrate on class scheduling, while the workers clamored away in the background. The day had flown and before I knew it, a piece of paper slid in front of me and David was in my office to collect me for the day.

"What's this?" I asked somewhat surprised by his entrance and shocked that it was already four o'clock.

"Just today's current breaking news," he chuckled sarcastically while he observed the work outside my office window. We had become accustomed to our regular security threat warnings. Yet this one stood out from the pack. As he silently observed, I picked up the paper and read, "International terrorist financier, Osama Bin Ladin, issued a statement outlining the goals of his organization, Al-Qaida (meaning "the Base"), which included a call to drive U.S. forces from the Arab peninsula, overthrow the Saudi royal family, liberate the Muslim Holy sites, and support other "revolutionary" groups around the world. This call encouraged his supporters to attack U.S. interests in Saudi Arabia and other Gulf states."

I continued and the same old reminder concluded the U. S. Warden's message, "The United States Government reminds all citizens living abroad to remain vigilant …yahda, yahda, yahda."

Not letting go of the paper, I looked up at David.

"Is this the guy that blew up the towers?"

"Not officially," David replied "but everyone knows he was behind it."

"What does it mean for us? Is this one different?" I questioned with heightened concern.

"It means he wants Americans – the infidels – out of Kingdom. But does it mean we need to do anything differently?" He turned from the window to face me. "No."

An extended silence followed and then David added. "By the way, there was an explosion in Bahrain today." He began gathering my bags to carry to the suburban. "A kid, well a student. American." He paused. "There was an IED (improvised explosive device) in the gas tank of his rental car."

"Oh my God!" My hand went to my mouth unconsciously.

"It's okay." David laughed at the perceived incompetence. "It failed to go off properly and the boy is okay."

"But still…David."

"I know baby, I know."

Even though we hated or refused to admit it, our security was an issue and becoming more so day by day. It was strange, but consideration of security had

ॐCreating Shamsiyahॐ

to be discussed with every decision we made as if it were as insignificant as which room to paint what color. Unlike DM18, the new center did not have a gate or a man to guard it. As a result, the decision was made for my *Maasai* to live on the premises.

When Madawi and I first assessed DM12 as our second physical shamsiyah, we thought of allowing Saleem to live in one of the four apartments. Yet we quickly ruled this idea out for two reasons: the women and the smell that would permeate throughout the center from his cooking of African cuisine. Consequently, I had to turn to Yacoub once again to build Saleem a room behind the building. All at no cost to us, but rather included in other base refurbishments.

Fortunately, a simple cinder block room, complete with wall to wall carpeting, a toilet inside, and a wash basin outside emerged between our building and our back wall. Approximately 8' x 12', Saleem's new apartment became his pride and joy. He had his own place, which was not the norm for TCNs in Kingdom. Typically, six to eight men would be housed in a room the size of Saleem's and none of them would be as nice inside. From the same compound as our floral furnishings, we were able to obtain a birch twin bed and a dresser for his use. We added one of the center's five televisions and I brought a bedspread and VCR from my villa as icing on the cake.

The days were long and hot, but the center began to take shape. Surprisingly, I began to feel as if we would make our deadline and I couldn't have been happier. With a little time to spare before our targeted completion date, I decided to give a bit of attention to our outside entry. Another reason apartment A was selected as the new facility entry was its larger courtyard space between the building and the security wall.

Shaped in a triangle, the far, narrow end of the courtyard cradled a tree that had obviously been shading it for years. It was huge and the children loved climbing its thick, low branches that almost completely shaded the approximately 20' x 35' space. As a final touch, I placed a plastic lawn table and chairs under the tree and one on the porch outside the art department to accommodate any students that may smoke or prefer the out of doors.

Conserving stones removed from the exterior wall when they made the new entrance, Yacoub's masons were able to transform the old three foot porch wall into a new stone planter box. We painted it the flat white of the wall and building and then filled it with 100 *SR* (approximately $25.00 U.S.) worth of perennials. Suddenly, the entrance came to life. Standing back, I gave it the nod of a job well done.

Pleased with my efforts and dripping in perspiration, I decided to give the lawn furniture a try and enjoy lemonade under the shade tree while I waited for David to collect me for the day. Surprisingly, the mere 105 degree heat felt comfortable as a soft, warm breeze evaporated my perspiration. Leaning back, I closed my eyes with exhaustion, when suddenly I heard the screech of the single wall door open. It was David, smiling because it was the weekend.

After showing him the planter box and a few other things I had done around the center that day, we gathered my bags and laughed with anticipation of the weekend while we loaded the suburban. Climbing up into the vehicle, I used the rag I kept there to hold the seatbelt buckle in order to keep from burning my hands when fastening it. Just as it clicked, David started the engine and casually mentioned, "Oh, by the way, there was another explosion today…in Bahrain. A car outside a hotel was firebombed."

Shocked, my head turned in his direction wanting details. "What?" My mood suddenly shifted from jovial to concern. "Which hotel? Was anyone hurt?"

"No. Fortunately the American was inside at reception, but I don't know the hotel. The report only said it was a 'luxury hotel' in Manama."

"Will it ever end?" I blurted rhetorically, revealing my exasperation.

"Not in our lifetime," he added and punched the accelerator.

As the end of September drew near, I knew I would be ready for Madawi's return in two weeks. With the grimy, physical work complete, I was free to return to my dresses, store the jeans for another day, and focus on my organizational duties as director. Each morning David would drop me at the center on his way to the base and then collect me on his way home in the afternoon. Stranded, I relied on my sack lunch or Lulu to bring me food from the palace only four blocks away. There was no such thing as commercial food delivery. Although I ate, I never left my work and continued to type with bites in between. It was grueling, yet exhilarating because I knew what I was doing was meant to be.

 Often when I needed to relax, to reflect, or seek inspiration, I would make my way to the secluded third floor of *The Learning Center* – the roof. Towering over all other buildings in the immediate area, the flat roof offered a gorgeous, three hundred and sixty degree view of **Al-Khobar** – the city of little pools. As far as the eye could see, in every direction, needle thin structures reached to the sky marking yet another Mosque along the Arabian Gulf or dotted throughout the city. During any of the five daily **Sallas**, the call to pray was heard in stereo on the roof of TLC and, at times, it was even majestic. With the open, clear sky above me, I felt free. On any given "pretty day," I could simply think there. I often dreamt of opening a roof-top café for the ladies. As I would subconsciously any sort problems at hand, I would walk off my dream café, think of decorating ideas, and analyze the costs involved. Ironically, my roof-top café was the only dream of the many dreamt that I did not see accomplished by the end.

Chapter 11
Unveiling the Dream
October 1996 - January 1997

Attempting to show my respect of Madawi's religion, I decided it would be a good idea to get a nice ***Quran*** and a stand to display it in the main salon – the heart of her dream. Placing it in the center of the bookshelf and straightening the pillows, I busied myself with last minute touches while I waited for her to arrive to see her new center for the very first time. Mohammed, the palace operator, had telephoned earlier in the day to tell me that ***Amity*** would be by in the afternoon. Anxious, I double checked with Lulu to make sure the tea was brewing when I heard the front door open. I stopped talking to Lulu in mid-sentence and made a beeline to reception. My Shamsiyah was back and I was thrilled.

Hugs and kisses dominated the first few minutes with both of us smiling beyond description. Obviously, she had missed me as much as I had missed her. Still beaming I stepped back and put my arms out to present reception and *The Learning Center* to Madawi.

"Well, what do you think?" I grinned with pride for my accomplishments and the future possibilities for my friend. Whirling in a circle, she exclaimed with pleasure, "***Marbrook ya mama!***" She clasped her hands to her chest in pleasure. "I just love it, Mrs. Teresa. Very nice!"

Even though we both wanted to enjoy our cup of tea and cap, we decided to take a quick tour of the center before relaxing and catching up on the last two months. Under her breath, she uttered various Arabic words of praise as she meandered through reception, smiling as if she had received the gift she had always wanted. After greeting Lulu in the newly tiled hall, she turned and walked slowly through the main salon, connecting with every detail, periodically touching as if confirming reality. When she reached the bookshelf displaying her Holy book, however, she stopped. Immediately, an awkward silence flooded the room. I stepped up beside her to offer an explanation without the question being asked, and I saw it for the first time. Without emotion, she spoke.

"There is no need for this," she stated with a stone face as her eyes starred momentarily at the religious display I had made. Then, her hand cut through the air to indicate its removal. Stunned by her obvious resentment, I reacted instinctively to remove the book and stand. Madawi, still talking, turned and said in a monotone voice. "Put it in the drawer. If someone wants it…they can get it" and she left the room.

After completing our tour, we returned to my office to enjoy some refreshment and simply visit. Madawi immediately gravitated to the overstuffed, floral chair by my makeshift desk, which is where she sat every time she stopped by from that day forward. Within a moment, Lulu appeared carrying a doily-lined silver tray with Madawi's tea and my cappuccino. We talked for hours catching up on all that had happened in each of our lives during the summer.

With personal details up to speed, our attention turned to TLC. She immediately announced we must have a party to unveil the center to the ladies of the province. Proud that I had thought ahead, I reached into my briefcase and handed her an invitation proof for her approval. Scheduled for two weeks later, she agreed the date would work but suggested this be an "unofficial" open house and that we "officially" open in the spring. For this term, she would simply "spread the word." Agreeing, I slipped the invitation back in my bag to save for another day. When I offered a sheet to show the class offerings I had scheduled for our first six weeks in the new center, she casually glanced at the paper and handed it back to me. "I think these look good, Mrs. Teresa. Be sure to put me in aerobics, huh." she replied and stood to leave.

"Most certainly." I stood as well, yet I had to share one more bit of news before she left. "I have to find a new receptionist."

She stopped, turning back to me to listen.

"MaryAnn's husband, Joe, has had another heart attack and they must leave Kingdom in December."

"Oh no," she replied while her face revealed concern. "I am so sorry to hear. We will miss her."

"Oh yes," I added. "And I am worried about reception. I don't know anyone to fill her shoes. I need someone that I can trust."

"And maybe speak Arabic, too, huh" Madawi added turning to leave once again. "You will find someone, Mrs. Teresa, **Insha Allah**. Do not worry."

With kisses and hugs, she assured me she would begin telling the ladies about the center that evening as she was attending a ladies party to welcome her return.

"It will be good," she concluded flashing her soothing, signature smile. "I will see you tomorrow, **Insha Allah**. Take care, huh." And she disappeared through the door.

With soft jazz playing in the background, I leaned against the wall and sipped my cap. Pleased, I quietly watched the ladies flow through the beautiful curved oak door and into our newly renovated facility. It was the first night of our second fall term registration, yet it served as the "unofficial" opening of the new TLC. The new Learning Center was an elegant, welcoming place that the ladies would soon refer to as their second home. The Saudi women and their desire to learn were gaining momentum and with each success—more steam.

As I observed the ladies and the friendship building interactions that were exuding from the room, the chatter of the women coming and going became distant to me. Unconsciously, I began to reflect over the significance of this budding phenomenon. I was still becoming accustomed to what was actually happening within the borders of this male dominated, incredibly conservative Islamic country. Honestly, in most countries of the world, what was happening before my eyes would have been seen as an every day event and nothing particularly special. Yet to place *The Learning Center* and the doors it was opening for women in the Kingdom of Saudi Arabia, and subsequently realize that this was perhaps the first opportunity some of these ladies had ever had to learn as adult women made the simple smiles and hellos of the evening historical.

Still using the wall as a brief reprieve from the arduous days I had had as of late, I continued to enjoy my coffee, rest a weary ankle one at a time, and observe. I saw MaryAnn, near the door, welcoming ladies with her Scottish accent and soothing smile as she greeted each and every woman that entered. What a blessing she was to join the TLC team as our first receptionist. She was always professional, polite, and calming, even in adverse situations such as the visit from the **Hiyah** in our old facility. With eleven years in Kingdom under her belt, she understood the Saudi culture and she knew how to work within its constraints, yet still achieve her goal.

In the center of the reception area, the most pivotal point in the room, stood Madawi welcoming her friends and exposing her fellow countrywomen to her vision. She beamed as the ladies passed MaryAnn's greetings and made a beeline for the princess. Standing tall with confident shoulders and naturally dressed in the latest Parisian fashion, Madawi took the time to personally connect with each lady and share her personal concern and happiness for them. She greeted in the traditional Arab way of kissing on each check, held hands, laughed, and with some even cried. Madawi embraced each moment of the unveiling of her dream's latest accomplishment as if it were a delightfully scrumptious desert that had never crossed her lips.

Ann stood near the reception desk just as absorbed in each lady she greeted as Madawi. Ann exuded a loving, maternal aura that the ladies gravitated unconsciously. Her eight year tenure in Kingdom coupled with her bubbling personality and determination to help the women made her invaluable to me, to Madawi, and to the success of *The Learning Center*. Ann had originally met Madawi when she stepped in to tutor for me at the palace during my son's birth three years prior, yet she quickly established her own unique relationship with Madawi. When Madawi and the family got to know Ann, they could not help but love her open, refreshingly optimistic outlook on life, her sincere respect for both cultures, her loving warmth, emotional support, and, of course, her wisdom. She had been there for me my entire life and she was now here for both of us as we unveiled Madawi's dream. It is no wonder that the ladies so fondly called my mom, Mama Ann.

I decided I needed to move rather than lean to ward off the looming exhaustion I felt from getting the center ready for this night. Knowing reception was in capable greeting hands, I began to mingle. I strolled down the hall and into the main salon. It was there that the ladies would eventually meet between classes, share a cup of tea or make plans to get together. It was where we hold student and staff birthday parties, staff meetings, holiday parties, and where we would even cried quietly at times with a close friend in the off hours of the center.

In the corner, I saw Mona sharing tea with a student and obviously enthralled in her conversation. Mona, the first teacher I had hired, had already established herself as a mainstay within the TLC team. Beautifully Lebanese, Mona was smart as well. She held a degree in engineering but taught French just as her mom had done. Mona was fluent in Arabic, French and conversationally fluent in English. With pride during our initial interview, she shared that both her mother and sister were French teachers and that she had been educated in a French school system. Even in Kingdom, she sent her children to the local French academy so they would be prepared to move back to Lebanon one day. Mona was quiet, yet passionate, professional and refined.

My thoughts of Mona were interrupted as a lady bumped me from the back. The center was crowded with ladies squeezing through this conversation and past the next, either looking for someone in particular or touring from room to room and meeting ladies along the way. Swinging by the center's kitchen where Lulu prepared the daily snacks and tea, I snagged a hors d'heurve and continued my mingling.

Energy rushed from the art department as the sounds of different languages filled the air. The women were excited to have such an opportunity available to them. Having it available in an elegant environment with the social elite of their community was simply icing on the cake. Before I saw Betsy, I heard her pitching her oil painting course to a few potential students. Typically Betsy, she had on her jeans and cowboy boots but had "dressed up" with a nice top. Her short blonde, wind-blown style hair suited her face and personality, accenting her eyes when she smiled. Over the shoulder of a potential student, Betsy saw me when I entered the room and acknowledged me with a smile. To help, yet not distract, I stepped into the conversation to meet and validate everything Betsy pitched. When it was appropriate, I graciously excused myself to continue my tour, leaving Betsy to continue fulfilling her commitment to the center.

To date, I had six teachers and three staff members on the TLC team. Staff members were paid a monthly wage and given a varying range of benefits, depending on their position and, unfortunately, their nationality. For example, Lulu, a Filipino indoor hostess, received more salary each month than Saleem, a Kenyan male driver, simply because she was Filipino. The center was required to pay their monthly wages, but their food, medical, living quarters, bonuses, and biannual vacation expenses were provided through the palace in the beginning.

The teachers, on the other hand, were contractual workers and paid a fee for each course/workshop that had enough paying students to make. The "contract" was more of a statement of understanding between the teacher and TLC so that everyone knew what was expected of the other. Because of the finite Western community and the pool of women from which I could find instructors, I worked with my friends. The statement of understanding kept us friends. It was signed and renewed each time the instructor wished to offer her course/workshop, which allowed an "out" for either of us. Now this is not to say I never had issues with instructors, I did. I am human. Yet, in over six years, I only had one disagreement with an instructor that the written understanding, our shared vision and open communication, could not resolve. Sadly, it was the disagreement that eventually led to my demise.

Among other things, the statement of understanding required the instructor to assist TLC in the promotion of her class(es). TLC would advertise through word of mouth and very limited flyer distribution to get the ladies there, but it would then be up to the teacher. The instructors simply had to be the ones to extend the hand. Saudis, by culture, are extremely private people and wary to open up and make friends. However, once they got to know you and accepted you as a "friend," typically they were extremely loyal. Considering our center was a new way of learning than most of our students had ever been exposed, the need for the instructor to work to build these relationships and trust became even more vital. It was a good feeling to walk through the center and see my teachers doing their job with such commitment and genuine sincerity.

The students, on the other hand, who came to the center behaved accordingly, seeking friends with their learning experience. They had to like their instructor to enroll. They would not register in a class based solely on the topic of the course, no matter how interested they may be in the information it would present. The flip side was that when they liked a teacher, they would then take everything the woman offered simply because they liked her, even if she were to teach underwater basket-weaving.

Because the Saudis are nocturnal, the center became more crowded as the night wore on. Working my way through the bottleneck in the stairway, I saw ladies moving up and down the steps like water in a river. All of them were joyful and smiling uncontrollably, with some even stopping me on the landing to ask questions.

I had been fortunate over the summer to find a replacement for Barbara when she felt she could no longer teach our computer classes. Our new computer teacher, Johara, was educated in the west and carried herself professionally like a western businesswoman would. I was thrilled I had found Johara. She was good and, honestly, I felt bad that I was happy Barbara had left after seeing Johara in action. She always wore a suit to teach and carried her brief case. Her documents, instructional material, resume, everything she produced was always presented clearly, timely, and professionally. So it was right in line with her personality for me to find Johara in the computer lab with each computer system and television on, scrolling various welcome messages, for our open registration. I smiled with approval when I saw Johara in her classroom explaining the curriculum to a potential student. Johara, a beautiful Egyptian woman, was married to an American on my compound. She was professionally fluent in Arabic and English and degreed in computer science. Although she taught in English – the language of computer technology – she was able to answer questions in the ladies' native Arabic language, which made learning much easier and comfortable for them. Initially, Johara offered typing, basic computer skills, and word-processing. As the students completed these courses, she went on to offer advance coursework to meet their instructional needs.

After a quick wave of acknowledgment to Johara, I sauntered through our two language classrooms to make sure everything was still perfect and ready for visitors. Unlike the downstairs, the language department was fairly empty without teachers in the classrooms. Ann, the English instructor, and Mona, the French instructor, were downstairs doing their public relations and the classrooms stood empty simply for display.

Walking quietly around the classroom, I sighed. DM12 was more facility than we needed. We had only opened our doors a year prior with 29 ladies and celebrated 70 ladies in the spring. In the old villas, 70 ladies filled the place up. Yet here, no. "In time," I reassured myself, "in time."

When I peeked into the big, aerobics room of apartment D, I saw Angela meeting ladies and promoting her classes for the term. I smiled while I watched the ladies' faces light up as they listened to Angela. Based on the number of names on the enrollment sheet at the front desk, it was already obvious that it had been a good decision to utilize the space to offer the ladies exercise classes, even if the rest of the apartment was in dire need of renovation. Yet again, TLC was clearing the path and launching another first by offering aerobics to the ladies of the Eastern province.

On my way to the kitchen to put my cup away, I saw Lulu directing the other Filipino nannies from the palace. Each of them scooting between the ladies offering hot, fresh hors d'eurves, iced Saudi champagne, and freshly blended fruit drinks. Their smiles as they served were genuine because they knew a surprise awaited them. The palace nannies loved being selected to serve at a palace dinner party or an event such as this because they would either receive extra pay or a gift of gold at the end of the evening for a job well done.

It was almost midnight before I called for Saleem to drive us to the compound. Most were gone by 10:30 p.m., but MaryAnn, Ann, and I remained to go over class enrollment and assess the evening's success over a final cup of cap or tea. We had 68 registrations on our first night. We discussed who had come and who we did not see. When we saw that several of our "regulars" were not there, we determined they simply did not know where to find us.

As expected, telephones started ringing around the Eastern Province once the ladies began to spread the word about the new TLC they had seen. By the time classes began three days later, we had approximately 100 registrations representing almost 75 students. Slowly, they were learning where we had moved. Although still manageable, it was obvious I would need an office assistant soon, particularly if Madawi wanted me to offer my communication workshops again. Unfortunately, the budget did not afford me the luxury of an office assistant at the moment. But, I knew finding the right woman would take time so I decided to start looking with the hopes of finding someone by spring.

Our enrollment system was simple, but efficient. Each class had an enrollment sheet in a three ring binder at reception. Once a class had five students, it was considered "made" and maxed with ten. Because of our November opening and the upcoming holidays of the Muslim's **Ramadan** and the Christian's Christmas, we only ran a short six week term. We offered our basic curriculum from before, which included English, French, Computers, Art, Business Management, Human Communication, and, our newest addition, Aerobics. Participation was light, but better because it was easier to manage until we got our feet wet in the new facility.

Just when things were going well and our spirits were soaring, Osama bin Laden reared his evil voice once again with his venom more directed. In a November declaration he called the recent OPM/SANG (1995) and *Al-Khobar* bombings (1996) "praiseworthy acts of terrorism," but denied directed participation. Exasperated, we all knew "direct participation" simply meant he didn't actually place the bomb or drive the water truck carrying it. He also reiterated his previous rhetoric against the Saudi royal family and America by calling, once again, for loyal followers to continue attacks against U.S. military personnel, yet he added that "if someone can kill an American soldier, it is better than wasting time on other matters." Naturally our security heightened once again, but I was beginning to become numb to these messages by now. I rationalized that he was after the military, not civilian women and children and I subconsciously could not accept the danger I faced. I guess in my mind I couldn't fathom these threats while in the midst of something so good and surround by Arabs that I believed to be genuine friends.

  Madawi always stopped by my office for a quick visit after her classes if her royal obligations permitted the time. One December afternoon, she dropped into the overstuffed chair letting out a sigh of relief after her aerobics class. I, on the other hand, had said hello but had not looked up from my papers. With the holidays just around the corner, I was working overtime to get everything done in order to take a few weeks off during our down time for my Christmas and the upcoming *Eid*, which would begin in late December. Just then, Lulu entered with her little silver tray holding my cap and Madawi's tea just the way we liked them. Unable to resist, I pushed my papers aside and turned my focus on my friend. As we touched on various issues with the center, I mentioned to Madawi that I wanted to start looking for an assistant. Honestly, I was sharing this to keep her abreast of what I was planning, not looking for the position to be filled. However, it turned out that one of our regular students, Hiba, had a daughter-in-law that was looking for part-time work. Naturally, my first thought was "oh great. It's one of *those*," and I guess my face revealed it.

"I don't know her, Mrs. Teresa, so I make no promises." She paused to put her teacup on the table and find her ***abaya*** in her bag. The silence was awkward.

"I've never met her," Madawi continued, emphasizing her distance to the lady with her hands. "But at least we can give her a try. Hiba says she is very clever." Madawi urged and soothed as she put on her ***abaya*** to leave. "If she can not do the job, you will look for someone else, huh." Gathering her bag, she added. "I'll tell Hiba to have her call you." She smiled and out the door she went.

Perhaps, "have her call you" got translated incorrectly somewhere in the communication chain, but bright and early the next morning, a young African-American woman in her early-thirties entered our door. Somewhat shocked to see a Western woman coming to the center, I paused at my desk to await

MaryAnn's report on the intercom. It was Hiba's daughter-in-law at the center for her interview.

It turned out that I was correct in my assumption of the communication breakdown. Although I had come to work in sweats only expecting aerobics students on a Wednesday (the last day in the workweek in Kingdom) not guests, I welcomed her, excused my attire, and the interview began. Maria was an American originally from Indiana. She had met her husband, Hiba's son, at a stateside university and fallen in love. They had been married for about ten years and had three children. She had her degree and previous office administration experience, which made her a perfect candidate for the assistant I envisioned. She and Yasser had moved to Kingdom about two years prior and Maria was overly eager to begin part-time work. Within a half an hour, I knew. She had the credentials and, more importantly, she had that intangible combination of personality traits that I constantly sought, could always sense, yet never define. Hence, I hired her on the spot, even though I was unsure how I would pay her. As luck would have it, she didn't want to begin work until after the first of the year, so it was a win-win situation.

Throughout the interview, she was rather reserved, yet very professional. After she was hired and all details set, I did, however, see the real Maria peek out when I asked her to participate in an upcoming staff event. Christmas was just around the corner and the Christian instructors had decided to have a little gift exchange in celebration. I knew it would be a terrific opportunity for Maria to meet the rest of the staff, and Maria was more than elated to be invited to a Christian celebration among other Christians. It had been over two years since her last Christmas party.

Our first fall term in our new facility had passed quickly and, before I knew it, I was hugging Madawi good-bye before she flew stateside. It had been a grueling fall for her with everything she had going on in her life. She was busy with *Al-Hamdi*, TLC classes and exercise, and her personal trials to boot. Her kids were anxious to spend their month holiday at their home in Mclean, so Madawi had agreed. Her face showed her exhaustion and I knew the change of pace would do her good. Madawi was not the only one that was worn out. I yearned for a few lazy days to enjoy holiday baking, wrapping, and some decking the halls. I need to recharge my battery and I knew it.

As hoped the three week break did the trick and I was rearing to go after we rang in 1997. Wanting to get as much done as possible before the manic days began with students in the building, I started going back to the center two weeks before I expected Maria to begin and the instructors to return. With the center still officially closed, I could slip on my sweats and work comfortably as I produced text books, brochures, contracts, and the like. Completely enthralled in my work, I was startled when Madawi popped into my office unexpectedly.

Instinctively, I jumped up to give my Shamsiyah a welcome home hug. It was a wonderful surprise to see her. After our initial hugs and hellos, she plopped into her favorite chair and nodded to Lulu for her usual cup of tea. I quickly scooted my papers to the side, turned my office chair to face her, and leaned back for a visit. Just as her tea and my cap arrived, Madawi began as she always did in the Arab way of asking about me, my family, and my holiday. The kids and David were fine and my holiday had been just what I wanted, a quiet, relaxing couple of weeks. Hence, the conversation quickly turned to her. After I sipped my cap, I began.

"So enough about me," I declared before another sip. "What about you? How did the girls enjoy their trip? How was Washington? What did you guys do?" The questions just flowed as I tucked my feet up in my chair to nestle in for the details.

"Oh, where to begin?" she rhetorically posed as a huge smile crossed her face and she threw her head back in obvious happiness.

"Well..." she beamed. "We did the usual." Her hands began to emphasize while she began to draw out the suspense that was so typically Madawi. "We went out to eat and took the girls to Bush Gardens again. We celebrated the *Eid* at the house..." Her smile indicated that the real news was about to spill. "... and we went skiing in Colorado."

"What?" I exclaimed. "Shoot" I jested as I snapped my fingers. "If I had known that I would have tagged along!" I added still smiling at her wonderful news. "When did you decide to do that?"

Well, *I* didn't…" the smile became broader. "Awad did." A grin emerged.

"What?" I was completely surprised, curious, hopeful, yet reserved. "Awad?"

She could stand it no longer and scooted to the edge of her chair to share. "Oh Mrs. Teresa," she beamed. "It was so romantic!" Her non-verbals kicked into high gear as every ounce of her being became involved in the retelling of the events. "It was the last night of the *Eid* …THE holiest night of the year for my faith," her eyes widened. "I was miserable. I was curled up…crying. I felt I could go no more and I asked God for peace." She paused, reflecting…"Just for peace." She paused yet again and a long moment of silence passed. "I had been asking for so long to have Awad back…but I could not ask any more. I simply asked God for peace. After the evening prayer, I went down to the meal. It's a special meal for us." She paused to make a connection for me, "like your Christmas dinner." Her hands continued to help her explain. "It was exactly one year to the night…exactly one year." Her face tightened to show the importance of the day. "Since the divorce… and for some reason, I did not sit in Awad's chair at the head of the table. I could not. It was strange because I had been there all week. But…not then, it did not feel comfortable. Rather, I took the chair on the right." Her reflective, more serious demeanor began to morph into nothing but joy. "Then just after we started to eat, Jackson stepped in the door and I knew." She beamed. "I just knew that Awad was there. I was so excited! And then there, standing in front of me was Awad. But.." She added as she came up from her chair to continuing sharing while she paced my office. "I did not want to get too excited. I just told myself the whole time we ate that he was there for the children. After dinner, he asked me to go to Colorado for a week."

"Oh my God Madawi!" I interjected, beaming as well. "This is so exciting! And…" my hands and eyes encouraged more detail.

Her seriousness returned. "I could not go, Mrs. Teresa."

"What?" I exclaimed in amazement. "Why not, for heavens sake? I know you wanted him back and there he was." My hands flew in response. "Why didn't you go?"

Her chuckle returned. "Of course I **wanted** to go, Mrs. Teresa. I just could not without permission."

Completely confused, "Huh?" was all I could muster.
"I am not married to Awad, Mrs. Teresa. I can not just go off and be with a man I am not married to." Her eyes showed she was amazed I would even think it was acceptable. "But I decided it was okay after Awad guaranteed no funny business." She continued with a chuckle. "He rented two chalets, one for him and one for me and the children. So I called Mohammed."

Confusion was really swirling at this point for me and she saw it in my face. "My little brother, Mohammed in Miami…you met him in D.C." She interjected somewhat surprised I did not remember.

"Oh…" I drew out as I recalled Mohammed. He was in D.C. on business and we met him and his girlfriend for lunch. Mohammed lived in the states and visited the Kingdom on holidays. He was young, handsome, and very westernized. It is no wonder Madawi would pick him to ask other than her other, more conservative male family members. "Yes!" I answered. "…but why did you call Mohammed to go with the Colonel? Were you planning to meet Mohammed there?" I was still lost.

"No, Mrs. Teresa," she chuckled. "I needed permission from a male family member and it was best to call Mohammed."

"And what did he say?" I asked in amazement that the call had to be made in the first place.

"Oh" she laughed deeply. "He said 'go for it sister'!" She clapped her hands together emphasizing her love of his comment.

Understanding and beaming again, I asked" And so…what happened?"

She returned to the edge of her chair and began to remember, using all of her body to tell. "It was so romantic! Awad sent me flowers." She grinned like a bashful school girl. "And…we had a romantic dinner on the very top of the mountain and then we skied down the mountain in the night." She beamed. "Awad was romantic and just the perfect gentleman."

"Oh Madawi!" I exclaimed so very happy for my friend. "I am so glad you two are together again! When will he move back to the palace?"

Her demeanor immediately changed yet again as her shoulders went erect and her back straight. "Oh no, Mrs. Teresa. He must marry me again. He must go to classes. He must work and prove to the courts that he should get me back." Her seriousness continued. "When he did this...he checked the last box." Her brows furrowed and her long slender finger emphasized the severity. "He checked the really bad one – no reconciliation." She paused.

Taking in what she was saying while I sipped my cap, I then asked. "So he has to attend classes to marry you again?"

"Yes, religious classes."

"So he has to really want you back, doesn't he?" A playful smile emerged as my brow rose.

"Yes." She beamed once again.

"Well," I laughed at the thought of an American man doing that, "then you make him work hard because you are worth it!"

"Oh yes" Madawi replied with a small mischievous smile "it won't hurt him to work a little." She winked and chuckled, obviously as happy as she could possibly be that her prayers had been answered.

After she left, I simply sat and reflected while I sipped a fresh cup of cap. What a romantic love story! The first time, Madawi and the Colonel married for a contract and to fulfill an obligation. Their union was a "business arrangement" made between their families. But, this time – the second time they would marry – it would be for love.

Chapter ١٢
Destiny Foretold
January – August 1997

We were two weeks out from the start of our first kids' *Winter Jamboree* in the new facility, yet the phone was ringing off the hook. People wanted to register their children. Not expecting such an overwhelming demand, I was in dire need of teachers and class ideas for them to teach. Of the teachers we had, only three were ready to work with children. The others were not interested and decided to take a break until the ladies' spring session. So in the ninth hour, I had to regroup the kids' program to accommodate the demand.

Ann decided to offer English and Drama, complete with a performance of "Little Red Riding Hood" in English, of course, for the moms at the end of the two weeks. Angela was on board for children's exercise, and Mirna offered French. I felt we needed to add at least four more offerings such as Cooking, Arts & Crafts, Art, and perhaps Music to balance the program. So back into my Western expat community I went in search of kid friendly ladies to become teachers for two weeks in only two weeks.

To begin my search, I stopped by the compound office and had them post job announcements on our inter-compound TV channel, which would place my need in 500 Western homes. I then started racking my brain as to who I knew on the compound that had the ability, a love for children, and who would be open to turning their personal life upside down for two weeks to teach. Almost immediately I thought of the compound preschool and *Dhahran Academy* teachers. They were on winter break and would be available during our program dates. Fortunately, the first two I called accepted enthusiastically to teach Cooking and Arts & Crafts.

As luck would have it, Mary, Mason's Taekwondo teacher, called me for an unrelated issue. But one thing led to another and before I knew it, she was on board to offer Taekwondo classes to the Saudi children. Because a martial art is not something you can package in a canned two week class, we decided to let the jamboree be a test study for interest within our clientele. If there was interest, we would meet again and coordinate an agreement for long term classes. I was ecstatic when I got off the phone. We were doing it again. The first in Kingdom to offer martial arts classes to Saudi children.

Many of our children's instructors came and went with the program. Perhaps we wore them out or perhaps they satisfied their curiosity. Whatever the reason, many teachers came, stayed a few weeks or months, and then were gone. Each touched the life of the center in some way, but only a few made an enduring impact.

Pat was one of those instructors. Originally answering my cry for help with the *Winter Jamboree*, Pat stepped into the center and made it apart of her and her apart of it. She dove into the mission with all of her energy. An incredibly talented artist, Pat first joined us to teach drawing to the kids. Pat was a unique, creative individual, operating outside the box as many of the TLC team typically did. She was attractive, tall in stature, and slipped very comfortably into the long skirts and tunics which were our attire while in Kingdom. Although she seemed in tune with the nature of humans, I believe at times she took her analysis of it to the extreme. However, she always sported a smile and looked for the best in everyone, even if she had to dig.

Just like our first jamboree, we allowed the children to select which courses they would take during the offered time period, setting age ranges for each. The children paid by the class and each had their own individualized schedule. Although it worked previously, it was a nightmare with the numbers we were running through the new center. Other unforeseen issues rose to complicate the situation as well.

The idea of adhering to the instructor's age range for any particular class was completely foreign to the majority of the moms. To them, their 5 year old would be fine in a cooking class with their 12 year old. The staff and I tried to hold firm to class age restrictions, but we simply couldn't draw the line in the sand, particularly with Madawi believing as the moms did. Furthermore, most of the children could not read or speak English very well and they were completely confused as to where they should go next. We managed through it by laying the burden on the instructors to help their students move onto their next class while Maria, Ann, and I wore our tennis shoes to catch up the slack. Honestly, I don't think I sat down for two weeks!

One afternoon nearing the end of the jamboree, Fawzia, one of our regular Saudi students with many children, was in the center to collect her crowd. I simply loved Fawzia. She was short and round with a smile that dimmed the sun. I just could not pass up the opportunity to step over and say hello.

"Well hello, Fawzia," I opened with a smile.

"Ah, ello Mrs. Teresa" she replied smiling broadly, but obviously still uncomfortable with her command of the English language.

Nodding and smiling, I continued. "Are the babies enjoying the camp?"

"Oh yes, Mrs. Teresa." She smiled even more as she clasp her hands in front of herself and then opened them wide as she commented, "He love it, Mrs. Teresa!"

"I am very happy to hear that Fawzia, We love offering the fun to the children."

An awkward, lengthy silence followed as we both looked to the kids flooding in and out of the door. Neither of us was comfortable with the language of the other, so our conversation was limited and coated with smiles. Fawzia, however, mustered the confidence to offer a request.

"Swimming, Mrs. Teresa. Can you make swimming for the babies?"

"Oh," I began hesitantly because we did not have a pool with this facility like we did at DM18. "I would love to offer swimming to the children, Fawzia, but we do not have a swimming pool." I chuckled as I modeled swimming motions with my hands and head shaking to emphasize my point.

"You will think of something…you always do" she answered.

"Oh Fawzia, I will have to see what I can do about a pool." I replied feeling guilty to offer false hope.

She smiled broadly taking my response as a "yes," and added. "Please see for woman too, huh?" With that and another smile, she scooted off to catch her youngest, Mohammed, who had run out of the door without seeing her. "***Ashufee baden, insha Allah***, Mrs. Teresa" she called out as she fled and was gone. Whether I was aware at the time or not, a seed had just been planted for another "first" to come our way.

The kids' program was emotionally rewarding and financially helpful to retroactively cover fall, but exhausting nonetheless. Consequently, I looked forward to the ladies' return. I busied myself with our official open house preparations and our spring term which lay on the horizon.

Although Maria was terrific with what she did, the two of us simply could not keep up with the demands on our time. Margaret's departure from Kingdom left a void in our team and I desperately needed to find a receptionist. Call if fate, luck, or divine intervention, but I was thrilled when an answer to prayer entered our Shamsiyah for the first time early one February morning.

Having heard about the center at a ladies' meeting on her compound, Amal entered our midst looking for part-time employment. As with me, she was tired of mindless compound gatherings and wanted to do something meaningful with her time while she was in Kingdom with her husband, Val. She was Lebanese, he was British, and the two made the cutest couple you will ever find. Amal was eager, energetic, personable, and qualified. As a bonus, she spoke Arabic and English fluently. The unanticipated interview lasted for over an hour, but concluded with her coming on board our team where she remained long after my departure many years later.

Our official open house in the spring of 1997 mirrored our unofficial one in the fall. The ladies flowed in the door to see and be seen, each wearing the latest from Paris or the best their closet held. They were immensely curious as to what our newest offerings would be and being seen with the few princesses of the province was icing on the cake.

Our mission was unveiling right before our eyes. The desperate need to socialize brought the ladies to our door, yet it was the exposure to new ideas and a little hobnobbing with the royals that kept them coming back. The TLC team was welcoming and ready to answer questions and explain the benefits of our different offerings while the servants served as before. The significance of the event, however, fell into another realm.

Although our doors had been open for business for over a year and a half, we had never had anything relating to *The Learning Center* duplicated professionally in a local shop. To this point, every single sheet of paper revealing anything to do with TLC had been produced by us because it was simply too risky. But now, we were beginning to find our legs. We were becoming stronger and unofficially accepted. Because our open house was a special event for us, Madawi gave the nod to have the invitations produced by a professional printer. It was her idea.

When re-designing my original invitation, I was allowed to put the day and the time. Yet, for location, I had to write "new location on Pepsi Road." The ladies would give details verbally when they presented the invitation to a friend. Even if we had wanted or been allowed, we did not have a formal street address to include. No dwelling in Kingdom does. However, we were printing 300 and a year prior I did not even consider having something professionally printed. Sometimes our successes were found in the smallest of events, but progress nonetheless. We had passed infancy and beginning to toddle.

During one of her after aerobics office visits, I had the proof for the open house invitations ready for Madawi's approval. Generally, she did not require I get her approval for anything regarding the center. But since this would be a document that would be left at a public place of business and out of our possession, she wanted to make sure we were not crossing the line. The line, however, was never defined and I never knew where it was until I crossed it – basically a gray area where I seemed to find myself often. After review, she made no suggestions and approved it as it was.

While we relaxed, we took time to reflect, discuss what we were accomplishing, and dream of what we wanted to do in the future. While the conversation was light and tranquil, I casually mentioned to Madawi about all of the help we had received from the husbands of our instructors and staff, including the Colonel. The idea of having a dinner party to thank our husbands for their help and support had been suggested at our last staff meeting. We were actually in the initial planning stages and I had never even thought to ask Madawi and the Colonel. It is not their custom for men and women to socialize, even if the reason for the socialization is business. However, the moment seemed right and I threw out the idea.

I began by telling her how much the staff wanted to do something for their husbands. The ladies wanted to thank them in a special way for all they had done. Unlike the states, we relied heavily on our husbands to do what we did.

Basically there were three ways for a woman to get around town: her husband, a taxi / private driver, or the compound bus. Any Western woman in the area that could help at the center had a husband or she would not be in the Kingdom. Ninety-five percent, however, did not have a private driver and taxis became expensive. Plus, we were advised to take the white taxis and warned not to take the yellow ones. Drivers of the yellow taxis had been known to hurt

Western women by taking them to secluded locations and raping them or worst. One yellow taxi driver in particular, when he was arrested for such crimes, admitted that he had aids and had hoped to infect as many women as possible before his capture or death.

The compound bus, on the other hand was safe and reliable, yet it usually did not stop near the stores we needed to frequent. Hence, it was on our husbands we had to depend. Our reliance was such that we even laughed and joked of having hats made for them that read "TLC Driver."

Madawi felt the excitement I felt about having a dinner to show our appreciation. Her eyes, her smile, her nods and "uhuhs" indicated she thought it was a great idea, so I used the opportunity to ask if she and the Colonel would join us.

"Oh no, Mrs. Teresa" she answered chuckling, I presume, at my even thinking she would attend a public mixed couples' event. Which in retrospect, I should have known better. But she added, "You may ask Awad."

"I can?" somewhat surprised.

"Of course, if you wish." Her hands reflected her indifference. "But let me know, huh?" She threw in with a smile and a wink.

While I was on a roll, I decided to toss out the other idea that had been nagging me as of late – swimming. I shared with Madawi what Fawzia had suggested and pointed out the success of the swimming at DM18 the summer before. She added that many of the women had private pools in their homes yet did not know how to swim. Given such, the pool idea was not a hard sell with Madawi. She immediately saw the need and agreed it would be a community service to offer water safety.

"Agreeing" and liking the idea, we laughed, was the easy part. The challenges still remained. Where to have the classes that would be private for the women and who would teach the classes?

"The pool is easy, Mrs. Teresa," Madawi began moving her hand to indicate it was essentially done. "We can use MD16. Awad will be moving back to the palace before the classes begin." She paused. "I'll ask him."

TLC was actually located right between the palace and DM16, which made our new pool option only a block away. Madawi continued, beginning to get very excited about the new offering possibility.

"But we still have no instructor." She said solemnly.

"Oh, but we do!" I started. "And you are never going to believe who," I added while lightly slapping her knee to emphasize her imminent surprise.

"Who?" She smiled broadly yet curiously.

"Cecilia!" I blurted out, laughing before I could finish saying her name.

Puzzled, Madawi just looked at me.

"Oh Madawi, you remember Cecilia from my compound. The hair dresser…the reason Pierre had to work on my hair before the wedding in **Riyadh**." I added to jog her memory.

Then I saw it hit her just as if she had just been hit by a truck. "Oh her!" she laughed and then questioned. "But….does she swim? Is she qualified? Will she be a problem?"

"Oh, no worries," I replied. "She is a certified life guard and swimming instructor. She is perfect for the job."

"But you two are not friends...she destroyed your hair!" Madawi interjected snicker obviously remembering the horrendous hair cut Cecilia had given me out of spite.

"Well that doesn't matter, for heavens sake. This is business." I responded nonchalantly and then added. "Plus…she's gotten nicer now that she's learned how things work on the compound."

"You Americans," she chuckled. "If it is good for you, then it is good for me." Standing, she reached for her *abaya*, which indicated our afternoon chat time had concluded. After our usual hugs and good-byes, she was gone and I was back to making it happen.

Using our staff communication boxes, I sent invitations I produced in-house to the teachers and office staff inviting them and their husbands to attend the appreciation dinner. Everyone was so excited because except for Yacoub, Mirna's husband, and David, the other husbands had not had the opportunity to meet the Colonel – a Saudi prince – and naturally, none of the Western ladies had met him. The Colonel, on the other hand, I called rather than send a written invitation. Being the jovial, westernized gentleman he is, he graciously accepted. Plus, he was "working." It could only look good to his bride-to-be that he supported her dreams.

Many of the Saudi women giggled like school girls when they learned we were offering ladies swimming and water safety – another first. Never in their wildest dreams did they think they would have an opportunity to learn to swim. But, in spite of their apprehension, they stepped onto the limb and took the risk. The water classes became very popular, very quickly. Poor Cecilia was working exhausting shifts to keep up with the demand, plus some private lessons she ran on the side. However, once the classes started, our anonymity became threatened. The constant flow of students' cars going in and out of a supposedly empty Western compound drew unwanted attention and spawned unanswerable questions. In response, we shuttled the ladies to and from DM16's pool only a block away. Their walking along the street was not an option. Again, we had side-stepped the barrier, found an alternative solution, and fostered another first in the Eastern province.

One afternoon I was waiting for Saleem to return from a swimming shuttle run so he could take me the local bookstore for supplies. While I waited in the courtyard behind our white, unmarked security wall, I thought of the empty lot directly behind the center's back wall and sandwiched between two fairly large private homes. Now it's not like this was the first time I had seen the empty lot. But it was the first time I took the time to climb on a lawn chair, look over the wall, and envision a swimming pool. The seed had been planted and now it was germinating.

Swimming was not the only success the spring of 1997 brought our way. TLC enjoyed a core group of ladies that always set the pace for the other ladies to follow. Most of these pace setters were among our original 29 students, and they were immensely committed to the center, its mission, and long term survival. These pace-setting ladies were both formal and informal leaders within the women's community of the Eastern province. A small few were royal but most were not. Yet, they were all open to new ways of thought and became very good friends, even if they didn't begin that way. Every course or workshop that this group enrolled succeeded.

French and English were going strong. Both Mirna and Ann enjoyed a loyal following of students. We were able to add Italian, which wasn't well received and lasted only two terms. Even though many of our ladies shopped regularly in Italy, they simply had no desire to learn the language.

Mirna's on-going French class, however, added an extremely influential female in the royal family – the governor's wife. Hence, her class was then made up of seven of the Princess's closets friends and Mirna never added a new lady to the group after that although many asked. This group began with Mirna in the spring of 1997 and were still meeting twice a week for French class when I left the country four years later.

Ann loved to teach English and it showed. She followed an older school of thought by emphasizing memorization and drilling of the basics. Her tactics worked, even with beginners that could not say a single word of English when they began with her. The ladies took to her teaching style and her like ducks to water.

Johara's computer classes filled quickly, yet her student's wouldn't have followed her through fire as Ann and Mirna's would have. The demand for computer knowledge was so great that we had to add several classes to accommodate, which began to take their toll on Johara before the end of the term. She was running ragged teaching two morning and two evening sessions four days a week.

Our art department held its own, but did not see a jump in enrollment as other classes did and only covered expenses. Actually, it was wavering for several reasons. Madawi had begun to enjoy supporting and appreciating art rather than producing it, which I believe thwarted the art program's growth, but only temporarily. Some students that had taken art before to be near the Princess no longer felt artistically inspired when they learned Madawi was not enrolled in the class.

Secondly, we were loosing Betsy and her regular art students were leery. Understanding their nature and reluctance to accept change, I hired a very talented, overly qualified British lady, Carol, to take over the art department after Betsy left. In the beginning, Carol took it slow and simply continued the general, leisurely curriculum Betsy had in place. But as time passed, she stepped forward to lead the charge for numerous "firsts" for our center and the ladies of the Eastern province.

At the request of several students, we threw out a cooking class offering to test the water. Through a friend of a friend of a friend, I had the privilege of bringing a delightful Iranian woman to the TLC team. Safa was the epitome of a refined lady. In a way, she reminded me of a young modern day, Arab Jackie Kennedy. Every hair was always in place, her posture always perfect, and her clothes flawless. Educated in England, her diction and conversation were impeccable and she possessed a soothing personality that lured people to her presence. And to top it all off, she was a chef of Arab cuisine.

The unique aspect of Safa as opposed to the other instructors was that Safa ran in the same circles as the students of the center. Most of the time, she spent more money taking classes than she made teaching them. She simply loved cooking and sharing her expertise with the other ladies. The four week workshop idea was a huge hit and the class filled twice during our eight week term.

In the spring of '97, we were six months into introducing aerobics to the ladies of the Eastern province. Although I am sure most had an understanding of the importance of exercise, I don't believe it was fully comprehended and the benefits obvious until they became involved. Because six of our pace setters had started step aerobics in the fall, the trend continued and other ladies followed. Our spring enrollment tripled our fall and we now had about 20 ladies attending aerobics regularly.

In early March, Nabila, an average Saudi woman who lived in the states but was visiting family in Kingdom, stopped by the center for a visit. Her claimed purpose was to contribute to the growth of the Saudi ladies by offering her services as an instructor when she was in Kingdom. Apparently, she had attended our open house with her sister, yet I could not recall seeing her. Throughout our first meeting, she was overly complimentary to the achievements of the center and even more so when it came to showing her intent to help. Naturally, as I was always looking for new opportunities for our ladies, I gladly accepted for her to join the team when she was available.

Although her demeanor attempted to indicate sincerity, I had mixed emotions when she left. I felt an ominous feeling deep in my chest, but I chose to ignore it by rationalizing the good of my ladies outweighed the nagging feeling I felt. It took many years and a lot of heartache for me to realize that a viper had entered our midst that afternoon.

With much anticipation, the day of our TLC appreciation dinner finally arrived. We were all so excited that we left the center immediately after classes in order to get home in time to devote extra effort to getting ready for our big night. Now, I must clarify. In the U.S., our dinner would have been no big deal. Simply 25 people meeting at one of a hundred restaurants to eat, distribute awards, grab a Kodak moment, and leave. Yet in Kingdom, it was a huge deal.

First and foremost, it was illegal. Men and women that are not of the same family do not eat together in public. In *Al-Khobar* at the time, there were very few restaurants that were available to us and even fewer that any of us would frequent to ingest the food they prepared. From the limited selection, we opted to hold our dinner at the local seafood restaurant, *Darrin's*, for several reasons. First, it was off the beaten path, literally, yet in the middle of town. You actually had to drive over a vacant, sand lot to get to the building. Although westernized, the restaurant ranked low on décor but high on tasty. Their seafood cuisine was simply delicious and incredibly affordable in comparison to stateside seafood prices. Plus, and most importantly, they were open to the idea of closing their entire restaurant for an evening so that some westerners could have an illegal, mixed couples dinner party.

The TLC staff and their husbands arrived on time and the Colonel, naturally, on his time. Everyone anxiously awaited his arrival because you just don't meet a prince everyday, even in the Kingdom. Many Westerners who call Saudi their home, for years even, never make a Saudi friend; much less dine with a member of the house of Al-Saud – dine with royalty. Hence, the anticipation was heightened. The workers stood at the ready to turn off the neon sign outside, lock the doors, and pull the blinds as soon as the Colonel entered the building. To be sure we weren't

Creating Shamsiyah

surprised with an unexpected visit by the **Muthawen**, the manager had one of his workers stand outside the front door and act as lookout. The idea was that he could warn us, if necessary, which would allow us time to separate by gender before the religious police could get passed the locked door. Jackson Westmoreland would whisk the Colonel out of the back door and we would all act as if nothing were amiss. The worker was instructed to lie to everyone else who came to enjoy dinner and tell them that the restaurant was closed for the evening due to a broken water pipe. For his service as watchdog that nameless worker received an extra 50SR at the end of the evening for a job well done.

Following the flow of a typical appreciation dinner, we began with a scrumptious carte blanch dinner and lighthearted conversation. The Colonel, a naturally excellent speaker, delivered a humorous praising speech upon acceptance of his appreciation plaque we had made for him. I was touched by his compliments and encouragement of our efforts, and I beamed with pride when he announced that "he wished he had more soldiers like me because I could move troops better than most generals he knew."

I have the utmost respect for the Colonel, now retired General. He was an accomplished pilot and successful businessman. He could have easily stepped in and paved the way for Madawi and her budding business endeavors. However, I believe he respected and cared for her enough to let her do it on her own.

He most certainly supported her, but he did so by letting her take the steps to her own destiny.

    In an attempt to supplement the center's overhead, I began to open the center during off hours for additional revenue streams. Targeting the children of our students during after school hours, we offered private English tutoring to those who needed additional help with their school studies. Taekwondo instruction for the Saudi boys was tremendously successful during our jamboree and Mary agreed to continue. We had two classes of young men with approximately 25 regular attendees meeting after school two days per week. Unfortunately, several terms later the program died. The American assistant we hired for Mary, who was also highly belted in Taekwondo, organized with her husband to teach classes on a Western compound and they subsequently pulled every student from Mary and TLC.

    The nature of the center was such that we never used a lady's title to refer to her. In other words, no one referred to Madawi as "Princess Madawi," and so on. Among the ladies, we did this to lower social barriers and encourage an atmosphere of equality and simultaneous personal empowerment. Of course the ladies knew who was royal and who was not, simply no one verbalized it. For the children on the other hand, the decision to not use titles went even further. It was a matter of security for the young royal heirs.

    Amazingly over the years with the thousands of women and children that came to our door, we only had one incident where this unwritten policy was broken and a confrontation ensued. One particular afternoon, the private British art tutor for the most powerful princess in the province and French student at the center, Princess Raja, arrived to pick up one of her royal pupils, Sarah. From the moment the lady entered the facility, it was "Princess Sarah this and Princess Sarah that" in this loud, boisterous voice that echoed through the halls. The woman was upset over everything Sarah's mom, Princess Raja, had scheduled and began to demand that classes be changed to fit Sarah's schedule as she felt it should be. Being the reserved person she is and because she was married to a Saudi, Maria was nervous to stand her ground too strongly with this overly assertive woman because she wasn't sure of the power this lady wielded. However, Maria did explain calmly and professionally several times that the class time could not change because of the other nine children already enrolled in the class. The Brit then attempted to pull a power play by indirectly threatening Maria with the influence of her princess. Because of the resonating voice of the British woman, Ann and Betsy had made their way to reception to investigate the commotion. Seeing Maria shaken, Ann moved into the receptionist's chair and began to tell the lady again why the class time could not be changed.

While the confrontation brewed, I was upstairs and unaware of what was occurring until Maha, Madawi's middle daughter, came running. "Mrs. Teresa! Mrs. Teresa!" she shouted as she took the stairs two at a time and landed in front of me completely out of breath. In her excitement and lack of oxygen, a mumble of words flowed from the child's mouth, but I couldn't understand a word. Dropping what I was doing, I turned to face her. In order to calm her so that I could gather more information, I knelt down, gently touched her shoulders, and made full eye contact with Maha. "Slow down baby," I encouraged. Still obviously anxious, she took enough deep breaths to continue.

"Mrs. Teresa, Mrs. Teresa," she blurted out. "The lady in the office wants to box Mama Ann!"

"What?" I exclaimed completely shocked that Maha thought a lady would want to physically fight with my mom. Exasperated because she felt there was no time to explain, Maha simply grabbed my hand and began to run towards the stairs and subsequently reception with me in tow.

Unwilling to take no for an answer, the British woman continued her ranting. Ann remained professional with each round of no until the art tutor began to attack the center's director on a personal level. In response, Ann got quiet, her back went straight, her demeanor tightened, and she replied with the sweetest of smiles in an exaggerated Southern drawl. "You know" she paused for emphasis. "THAT is MY baby," she concluded by pointing to me when I landed abruptly by the desk after being literally pulled from upstairs by Maha.

Even though I was unsure of what was happening, I knew the first thing I had to do was get this disgruntled woman out of reception and away from watchers. Politely, I asked her to please step into my office to discuss the matter further. Indignant she refused at first, yet I persisted and refused to continue the discussion until we were out of the public forum. Finally, she acquiesced. Graciously, I motioned to allow her to enter my office first while I turned to Maria and requested tea be delivered to my office immediately. I then followed the lady inside and closed the door behind me. Wanting to resolve this peacefully and professionally, I offered her a chair with my hand and moved to sit behind my desk. Even though I was unclear on the schedule issue, I was completely aware of her use of titles because of the numerous complaints I had received as of late. Believing she would have no problem with our policy once she understood its purpose, I opted to begin with this issue in order to get a good rapport going with her before I addressed what I thought would be the bigger issue – scheduling.

Well blow me down and paint me pink, the woman simply could not understand the purpose of the policy even after I tried numerous times to explain it. She then became belligerent and obviously resented me for telling her who she could call what. As she continued to unleash insults upon me, she came out of her chair towards my desk. Unconsciously, I came to my feet as well. The barrage continued.

"WHO do you think YOU are to tell me that I can not call Princess Sarah, princess? She IS a princess and should be titled as such."

"I realize her position and I respect it immensely. However, it is for her safety that she not be identified by a title while she is in the center." Trying to calm the situation yet again and appeal to her compassion, I continued. "Plus, labeling her only sets her apart from the other children and makes her different. At least here she can be a regular ten year old."

Tightening her jaw and crossing her arms, she replied, "Well, I WILL call her princess whenever I refer to her whether you approve or not."

Miffed, I answered slowly and firmly, "No, you WILL NOT use her title in my center."

Attempting the power play with me, she continued. "Oh right then, why don't I just tell Princess Raja that YOU said I can not call her daughter a princess."

Completely annoyed at this point and ready to end this ridiculous squabble over a simple request, I retaliated. "NO." I leaned over my desk for emphasis, placed my hands firmly in the middle with my elbows locked, and glared straight into her eyes. "Why don't *I* tell Raja?"

Surprised, she had no idea that I could speak with Raja directly and her ploy was immediately foiled and her threats powerless.

"Well," she began backstroking to make a speedy exit from my office and the confrontation. "You just do that" she added crossly as she opened my office door and ran smack into Lulu who was carrying a tray holding our requested tea. Instantaneously, tea went everywhere. With no apology for the spilled tea or her behavior, she didn't even break stride and left the building.

My adrenaline peaked and I started shaking once the door closed and silence filled the room. I then collapsed into the overstuffed chair and the whole room began to chuckle. For the next hour over fresh cups of tea, Ann, Betsy, Maria, Lulu, and I sat and discussed the woman and all that had happened. Maha jumped around the room joyfully because she felt as if Mrs. Teresa and Mama Ann had "beaten" the bad lady. Betsy laughed deeply as she retold Ann's response to the lady's insults about me in her county accent.

"I could have just died when Mama Ann told her 'THAT's MY baby'" She laughed, clapping her hands to emphasize her take on the comment. "You know guys, that's basically southern lady talk that really means 'talk about my daughter again and I'll kick yer ass.'" Our mouths fell open and our eyes went wide with Betsy's analysis of Ann's message and then we lost it. We all laughed until we cried.

It wasn't long before Madawi arrived for her aerobics class to find us all lounging in my office reminiscing about the afternoon's confrontation. When she asked the group what was so funny, they each made an excuse as to why they had to leave and made their exit. After the room emptied, I proceeded to tell Madawi what had happened.

Even though Madawi had demonstrated her attitude towards this issue in McLean when she fired the driver on the spot for calling Nora "Princess Nora" in public, I still was not exactly sure how she would respond to my position in the altercation. After all, I was in Kingdom and Princess Raja out ranked my Princess. Perhaps the British woman had more influence with Raja than I assumed. Either way, I was a bit nervous. I had a feeling one of the Western tutors would loose their position over this, but I didn't know it would not be me until I heard Madawi's response. She totally agreed with me and insisted I had done the right thing. Announcing she would speak with Raja, we dropped the subject and no one at the center ever saw the British tutor again. In time, we heard rumors she had left the country "exit only."

    One afternoon when I was working out of doors, I looked up to see Saleem smiling at my progress with the new perennials in the planter box and a skinny stranger standing behind him. Flashing his big Kenyan smile, Saleem introduced me to Riaz, a hold-over *hajji* that had ducked under immigration to stay in Kingdom and find work. Harboring him at the palace unbeknownst to Madawi, Saleem was eager to help him and when I saw his sincere face, I was too. Although I knew our budget was tight, I felt the mere 250 *SR* (approximately $50.00 U.S.) per month he would cost the center would be worth it in the long run. After all, we could use another man around when Saleem was away driving the ladies, and Lulu could use the help inside the center when cleaning as well. Standing, I dusted my hands on my jeans before welcoming Riaz to the TLC team. Even though I know he didn't understand a word I said, he knew by my smile that he had the job and was ecstatic.

In May, Nabila returned and offered two different seminars at TLC: *"Dealing with Stress"* and *"Understanding Depression"*. The progressive, pace setting students that were keeping a close second behind Madawi in their personal growth, stepped up to attend these culturally radical seminars. Nabila's popularity was almost instantaneous. The ladies were overjoyed to be introduced to topics that fell so close to their hearts and a need we had not attempted to tap or meet at this point through the center and its offerings. All went well her first term with Nabila, and I was thrilled to see the women so engaged. Per our standard TLC statement of understanding, Nabila was compensated approximately $1,600 for 16 class hours of instruction.

Before I knew it, our ladies' spring term was drawing to a close and I had not stopped to think of the social aspect of our mission statement. Hence, it was time for a party. We were enjoying tremendous spring weather that beckoned us to enjoy, so I decided to take the party in a different direction - one that most of our ladies had never had the privilege to experience. We would have a beach party! Madawi and the Colonel had just purchased gulf waterfront property and began construction on what we would soon refer to as "the beach house" which was, in fact, more of a beach compound. Located directly on the Arabian Gulf, the beach house was situated on approximately 30 acres with an estimated quarter mile of water frontage in a private cove. When complete, the beach house would be approximately 50,000 square feet of living space, complete with a main house, the Colonel's house, Fahad's house, a guest house, garages, servants' quarters, gardens, a pool, and tennis courts.

In such an expansive, private setting, our spring social was primed for success. Women can not drive in Kingdom, not even bicycles, but they could ride until their hearts were content at our party. Given Saudi women do not typically swim in public, even the ones that actually knew how from our classes, the opportunity to swim and drive the jet skis was simply exhilarating. The two rare times I had seen women swimming off shore from a public beach along the Corniche, they wore their ***abayas*** in the water, resembling a black jellyfish that could only weigh them down and be potentially hazardous.

Even though most of the beach house buildings were still under construction at the time, we were able to use several bathrooms in one of the villas for the party and we rented a few portable units to place periodically around the property. We set up a beach volleyball court in the sand by the water with a Bedouin tent just behind to act as the central location of the event where the ladies could sit and talk, dance, eat, or just hang out if they weren't busy with another offered activity. I borrowed every bicycle I could find on my compound and had the palace drivers take them to the beach the morning of the party. Madawi had the drivers prepare and deliver their jet skis for the event, and we set up a bonfire beside the water for later in the evening. We took fishing poles, beach balls, and Frisbees. Simply anything that we could think of that is typically associated with a beach party and that we could acquire in Kingdom was available at the party. To make it easy on the ladies to attend, to monitor attendance, and to make sure we didn't have a *Muthawen* come unknowingly, David secured two buses for our use. We had the ladies meet us at TLC and we shuttled them back and forth from the beach house to the center on hourly runs.

As the evening sun made its final appearance on the horizon, Madawi and I sat in quite respect to watch it melt into Half Moon Bay of the Arabian Gulf and say good-bye to another day, just as we had done in Cannes four years prior. Sitting on the grassy knoll to the east of the main house, Madawi and I enjoyed the coolness of the imported grass that had its own gardener to keep it alive through the rigorous dry heat of the desert. We found it a lush pleasure among the sand. As the sky became gray for lack of rays, the silence was broken when she spoke.

"*Shamsiyah*," she said solemnly still watching where the sun had been as the warm, salty sea breeze blew her straight raven hair across her face. "I will name the beach house *Shamsiyah*," she repeated as if confirming her decision, while she continued to gaze meaningfully toward the Western sky.

The beach party was a grand success. Women were everywhere doing their own thing. We had some ladies learn to ride a bike and others the steps of the popular dance craze, the Macarena. Some played volleyball while others grabbed a book and settled in on the grassy knoll partially encircling the private cove by the water for a little quiet time of reflection. We had students fishing as the palace cooks flipped burgers while other women relaxed in the tent listening to music. Honestly, to hear the giggles as a lady first balanced on a bike for the first time made the entire effort worth the while. Until the wee hours of the night, the women talked, laughed, ate, and played.

Because it had become routine for Madawi to stop by my office after aerobics, I started to look forward to her visits. Some days, we had much to discuss relating to the center and found it to be more of a business meeting rather than a time to grow our friendship. Yet, there were days when we simply sipped our beverages and talked about indiscriminate topics, which is so necessary for women to do every now and then. On this particular day, however, it would be an impromptu meeting because we both had things to share and discuss.

Madawi could hardly wait to tell me her news, so I let her go first. Wafa, one of our pace setters and good friends of Madawi, had enjoyed Safa's Arab cuisine workshop so much that she offered to help renovate the upstairs kitchen in apartment D so that we could continue to offer cooking in a more pleasant classroom environment. I was ecstatic. Wafa's husband's company would supply the materials at no charge, but we would have to coordinate and oversee the actual construction. Madawi wanted David to contact Yacoub to provide the workers, free of charge of course, and to contact Mr. Abdul for the man's name that would supply Wafa's gift.

My news was less concrete than hers and inspired by Fawzia's seed. After explaining the financial success of our swimming program and the challenges of holding the classes on DM16 to Madawi, I posed the idea of acquiring either the vacant lot to the side of the center that faced the main road or the vacant lot behind the center between the two homes to build an indoor swimming facility. Instantaneously Madawi liked the idea.

We walked outside and viewed both lots, discussing the feasibility of each. In no time, we ruled out the side lot and felt the one behind the center would be better to attach to our current center and, more importantly, less conspicuous. Returning to my office for our typical tea and cap, Madawi gave me the mission to investigate the cost involved in such an endeavor and she said she would look into ownership of the lot.

Excited about both "firsts" that were now in motion, we set our plan. With the children's program starting the following week, we decided to close the center after the children's program to renovate the kitchen and unveil it to the ladies in the fall. I, on the other hand, was to have Yacoub build a temporary fence around the vacant lot and let it sit in the hopes that no one would come by and claim it as theirs.

With June came the start of the kids' summer program and a prayer that enough children would attend to cover our deficit from the spring term.

Fortunately I was not disappointed. The program laid out much like the first and included all the activities normally associated with summer camp.

When the books were closed on our second kids' summer program, a trend began to emerge that I did not understand as a trend until later. The successful kids' program covered the ladies' retroactively.

Our financial situation seemed to find itself in a catch 22 from the beginning. First and foremost, we remained underground which allowed for no advertising. Hence, we could not draw students that did not know Madawi or another already accepted student of the center. This severely limited us because word of mouth could only move so fast and Madawi's circle of friends only held so many people. Our tuition had to remain affordable for the "regular" Saudi woman because we wanted to reach them all.

Our Western instructors, however, had a base level of pay they would accept. And even though the majority of my instructors did what they did because they believed it in, they still had to be compensated for their time and expertise. A class was considered "made" with five students, which basically covered the instructor's wages, even with them set very low on Western standards. Consequently, a class of six left very little to contribute to the overhead cost of a center. We were a not-for-profit organization and Madawi wanted nothing in return from the center. However, she did not want to add additional funds either. As with our first one at DM18, *Summer*

Spectacular 1997 balanced our bottom line and we were able to continue floating.

Although exhilarated from what we were accomplishing with the ladies, I was drained and I had not been stateside to visit family in ages. With the traditional mass exodus of women from the Kingdom during the incredibly hot summer months the desert offered, we opted to close the center following the kids' program to save on expenses and to renovate our newly gifted kitchen. While I was stateside with the children, David and Yacoub took the reins and surprised me with a beautifully redecorated cooking classroom upon my return in the fall.

Personal tragedy hit me and my family while I was celebrating the Christening of little Madawi in the states in the summer of '97. My Dad was struck with an aneurysm and subsequent brain surgery while he and Ann were on holiday in the states as well. It was an emotionally wrenching time in my life as it had been when my Mom faced a similar life and death situation two years prior with her heart attack. Softening the strain, Madawi and numerous students from the center flooded us with telephone calls of encouragement and well wishes. I can remember squatting on the floor beneath the public phone in the hospital, crying as my Shamsiyah reminded me of my faith and assured me that God would pull **"*Baba*"** John through, **"*Insha Allah***," she would repeat. Fortunately, she was correct.

Chapter ١٣
Recharging
September- October 1997

In spite of the pile of paperwork that lay before me on my desk at *The Learning Center*, it still felt good to be home. As I leaned back in my chair, Lulu served my much missed morning cappuccino on its usual doily-lined tray, as she had done so many times before. It had been a grueling summer and I was thankful to be back at work. With the shock and exhaustion of Daddy's surgery coupled with the international travel of two kids and a servant in tow, I was physically and mentally drained. Fortunately, some semblance of relief was beginning to peek through, even though the stacks of paper before me still reflected my late return to Kingdom in the fall of 1997.

Arriving in late September, I only had two weeks to solidify the fall term plans I made before I traveled stateside. However, this was not difficult because the center was energized even before our classes began. We were moving and shaking and could no longer be equated to a toddler because we were breaking ground with each new endeavor.

Our latest idea began to gain speed when we learned that Mr. Abdul, Madawi's house manager, discovered that no one was listed on any public documents as owning the vacant lot behind TLC.

Hence, we immediately implemented "squatting rights" by having Yacoub build a stepped entryway through the wall separating the two lots in addition to the wall he had erected. Madawi's latest dream was just around the corner.

In an effort to confirm everything for the start of classes, I telephoned Nabila in the states and questioned the fees she had requested in several faxes to me over the summer. In spite of my effort to explain that we were not-for-profit and existed solely to further the personal development of Saudi women, she still demanded more. She refused the fee schedule used by all of the other TLC instructors. The same schedule she had accepted just four months prior, which now I believe was simply a means by which to get her foot in the door. Although I felt her requested fees were high given the center's situation and mission, I knew the ladies wanted the information and I acquiesced after she reduced her stipulated fees by a minimal amount. The little nagging feeling I had felt in March returned, but I repressed it again for what I thought was for the good of the center – the good of the Saudi women.

Agreeing to the other points of our standard TLC statement of understanding, Nabila confirmed she would be at the center from October 8 to November 11. During which time, she would conduct programs and deliver therapy in Arabic to the women and their daughters. Her biggest program was a cognitive enhancement program for women that would take 24 hours to complete in 12 two-hour sessions. Basically, it was a structured group therapy program based on research with cognitive-behavior principles. The program addressed such topics as the purpose of women's feelings and moods, building self-esteem, relation to self and others, family of origin, body image, conflict management, and sexuality. Much of the information in this program was presented through our human communication workshops previously, but I presume the ladies were more comfortable investigating these issues in their native language with an individual of their own faith. In essence, this foretold the destiny of TLC and the inevitable evolution of things to come.

In addition to the 24-hour program, Nabila would offer three different four-hour seminars. These short programs would focus on such topics as anxiety, phobias, depression, anger, jealousy, guilt, and shame. Once Nabila arrived in Kingdom, she added the offering of career counseling to our students' high school daughters who were in the process of making decisions about their major field of study or future college education. Widely used in the states, the tests assess personality types and match them with major fields of study or potential professions that the individual is interested in and capable of pursuing. Typically administered by schools stateside, Nabila offered these tests to the daughters of our students for a substantial fee per student.

Most of our instructors from the spring returned and offered the classes and workshops in their area of expertise. Mama Ann, however, was still stateside tending to my father's recovery and her students were devastated. Fortunately, I was able to find a delightful, well educated Iranian lady named Ruby who stepped in to take our English program. Fortunately, the ladies finally warmed up to Ruby, but they missed Mama Ann and anxiously awaited her return.

Because of student requests and my good fortune to find new class ideas and teachers to teach them from the dreaded coffee mornings, TLC did, however, open several new courses and workshops for our students as we pushed into our second year in the new facility and our third fall term of TLC's existence.

To help our art students get to know Carol, our new British art instructor, and to make their transition to her easier, Betsy agreed to stay on board until she left the Kingdom "exit only" with her husband to pursue stateside career options in mid-November. Fortunately, the ladies took to Carol immediately and all the worries I had had dissipated.

Proudly, we showed off our newly renovated kitchen. It was new, thus exciting, and the ladies wanted more cooking classes as a result. On demand, Safa offered Arab Cuisine again and the workshop filled almost immediately because the pace setters recommended it. To make maximum use of Wafa's gift, we added Italian cooking and a Scrumptious Desserts workshop.

For me, an unexpected benefit to our cooking classes was the eating. Throughout the term, I enjoyed delicious food and sweets cooked by our students who absolutely loved bringing me a plate of the day's latest creation to sample. I found this to be quite a treat because I didn't have to worry about bringing my lunch to work on cooking class days. Unlike the states, fast food was rare, very rare. Food delivered to your door was a foreign concept with the only delivery food I could rely was whatever I could send Saleem to retrieve. And if I didn't think of organizing him to get the food before noon, we were simply out of luck until at least 4:00 p.m. when the local restaurants would reopen for the evening.

    Originally, I had not wanted to offer kids' programming while we had ladies' classes in the center. Yet after offering Taekwondo in the spring and the popularity it enjoyed, I had to continue with it in the fall. In addition to her ongoing afternoon Taekwondo classes for Saudi boys, Mary decided to offer Taekwondo and self-defense to the ladies as well. The idea of a woman being able to physically defend herself was new and of no interest to many of the Saudi ladies. A few, however, embraced the opportunity and began their martial arts training.

    Many times, a husband would want to come to the center with his wife the first time she enrolled. However, only ladies were allowed inside our wall. So to accommodate the husband's wishes and, hopefully, have his wife as a new student after his inspection, we would organize a time during our afternoon off hours for him to visit when no Saudi women would be in the building. I would, of course, be dressed conservatively and welcome the couple with open arms as Lulu served the tea. I would give them a tour of the facility, explaining the classes we had to offer and the benefits of each. Amazingly, some husbands only made it to reception and gave the okay for their wives to enroll. With these "quick inspections," I often laughed and said he just wanted to make sure we weren't a brothel.

At one time, there was in fact a house of ill-repute located south of Al-Khobar. I, naturally, never saw it personally but was told that it was a thriving business located under a battery factory in the industrial park. We were told that the business was discovered and subsequently closed because of the heavy flow traffic – go figure.

With two years of offering educational opportunities to Saudi ladies under my belt, I had begun to understand the nature of our students' husbands. Yet, I was unable to categorize them until we started to offer self-defense. I found that I could sort the Saudi husbands into one of three groups.

First, there were the Colonel's of the Kingdom, which were the majority by the way. These husbands were incredibly westernized and open to educational opportunities for their wives. They men saw what we and their wives were doing was good. They did not see it as threatening in any way and enjoyed seeing their wives sink their teeth into something, so to speak. On different occasions, several of these husbands indicted how much it improved their marriage to have their wives so intellectually engaged. These husbands respected their wives with carte blanche with whatever they wanted to take at the center. These men did not ask to visit the center.

The second group moved more towards the middle, balancing new opportunities with old ways of thought. These men were essentially open to their wives being educated, but would only let them enroll in classes that are typically seen as female and non-threatening, such as language study, cooking, and painting. However, this group was adamantly against their wives' participation in any class they saw as "threatening," such as computers and self-defense. It was this group that seemed to always want to visit the center before giving their blessing.

The third group was the group I personally would love to eradicate. These men were completely closed-minded and against their wives even affiliating with women of the center. I did not meet these men so I can not make assumptions as to why they held the attitudes they held. After all, it is not against Islam for women to learn. Yet, there were several times I sat in my office with students who shared stories. One even cried for over an hour as she told me about her best friend whose husband said he would "slaughter her like a lamb" if she attempted to come to *The Learning Center*. Sadly, he always kept her locked in the house to make sure she complied. Obviously these men had self-esteem issues.

With a massive hustle and bustle, we managed to begin our new term with smiles on our faces and band-aids lining our high heels. From the manic pace of getting the center ready coupled with my challenges with Nabila and topped with hold over stress from my father's brush with death, I was exhausted emotionally and physically.

One early October morning, I enjoyed the calm of the center and the relaxing background music as I sipped my cap and focused on the day ahead, which was officially scheduled to begin in less than an hour. I looked at my clock as the ring of the telephone broke the peace I was enjoying. It was Madawi, up earlier than usual.

"**Sabah al-Khair**, Mrs. Teresa," she pronounced sounding rested and employed in a mission.

"Hey, Madawi," I replied in my Southern voice, truly happy to hear from her. I could tell already that it was going to be a good day.

"Have your bags ready for Saleem tonight," she announced. "We want you to come to the opera with us."

"Luxor?" I questioned with surprise and excitement.

"Yes, Mrs. Teresa" she replied with a chuckle. "We leave in the morning, and you need to prepare your bags today. It will be you and me and the big girls only, a special girls' time for us."

Astonished, I replied, "Oh my heavens, Madawi! You are kidding? But," I hesitated. "You and Mom were going to do that trip." I continued as my excitement rapidly deflated thinking of my mom stateside and all that she had been though over the past two months. She of all people needed a weekend in Egypt.

Ignoring my protest, she continued. "You need a break, Mrs. Teresa, and this will be the perfect thing. Saleem will collect your bags tonight and you at ten in the morning." She paused for a moment to confirm my compliance. "Yellah," she added, "don't worry, we will have fun and Mama Ann would want that. *Ma'assalaamah.*"

As I returned the receiver to the cradle, a huge smile broke across my face, as I thought about what was happening to me yet again. Oh, a weekend in Egypt to see the Opera Aida! Even after six years with my princess, I was still amazed every time one of these once in a lifetime, wonderful opportunities reared its head.

Full of energy, I set to task. I worked like crazy until the afternoon so that I could get as much paperwork done as possible to personally justify jet-setting off for the weekend to Egypt. All the while, my spirits soared. I was home, back to the life that I had become so accustomed. The challenges of the summer were history now, and it was time to move forward.

My excitement was overcome by the exhaustion of my preparations. While the day was spent preparing the center for my absence, family and personal details took up the evening. I had to list out our schedule and childcare details for David, organize the servant, and pack. Even so, by 10 a.m. the following morning, I was set to walk out the door. As usual, ten o'clock did not mean ten o'clock with Saleem, nor with any of the other drivers for that fact.

ॐ Creating Shamsiyah ॐ

This irritant no longer bothered me, however, as I now saw it as an additional opportunity to play with my little ones for a few more minutes.

I took in a deep breath of hot, desert air as I stepped out of the villa to the waiting 720LI BMW where Saleem held the door for me to enter. With Arabic music rolling through the interior of the cooled Beamer, I reached for my bag as we moved through the compound as swiftly and quietly as a mouse. Slowly, I slipped on my sunglasses, mentally stepping into traveler mode, while we whizzed toward my next adventure.

My excitement was tempered by reality, but only for a moment. I thought of the 9 German tourist and Egyptian tour guide who perished only a few weeks earlier. I remembered reading the warden message over my morning cap on the veranda, yet I had not given it another thought until now. On the 18th of September, terrorists launched a grenade attack on their tour bus parked in front of the Egyptian National Antiquities Museum in Cairo. The two Egyptian gunmen, however, claimed to support the Egyptian al-Jihad but were not found to be linked to an established terrorist group. Oddly, the thoughts passed quickly because I felt immune.

Leaving my things in the car, I hopped out and zipped into the salon the moment the Beamer came to a halt inside the palace's inter-sanctuary. Unlike ever before, I found the smallest of entourages when I arrived. Only Madawi, the "big girls", Nora and Fatma, along with only one nanny, Susan, Jackson, and I would be traveling for the weekend. To my amazement, neither Sabre nor Saleem joined us up the stairs of the Boeing 777. Actually, they did not get on the plane at all this trip. It was just the girls, and of course the security guy and servant, off for the weekend.

As we entered the plane, the females found their seats in the first class cabin and started to settle in as Jackson continued to business class where he could keep eye on his charge from a distance. Even though our group was smaller than usual, the level of excitement and flurry to see the newest, best from the west in the duty-free catalog simply did not wavier from previous flights. Before we were barely off the ground, the girls and I had already gone through the entire catalog with a fine tooth comb, each identifying our favorite item complete with commentary. Once airborne, the exhaustion of the previous twenty-four hours hit me full force, and the need to sleep overtook me. Saying my good nights to the girls, I spread out in the leather, first-class seating, nestled with my blanket, pillow, and headphones playing a soft jazz to grab a quick sleep before the next step of our adventure began.

As it always seemed to happen with me, I awoke startled to the echo of a man's voice speaking in Arabic. It was the pilot, naturally, announcing our arrival to Cairo's international airport. Stretching and peeking out of the window, I found nothing unfamiliar and interesting since the climate and terrain is the same as Saudi's. Incredibly blue skies with no clouds in sight held high over the reddish brown, blistering sands of the desert. Haze filled the air, indicating the amount of sand being blown above the parched surface, blowing the palm trees and stirring the heat into what would feel like a suffocating, yet intoxicating fan.

Once on the ground, we all giggled as we anticipated our arrival and the things we were about to experience. As we taxied endlessly down the landing strip, the girls' giggles quickly turned to laughter as their suddenly outstretched arms presented me with a duty free bag. Surprised, I looked deeply into each of their faces, revealing my appreciation with my eyes before I even touched the bag. Inside I found my selected favorite from our preflight shopping at the beginning of our trip: a Rado wristwatch with a black leather band and gold face. Surprise flooded me as I took the watch from its box. I was overwhelmed. Looking over at Madawi, I could only say thank you as I was touched beyond words. Halting my thanks, her hand gracefully raised as it always did when she wanted to make a point with no debate, and said, "I wanted to give you a little something to pick you up. I thought this would do the trick." She smiled that special smile of hers, and I couldn't help but give her a hug. Instinctively, Madawi always knew just what to do when I needed it the most.

Still smiling, I realized that this was truly the longest taxi I had ever experienced on a flight. We all sensed the unusual length and, after several minutes, we actually began timing our roll. Another twenty-one minutes passed before we arrived at the old, weathered terminal.

Disembarking the plane down the stairs to the tarmac, I soon realized our little entourage and lack of male guardianship was short-lived. Five men in three-piece suits met us at the bottom of the stairs, greeting Madawi, with obvious respect, in Arabic. After a brief exchange, they encircled us and we quickened our step to the terminal. This small exchange sparked my internal red alert, because it was quite out of the ordinary. While we walked toward the terminal, I surveyed my surroundings since I had become accustomed being a defense contract expatriate in the Middle East. Terminal entrance straight ahead, four armed security in the distance off to my left, our plane behind me, another jet to my right that had taxied in as ours did with a half dozen people at the bottom of its stairs. Oddly, what looked like three television personnel, a cameraman, or a photographer were positioned near the entry to the terminal just behind two additional armed security men.

As I surveyed my surroundings and struggled to keep stride with Madawi's long gait, I could not help but chuckle at all of the excitement with our arrival. In jest mingled with curiosity, I commented, as I almost broke into a jog to keep up, "Wow, all of this security for you!"

Without breaking stride, her head turned to me and replied with a naughty smile on her face, "Now, Mrs. Teresa," she chuckled, "You look more German than I do."

Before turning her head forward again, she quickly flashed the smile I had grown to love and trust, as her wind-blown hair streamed across her face, reassuring me of my safety with her.

It was at that very instant did a not-too-distant, but forgotten, memory flashed before me: nine German tourists, along with their Egyptian bus driver, were killed on their tour bus by flying grenades outside the Egyptian National Antiquities Museum in Cairo less than a month prior (18 September 1997). Typically, I would have been very aware of something like this before I landed in a country, but with Dad's surgery and a long and grueling return flight to Kingdom, current and global news were not at the forefront of my consciousness.

Once inside the terminal, the girls and I stood by a huge glass wall overlooking the landing field as Madawi stepped to the side with the suited gentleman that seemed to be in charge. Two servants appeared offering tea to the weary travelers, and we accepted with gratitude as we were parched from our short walk into the terminal. As Madawi spoke with the man, the girls and I noticed several massive construction projects dotted outside the terminal. It was no wonder it had taken us so long to taxi around all the barricades after our landing.

Shortly, Madawi informed us that we had a four-hour layover before our flight south to Luxor. Unwilling to sit in such a boring terminal for that long, she informed us that we would take a drive through Cairo, have lunch, do a wee bit of shopping, and then head back to catch our plane. Excited about the idea of the layover, I questioned the chance to get a glimpse of the pyramids, only to find out that they were located too far from the airport to get there, see anything, and get back in time to catch our flight. I wasn't disappointed, however, since everything we were doing was new to me, and I was simply happy to be there. With the plans announced, we grabbed our bags and were escorted to the waiting vehicles, naturally cooled and ready for departure. And in a zip, we were off for a quick side venture along our journey to the opera.

With the exception of Istanbul, I never thought driving could ever be any worst than it is in the Kingdom of Saudi Arabia. Until Cairo. Even with my long-acquired passenger nerves of steel, I could not keep my head out of my lap in Cairo. The leaning over coupled with the manic sway of the car made my head spin, and I had to sit upright. To do so, I had to close my eyes and attempt to distinguish the sounds around me, praying that the forceful braking and skidding sounds would remain in the distance.

Thankfully, as I opened my eyes, the car finally came to a stop on the corner of a very busy street, lined with large trees, which somehow looked out of place. The restaurant that the gentlemen had selected to take her highness and friends was on the second story of a flat-roofed stucco building with half the seating on the open-air roof. The uneven cobblestone flooring was topped with rustic wooden tables and benches. The room was dotted with useful Arab whatnots, such as ***sheesha*** pipes and ***ghawa*** pots all brought together with greenery throughout. Because of the exhaust fumes and screeching car noises on the open-air area, we chose to eat inside. As time passed and courses came and went, we were all finally satisfied with wonderful Lebanese cuisine. I believe it was because of Mama Soha's influence that Madawi loved Lebanese food and always seemed to ask for the flavor every where we went.

  After a filling, delightful meal, we all decided that we needed to walk it off a bit, so we were off to the mall. Fortunately, it was a short drive so we came close to sudden death only two or three times. From the outside, the mall did not look like it contained anything special inside and simply blended in with the other dilapidated-looking stucco buildings on either side. However, the inside revealed quite the contrary. Everywhere you looked on three floors was designer stores: Givenchy, Luis Vutton, Hilfiger, and more. You name it and it seemed to be there, and we walked all three floors in less than one hour. It wasn't long before my feet began to beg for mercy, and I found myself happy to be in the car again heading back to the airport.

  Fortunately, the hop to Luxor was a rather quick flight, only about an hour, and our Mercedes was soon pulling into the valet of the *Sonesta St. George* Hotel, a newly opened five-star resort on the east bank of the majestic Nile River. We were assigned the T-shaped wing of the second story on the north end of the hotel. It was decided that Madawi and Fatma would share a suite, and Nora and I would double-up, with both suites complete with balconies overlooking the Nile. The nannies were given the first hall room to our right and Jackson to the left. All of our rooms were conveniently bunched together at the T for easy access back and forth.

After a delightful dinner at The St. George's *Isadora*, a fine dinning experience of European cuisine, we all elected to call it a night and prepare for the morning. Once in our suite, Nora and I cranked up the music, flew open the balcony doors, and danced around while we took turns with the bath. Once in pjs and housecoats, we curled up on the balcony with the freshly ordered room service cappuccino. We chatted about our flight, Cairo, and what we would do the next day. We were scheduled to tour The Valley of the Kings in the morning and the Opera Aida in the evening. We giggled at the thought of our tomorrow as neither of us had ever experienced Luxor.

As moments of silence invaded our conversation, I could not help but enjoy the breathtaking beauty before me. Lit only by the full of the moon, small boats, with hand-made sails drifted majestically on the Nile River, lined with a backdrop of black palm tree shapes. There was not a cloud in the star-speckled sky and the warm, yet moist night, air made my cup of cap seem even more delightful.

After a bit of silent pleasure mingled with personal conversation, we decided that Madawi and Fatma needed to be enjoying this as well. So we hopped from our loungers, grabbed our cappuccinos cups and scurried off the balcony toward the door. Behind Nora, giggling, I stopped momentarily to flip the lock backward so the door wouldn't close and lock behind us, an act I had done a hundred times before with the family. Turning around to continue to follow, I rounded the corner only to run right into the back of Nora, spilling my cap all down my robe and hers! Ignoring the spill, my attention went to the cause of my accident, and I looked up over Nora's shoulder to see a strange man in a three-piece suit sitting in a hard backed chair in the middle of our wing. Positioned so he could see down the longest hall leading to our T of rooms, he sat ridged and was seemingly shocked by our appearance. Quickly Nora spoke to him in Arabic with her voice elevated slightly, revealing her surprise as well. The unusual sight got my attention and curiosity immediately.

  After the short exchange, I followed Nora's lead to her mom's door. Once inside, Nora and I could not help but talk over each other, each trying to tell Madawi first that there was a man sitting outside our doors. After chuckling at our cappuccino-washed appearance, Madawi smiled and dialed the phone for our robe replacements. Meanwhile, Nora and I attacked their room service tray to nibble on what they had fancied.

  Once settled onto loungers in their mirrored suite, Madawi explained that the gentleman outside our door, and down the hall, was security provided for us by the Egyptian government.

"Awad," she commented before turning back to the view, "told them to take care of us."

After I ingested what she had said, I felt a little more at ease, and as I gazed back upon the Nile, my thoughts rationalized. Naturally with Madawi and the girls being diplomats and in lieu of the recent terrorist attacks in Egypt, the additional security was probably a good idea. Yet, it was very strange to have these men so close to us 24/7.

Realizing the time, I knew I had to sleep, although I would have preferred to stay up a bit longer. However, we had a big day ahead of us, and I did not want to miss a minute of it.

After exchanging our goodnights and confirming the morning meeting time, I scurried back through the hallway to our suite. Passing the suited man, I cordially greeted him in Arabic. I thought it best that I get to know the individual to which I may have to call out to for help. Oddly, he did not respond, only sat and looked.

Uncharacteristically, my eyes popped wide open, bright and early the next morning. I was so incredibly excited. Knowing that Nora had my normal morning tendencies and could sometimes be difficult to wake, I flung open the thick curtains exclaiming "rise and shine!" After a few mumbles on her part and a few chuckles on mine, she was finally upright.

I could not help but be excited about the day that lay before me. The highlights would include a tour of the Valley of the Kings and the funerary temple of King Montuhotep, with other adventures yet to be uncovered. We would then end our evening with the 125th anniversary performance of Giuseppe Verdi's "Aida," open air at the Temple of Queen Hatchepsut.

Perhaps it wasn't the wisest idea for Nora and me to bunk, since we have the same tardy tendencies. Finally, with the room looking like a hurricane victim, we flew out the door for breakfast as giggles heightened our anticipation of the day. Suddenly, the giggles stopped when we saw the man again. After an awkward moment of silence, we said hello and he looked. We walked and he followed.

We grabbed a quick breakfast on the fly from the café's buffet and ate with maddening speed. We both knew from experience that this crowd didn't wait for anyone, except for Madawi. Laughing at our hurried state on yet another adventure, Nora signed the tab and we were off to the waiting caravan of Mercedes followed by the three-piece suited men on our heels.

Walking without breaking stride as door after door was opened by gentlemen in white coats and black trousers; I stepped outside the St. George, slipping on the sunglasses while in stride. Suddenly, the moist heat hit me, spiraled with a warm, yet comforting breeze. It was, of course, another pretty day in the desert with not a cloud in the sky. As indicated by several outstretched arms, as we were the last to arrive to the cars, I took my place in the backseat of Madawi's Mercedes. Still settling in as the car began to roll; I greeted Madawi for the first time that particular morning. She could not help but grin slightly, even though she was trying to be upset with Nora and me. After my apologies for our tardiness, she gave me that forgiving, yet topic-closed look, and we laughed in response.

Periodically along our route, I saw jeeps with military men in the back wielding M16s at the ready. I noticed this and thought it odd, yet not alarming given the recent attacks in Egypt. With security vehicles in the lead and rear to protect the people in between, our motorcade rumbled down the uneven pavement nestled under the palms along the flood plain of the Nile. As we neared the entrance to the Valley of the Kings, I dug through my backpack to retrieve my white Egyptian cotton head scarf, which is a much-needed item in the intense sunshine and blustery wind.

Unlike stateside national parks and the like, there was no paved and lined parking lot, only space cleared in the sand. No real commercialism to speak of except for the nomadic retailers dressed in traditional attire that carried their wares on long sticks high in the air as they meandered through the flood of tourists. Our car came to a stop at the furthest point of the drive, and the doors opened. Stepping back into the elements from the overly chilled car, Madawi and I took a prominent place at the entrance so that the passengers of all of our party could assemble for our tour.

It was a privileged time to visit the ancient Valley of the Kings in October of 1997 as it was the 75th anniversary of the discovery of the tomb of the young Pharaoh Tutankharnun, which made the valley

ॐ Creating Shamsiyah ॐ

an even more enticing morning. Winding up, around and over the sand-laden rock mounds, we fought the elements of wind and heat to study the map guides, find the tombs, and enter only to stand in awe at the history we found in each. Although all of the tombs we entered were fascinating, it was the tomb of King Tut that was the highlight of the tour for me.

Unearthed in 1922, the tomb of the young king is noted as one of the most momentous discoveries of the Twentieth Century. As one of the most complete royal burials ever discovered, the tomb of Tutankhamun provides a unique insight for mankind into the life and times of the 18th Dynasty (1500 BC – 1319 BC) in Egyptian history.

Wanting to see more, we pushed ourselves until we felt we could go no longer with out sustenance. We needed lunch and it simply wasn't available at the valley. Reluctantly, we loaded into the waiting motorcade.

Following a delightful lunch in a local establishment organized, I presume, by our diplomatic security tour guides in the three-piece suits, we loaded the motorcade once again. Our next stop was a little more difficult for me to enjoy than our morning tour. We visited the temple of King Montuhotep, a spectacular structure that inspired the design of Queen Hatshepsout's temple. Unfortunately, I knew very little about King Montuhotep before my visit, which hindered my enjoyment. Plus, our temple tour guide wasn't that fluent in English. Then again, he was better in English than I was in Arabic. In spite of this, I couldn't help but gasp at the enormity of the towering columns, carved with depictions of a king and a time that lives on in infamy as a result of their construction.

Hence, I was easily distracted from my Egyptian history lesson when Nora and Fatma decided to tempt me with a game of hide-and-seek. Glances and devilish grins exchange between us indicated the start of our play. Sliding silently away from the group, Fatma took the lead to begin the game, which was a typical move for Fatma since she loves mischief. Pretending to be the supervising adult, I slipped away right behind her with Nora tight at my heels. Once out of reach of Madawi, the guide, the nannies and, of course, the three-piece suits, we giggled as we popped around the maze of massive antique columns. Our game continued until we heard the call of departure from Susan in the distance. Still giggling as we made our way to the waiting caravan, we relished the fun of the day.

As we pulled away from the temple, Nora was insistent with her mom about something. I listened as carefully as I could, yet could not get the full gist of the conversation. I did, however, pick up that Nora wanted to do something badly, and she was attempting to get her mom's approval. Yet, due to my lack of Arabic vocabulary, I did not know what it was.

Believing that we were returning to the hotel, I was somewhat puzzled when we came to a halt in front of two dilapidated, make-shift looking structures. With a big smile and an Arabic thank you, Nora hopped outside of the car, not waiting for a driver to do the honors of opening the door, and she beckoned with excitement for me to follow. Madawi remained in the car and showed no sign of moving as we clamored out to meet up with Fatma from the car behind us.

Once outside the car, it became obvious that the structures were in fact barns, and we were at a stable of some sort. With the all cars still running to keep the interiors cool, I noticed the three-piece suited men bunched together at the front of our car. They were obviously debating something, and I asked Nora what was going on.

"Horses, Mrs. Teresa," she exclaimed as she snapped her fingers and clapped her hands the way she always did when things were going great. "We will ride horses today!"

Caught in her excitement, Fatma and I exchanged a high-five in anticipation of our ride. Giggling, we quickened our step as we followed Nora to where the Egyptian farmer dressed in traditional attire with dirty sandaled feet stood holding three somewhat unkempt horses, saddled and ready for riding. Nearby stood a young relative of the old man, smiling like crazy to see the tourists as he held an additional two horses also saddled and ready.

My attention was pulled from the site of the child by the increase in debate among the three-piece suited men in front of the Mercedes. Their voices continued to rise for another moment and then, suddenly, their conversation ended abruptly, and two of them headed toward us. Observing this, it became obvious who must have been selected to follow us and who had been selected to stay and guard the remaining. With that issue solved, I turned and mounted the horse held out to me.

The girls mentioned that they had ridden before, and chances were that they had as Madawi goes to all lengths to allow her girls to truly experience many things in life. However, I still felt compelled to give a quick verbal review as the horse spun around while Fatma tried to mount. The old man was of little use because he would never come close to touching the young princess. Giggling, yet listening, she had that left foot in the stirrup and leg over the back in a matter of minutes. Smiling with pride as she settled into the saddle, she encouraged Nora to follow her lead.

With all three of us saddled, I noticed we had no one else except for the two guys in suits thirty yards behind still attempting to get on their horses from the incorrect side. Curious, I asked Nora since she had been the coordinator of our side excursion. Obviously not having thought of it either, she turned and yelled something in Arabic to the old Egyptian man, and he replied. Satisfied, she gave a little nudge to her stallion and started down the not-so-trodden path before us. Even more curious as I saw us leaving all other humans, without a guide to a place unknown, I questioned again. Raising her voice to be heard, Nora replied, "**Mofie mushkala**, Mrs. Teresa. "We follow the path and when we are tired, we turn around," she interjected nonchalantly as all three of us looked to our rear to see the two men in suits try to ride a horse and follow us.

Seeing the comical event begin to unfold before us, all three sensed the need for a bit of mischief as was revealed in our exchange of glances. To confirm, I asked, "Shall we ladies?" with a huge grin across my face.

Breaking into smiles themselves, they agreed and we all gave our steeds a quick kick into gallop. As soon as comfortable with the new gait, each of us turned to see the men behind, doing their best to do their jobs of protecting, yet obviously lacking in riding experience. I felt as bad for them as the horses pounded their behinds while enduring the Egyptian heat in three-piece suits. It only took a few moments of this sight for my laugher to turn to pity for these poor men.

For almost an hour we rode, galloping and walking, along the edge of the Nile, shaded by the trees of the river bank. We rode by huts, constructed of old lumber, with openings for our view revealing a family living in the one-room, bathless shelter. We rode along an antiquated railroad track going, it seemed, to nowhere. Along our return ride down the path, we began to pick up a parade as we rode. Many children started following the horses, laughing and calling to us, obviously happy for our diversion. Excited by the children's joy, Fatma began to speak to them in Arabic, exchanging cordial greetings. Then as she always seemed to do, Fatma felt compelled to give them something, as she has such a giving nature.

Digging into her jeans' pockets and insisting Nora and I to do the same, we were able to come up with about 500SR (125 U.S. dollars). Delighted, Fatma leaned over from her horse and started handing the money to the children, joking and laughing with them until the last riyal was distributed. Satisfied with our making of new friends, we continued our way back to our waiting caravan.

Sweaty, dirty, and almost pooped, we decided to head back to the St. George to rest and then ready for the highlight of our weekend. To commemorate the 75th anniversary of the discovery of Tutankhamun's tomb and the 125th anniversary of the world premiere of Verdi's opera, *Aida*; a special production of the opera was created and to be staged at the temple of Queen Hatchepsut for five days only (12 to 17 October 1997). With seating of 5,000 per performance and limited performances, we were among the select to get to experience such a magical event, and I didn't want to miss a moment of it.

Room service, the nap and dressing, all seemed like a blink as we found ourselves yet again in the hallway pushing the button for the elevator. Yet this time there were no sneakers, jeans, and tummy pouches—rather, long dresses, high heels, elegant jewelry, and evening bags. And in another turn, we were zipping off in our motorcade to the Valley of the Queens and the temple of Queen Hatchepsut.

An official lead car cleared our path of pedestrians as we approached the temporary risers built specifically for the event. Pulling to a stop as close as possible, our doors swung open by the unseen hands, and we stepped onto red carpets, which lay on top of the sand, lined from the car-stop to the seating entrance. As we made our way, I noticed our small entourage of ten quickly doubled as we were joined by Egyptian diplomats, obviously hosting Madawi to this historic event. Never breaking stride nor showing a ticket, as was typical when traveling with Madawi, we made our way to a row of roped seating. After all the chair swapping and moving around, I ended up enjoying the opera with Madawi to my right and Fatma to my left, the three-piece suits on the row below, and a group of American tourists behind.

  The risers were filled with conversations of many languages, each trying to speak over the next, and the smells swelled around with each designer perfume and incense imaginable. Excitement was in the air, and we enjoyed a warm breeze under the star-lit sky. It was a magical night, indeed.

  Soon, with the clamor of the orchestra and the brilliance of the lights as the darkened stage illuminated, quiet fell over the entire throng. The opera had begun and we found at our feet the most spectacular staging, sets, costuming, and performance for the next three hours. Behind this unbelievable stage, stood the 3,000-year-old majestic back drop of Queen Hatshepsout's temple, set directly into the cliff-face near the Valley of the Queens. Honoring Egypt's only woman pharaoh, the temple is considered by experts to be one of the finest ancient Egyptian temples in existence.

Verdi's *Aida* is hailed as one of the great operatic favorites with its story of the doomed love between Aida, the Ethiopian slave, and Radames, leader of the Egyptian armies. In spite of not understanding the words, I was enthralled with Aida, feeling every emotion and sensing every thought as the tale unfolded.

Before the applause diminished marking the first intermission, Madawi and I could not help but chatter about all that we had just witnessed. As Nora entered the discussion, I faintly heard a voice that seemed noticeably out of place. It was a female American's voice with a Southern accent, saying "excuse me," repetitively. Unable to ignore the sound of home, I turned to find a lady looking right at me, wishing to gain my attention with her "excuse *mes*." When I replied, "hello," I unknowingly opened the flood gates for questions. Looking from me to Madawi and back, obviously puzzled, the lady began. She asked if I was enjoying the opera, and general questions obviously trying to sort out why I was with a group of Arabs rather than Americans at the event. Sensing her over-abundant curiosity, the mischievous side in me could not help but rise up, and I found myself offering vague answers to her questions, which only served to make her more curious.

As the orchestra sounded to begin the next act, I leaned over and quietly shared the exchange with Madawi and peaked her sense of good fun as well, and we decided to continue the charade with the next intermission.

Creating Shamsiyah

Much to my surprise, Madawi was ready for the next intermission, offering things for me to say to the stranger, which would only create a greater sense of curiosity. With the expected "excuse me," I turned to face the lady again as Madawi stretched to listen as I continued with the cloak-and-dagger conversation. In a few short minutes, I learned much about my newfound friend. From Birmingham, Alabama, she was with friends on a two-week Nile cruise tour that originated in Alexandria. She told me where they had been and where they were going, which was a horrible practice for good security when traveling, yet very entertaining for me.

Even so, by the end of the intermission, she was even more frustrated because all she had learned about me was that I was from Georgia, living in Saudi Arabia and there for the weekend to see *Aida*. Bless her heart, the woman never knew, never had a clue that she enjoyed the evening with Saudi royalty.

The weekend had been all we had hoped it would be and more within the splendor and glamour of an ancient setting beyond belief. I thought of Luxor often in the days that followed as I tackled the pile of paperwork left from the week before. I loved my life, yet I understood the two-sided nature of the sword. I lived in an unbelievable world of the rich and famous with the evil side of humans always looming. Consequently, I often counted my blessings, prayed for safety, and kept focused on my purpose.

Chapter 14
Coming of Age
November 1997- July 1998

As luck would have it, the idea for our fall social walked into my office my first day back from Egypt. Huda, a delightful elderly woman from Columbia, South America had heard about the center in the expat community and was interested in teaching South American cooking. She was interested in the center having a dinner party so that she could cook for the ladies and allow them to try her motherland foods. It was the perfect idea! We would have a South American evening. With the idea set, the details would follow and we set the date.

The term had just begun and the staff was already tiring. We needed additional help to maintain the extended open hours and manage registration. Desiring the same qualities and professionalism we had in Maria and Amal, I looked to Madawi once again. The first time she had suggested a relative of a friend, we hit the jackpot. Consequently when she suggested it this time, I felt for sure we couldn't be so lucky a second time around. Yet, there is something to be said for nepotism. Nada, a daring, educated, smart young woman entered our shamsiyah. She was Maria's sister-in-law and Hiba's daughter. I honestly didn't know what to make of Nada when she arrived for work the first time. With purple lipstick, shadow, and nails accented with a flower tattoo on her shoulder. Yet beneath that once the young professional woman began to emerge, I found another committed go-getter. Nada was a perfect addition to the team.

The 11th of November rolled around and Nabila's offerings came to a close. Enrollment in her classes had been superb in comparison to many of our other classes because the pace setters had had plenty of time to promote her since her initial visit in May. She enjoyed 41 students in her five four-hour seminars, and in her 24-hour program she had 10 enroll and 9 complete.

The pace setters could not get enough of her programs. However, Nabila's classes did touch the deepest fears and emotions of her participants, and it was probably the first time any of them had ever been exposed to this type of information. Many of our students were fearful of such personal exploration and shied away.

About five weeks later, Nabila walked out of the center with almost $17,000 in her hands for 52 class hours of "helping" the Saudi women, plus an additional $2,000 for 19 private counseling sessions given between her classes. She had found a cash cow. Granted it was a thirsty cow – thirsty for knowledge – but a cash cow nonetheless and she knew it.

Honestly, I resented handing her the envelope of cash. Even though she was a very educated woman and her fees were probably in line with stateside pricing, I could not get over the fact that the Western, Christian women of TLC, many of whom held degrees as good as Nabila's and most from more reputable universities, worked long hours for little or no pay because they believed in the mission of the center and in the potential of the Saudi women. Whereas one of their own only seemed to be interested in personal gain as she smiled to their face and dug deeper in their handbags.

I feel I can make this postulation of Nabila's agenda because of many comments she made and behaviors she exhibited over the time I had to associate with her. To me, one incident in particular that occurred during the course of her first fall term clearly shows her loyalty to the almighty dollar rather than the betterment of Saudi women.

One long time TLC student attempted to take Nabila's 24-hour program. Whether it was a scheduling conflict or her inability at that time to address the personal issues presented, I don't know but the lady dropped out of the program. She had only attended the first hour of the initial two-hour session and probably received no benefit for doing so. Within the center, this should not have been an issue. Yet, it became one.

From the day we opened our doors in November of 1995, we knew what we were doing through the center was new and to most, unfamiliar. Consequently, we always held the policy that a lady was more than welcome to attend the first session of any class to see if it were something she would like to take or not. If not, she was never charged for the single, investigative session. Immediately, we found this policy fostered an atmosphere of non-threatening, risk-free exploration by our women and no TLC instructor had ever had a problem with it, until Nabila. She insisted the student pay 333 SR / $ 89.00 for the hour and flatly refused to leave without it. I could have never argued to that extent over $89.00 with $19,000 in my purse, particularly if I cared about the cause. Obvious from her staunch debate in my office, I knew I had to pay her if I were going to get her out of the center. Yet, I simply could not ask our student for the fee. Rather, I paid it out of my own pocket to appease Nabila and to keep our courageous student coming back for additional learning from which she could derive benefit.

With all that was going on with the center, both the exciting and the challenging, I rarely noticed the world outside of my world. I would read the regular warden messages, ponder for a moment, and then move on. Subconsciously, I still felt immune. However, the night of the 17th of November altered my perceptions and brought my reality a bit closer yet again. Six gunmen methodically murdered and knifed fifty-eight foreign tourists, three Egyptians officers, and one tour guide for 30 minutes in the Hatsheput Temple, where I had walked only four weeks prior. Reports indicated it was the largest terrorist attack ever committed in Egypt.

At the end of our previous term, one of our students asked that I see about offering yoga in the fall. Yoga, for heaven's sake! Where in the world would I find a female yoga master in Kingdom?

Believing it to be an impossible task within the confines of my desert domain, I simply asked the teachers to keep their eyes open and I took no further action on the matter. However word of mouth goes a long way, particularly in Kingdom, and before I knew it I had a yoga specialist from the country of India in my office applying for the job.

    Luwa was very well qualified and a delightful person to boot. Plus, she had all of the required qualities. After the interview, I offered her the opportunity to offer a class or two. Yet, she had reservations about the Saudi women although desperately wanted to teach. In Kingdom, whether anyone wants to admit it or not, a mutated version of India's Cass system exists. Foreign workers are paid based on their nationality, not their level of expertise or education. Unfortunately, Indians rank rather low on the ladder. Consequently, Luwa was afraid the students would see her as a servant rather than a knowledgeable instructor with much to share.

    Understanding the Saudi culture, I could empathize with her concerns, yet I reassured her that the ladies of the center were an exception to the norm. Even so, she was still reluctant. Not wanting to loose such a valuable addition to our team, I encouraged Luwa to attend our upcoming South American dinner fall social. I knew for sure our TLC ladies would welcome her with open arms and treat her as an equal, but she needed to experience that in order to feel comfortable stepping in her new instructor role. For the final push to get her to come, I promised that if she still didn't feel comfortable after the party, I would understand and the center would go on without the offering of yoga. Luwa agreed and planned to attend the following evening.

    Typically, late November weather in Saudi was incredibly pleasant and the idea to utilize the vacant lot for our South American evening was perfect. Huda could prepare the meal in the new kitchen and the ladies could have access to the center, yet make their way to the empty lot via our newly built stairway entrance between the two. We couldn't however have two hundred ladies standing in the sand sporting designer dresses and matching shoes with no shelter for the evening, so I rented a small Bedouin tent to serve as the buffet and a large one for the festivities. I borrowed Madawi's camping carpets, which are huge, and used them as flooring in each tent and runner carpets to connect the two. There was no need to step on sand unless you desired. Lights strung from the support poles of the tent were included in the rental charge and I added a piñata for fun later in the evening.

    To carry the theme, I had five palm trees delivered and placed strategically around the tents to hide the ugly metal wall that was accomplishing our squatting for the lot. Throughout, I added bamboo tikki torches which gave the entire setting a warm glow and festive feeling. I had Saleem and Riaz place enough birch dinning room tables and chairs in the big tent to accommodate all of our guests to sit down for their meal, leaving an open space between the tables for dancing. I grabbed our biggest boom box and we were set for a night of fun.

As the music blared and I boogied with the ladies, I felt someone bump against me. Still dancing, I looked to my side to find Luwa moving and shaking just as much I was. Out of curiosity, I inquired.

"Well, what do you think?" I shouted with a smile as I began to do the twist.

"It's wonderful!" She shouted back. "But I haven't seen a princess yet."

Laughing I answered, "Heavens Luwa, are you expecting for them to parade around with a crown? Just keep dancing! They are all around you!"

For years to follow, Luwa and I laughed about our quick exchange that evening. I think she expected more pomp and circumstance. Perhaps she expected horns to sound and the princesses to parade in with crowns gleaming and capes flowing. When in fact, Luwa learned that our princesses were no different than any other women and that they slipped on their high heels one at a time just like everyone else. When it came time to smack the piñata, the women were like children experiencing Disney world for the first time. In designer dresses and expensive jewelry they swung the bat and cheered with glee. They had more fun with that piñata than I could have ever imagined. The evening was a grand success and the ladies had a ball! The food was scrumptious and, as usual, we danced until the wee hours of the night.

As 1997 and our fall term came to an end, I found the center in financial stress once again. Now although I am not a business major, it has always been my understanding that any new business takes a few years to get rolling. This estimate, I assume, would be applicable if the business were able to advertise to attract new students, and implement other standard business practices. *The Learning Center* however was not a typical business. We were operating under the radar and unable to apply tactics that legitimate businesses enjoy.

In our initial years, we had prepare and renovate two facilities and maintain the standard of learning and social offerings that our students had come to expect from TLC. We then compounded these challenges by the introduction of Nabila to the mix. Her demanded fee structure did not allow for any funds generated from her classes to be applied to the overhead of the center. Additionally, Nabila insisted her seminars be held in our fitness room which eliminated some of the fitness class times – a strong upcoming revenue stream. With this reduction of income from the center's precious class space, coupled with the ladies taking those classes instead of TLC's offerings, it is obvious why our bottom line fell red. When presented with this situation, Madawi reluctantly put $5,000 into our capital so that we could cover our fall term expenses and stay solvent to continue.

Fortunately, January brought another *Winter Jamboree* and the kids into our mists. The ladies were joyous as the New Year arrived and with it, Mama Ann. Returning to Kingdom after an extended stay stateside while my father recuperated, Ann jumped right in to help with the children, just as she always did. Offering the typical kids programming, we were able to add outside activities because the South American dinner had showed us how beneficial the adjacent vacant lot could be. The children giggled with delight with a good old fashion game of kickball on the open-air sand lot.

Unfortunately, January also brought an end to our Taekwondo offering for the Saudi boys. Not one child registered to take the class for our *Winter Jamboree*. None of us could determine why. Later, we discovered that Susan, a lady Mary had solicited to assist her with the classes, had had a hidden agenda. Susan and her husband were both black belts in the art and were able to pull all of the boys in the program to another location where they were the instructors, effectively cutting Mary and TLC out of the loop. Mary did continue for a while with her ladies however interest soon died in the class that wasn't seen by most of the Saudi ladies as something they would benefit.

In late January, Nabila called and we began organizing the schedule for her anticipated spring visit. Our negotiation of her contract went well into March and concluded with her commanding the same disproportionate fee structure from the other instructors. Surprisingly, this did not bother me as much as something else. Unlike the fall, she flatly refused to sign our 12 month non-competition clause, which was standard in all TLC contracts. No other instructor ever had a problem with the clause, but Nabila responded by saying, "I have no plans to undertake such in the near future but cannot accept this type of limitation on my professional freedom." Because of her immense popularity with the pace setting ladies and Madawi's budding loyalty, I acquiesced yet again. I knew however that this was the beginning of the end, but I was powerless to do anything about it.

Near the end of February in 1998, a series of public decrees surfaced among our regular U.S. Warden Messages from renegade Saudi terrorist financier Osama bin Laden. Publicly he threatened to attack U.S. forces in the Kingdom in an effort to drive the United Sates and its allies from Muslim counties. In doing so, he encouraged that it was a religious duty for all Muslims to wage war on U.S. citizens, military and civilian, anywhere in the world.

I often wondered if this was *"the man"* that the women in the center spoke of often in those days. Whenever a terrorist attack or public threat surfaced that could remotely be related to bin Laden, the ladies would speak of the event with what seemed like heavy hearts. Each time the current attack discussion would begin to fade, they would conclude by whispering, "Oh Mrs. Teresa, there is *this man*" and they would shake their heads as if saddened. With each new message or current warning, I knew history was unfolding and we had a front row seat.

Our core courses grew and our fitness exploded. We were running four fitness classes per day with our maximum of 6 ladies in each, limited only by the room. In the fall, aerobics had enjoyed the favor of our pace setters, yet by spring the word was getting out and ladies we had never seen were starting to appear. For security, Madawi subsequently requested to review our fitness membership list. What or who she was looking for, I am unsure, but she checked it daily for about a month. That was the only time she ever became involved in any of the daily operations of the center. To accommodate the growing demand and Angela's desire to work part-time, we decided to hire an additional fitness instructor. Terri, a striking American blonde, had not been in Kingdom long, yet she was enthusiastic to become involved. Because of her recent arrival, Terri was abreast of all the new fitness crazes in the states. Fortunately, she was eager to share and be responsible for bringing yet another first our way.

  She told us about the latest stateside rage called "spinning." It was created by world-class cyclist "Jonny G." Goldberg as a convenient and quick way to train for races. In 1989, he and John Baudhuin opened the first spinning center in Santa Monica, California and then developed a program to certify other spinning instructors. Spinning is an aerobic exercise that takes place on a specially designed stationary bicycle called (obviously enough) a spinning bike. In a typical 45-minute workout, a lady could burn up to 450 calories. The appeal of spinning, however, was that it incorporated the mental with the physical. As you pedal, motivating music plays, and the instructor talks you through a visualization of an outdoor cycling workout: "You're going up a long hill now. You can't see the top yet...." During the class the pace varies, pedaling as fast as possible one moment and possibly cranking up the tension and pedaling slowly from a standing position the next. Madawi was very excited about bringing spinning to TLC and immediately offered to bring two spinning bikes back for us from her stateside summer holiday. Even so, I think she was shocked to find they cost over $800 per spinning bike, plus international shipping, but she purchased them nonetheless.

 Our art department started down a new path as well in the spring of 1998. Carol with her delightful, encouraging personality had become a pillar on the TLC team in just a few short months. The ladies interested in art fell in love with her for many reasons. She was talented, well educated, and most importantly she saw the potential of our women. In such, Carol went the extra mile and she was able to secure the inclusion of coursework and subsequent certification for the ladies from a prestigious art school in Britain, *City & Guilds of London Art School*. The requirements to affiliate with this esteemed program were stringent, but Carol guided our curriculum so that TLC could meet those requirements. The inclusion of *City & Guilds* was a huge success for the art department, but it was even bigger for TLC because it was our first validation by a legitimate institute located outside the Kingdom's borders.

 Although she did not take art classes at the center any longer, Madawi's interest in art continued to grow. In March, she decided we should travel to

Jeddah to view the work of a local artist, which was the trip we had planned to take almost two years prior but canceled due to the bombing of **Khobar** Towers. Much to my delight, Madawi invited David and the children to come along as well and she brought her girls to make it a family weekend.

  And what a weekend it was. To accommodate our group, Madawi rented three beach front condominiums at the Holiday Inn situated on the shore of the Red Sea. It was a five-star resort complete with two indoor swimming pools, one for men and one for women. The beach however allowed for mixed couples to be there, yet I was the only one wearing a swimsuit with a long shirt rather than an *abaya*. In the heat of the day, the beach was empty of Saudis and our party essentially enjoyed the run of the place. Madawi, wearing trousers and a tunic top, laughed as she lounged on the beach chairs and watched me and the children run from the minimal wave action the sea provided and then chase it back again. We built sand castles and the children rode ponies in the surf.

  Amazingly, two TCNs were operating a Jet Ski rental business right outside our condo. David decided to take advantage of the rare opportunity and took one for a spin. Jealous, I wanted to ride too and David knew it. When he returned, he asked the worker if I could ride. Of course the man did not understand David's request, but he nodded and smiled as they typically did whenever an American spoke to them whether they understood the speech or not. We knew this, yet we accepted his head nod as a "yes" because I wanted to ride so badly. Before I jumped onto the Jet Ski, David whispered to me. "This is an inland bay. Go west. If you go east, you will run into other boats and people will see you." He paused. "Be careful."

With my instructions clear, I smiled at the gentleman and then jumped on the Jet Ski and hit the gas. It was at that moment the worker fully understood what David had requested and went ballistic at my being on his Jet Ski. I could hear him yelling in his native tongue as I zoomed away. This was illegal on many levels. Not only was I **driving** the Jet Ski, but I was doing so with very little clothing and definitely showing more than my wrists and ankles.

It was exhilarating. The wind in my hair and the salt spray in my face made me feel alive. For that short ride, I was no longer submersed into a radical Islamic country, rather I was free. When I returned the man was still yelling, and David said he had not stopped since my departure. Ignoring him, I went to join Madawi on the lounge chairs and David compensated him an additional 100SR for his stress. Later that evening, I thought of the man and felt guilty. I should have not put him in the situation I did. Had I been caught, he would have been punished for letting me get away with it. He could have been flogged or imprisoned, and it was wrong of me to endanger him for that brief "stateside" feeling.

I was quite taken back with what we found when we went to see the artist Madawi had raved about. Expecting his art to be in a gallery of some sort, I was a little leery as we were led through the tight, dark alleyways between the dilapidated buildings in downtown **Jeddah**. Eventually, the winding path led us to an open air area between the buildings that appeared to be some sort of a courtyard for the surrounding apartments. There, the artist had made his gallery and on the walls, his creations. Plaster, pots, paint, and brushes were the tools of his trade. I was surprised to see the creativity that emerged from the cracked walls and wound its way around the piping and windows that existed on the façade. The two dimensional depictions incorporated a Bedouin flare in style and color while the 3-D areas took my breath away. I fell in love with one particular section of the wall where the artist had taken Bedouin clay pots, cut them in half, and plastered them onto the wall reaching at least twenty feet into the air. After the privilege of seeing this, I often dreamed of doing the same on a wall of the center, but never had the time or the funds to make it happen.

After our trip to **Jeddah**, Madawi decided that we had sat long enough and we set our sites on incorporating the vacant lot behind the center. We were doing it again…the impossible. Yet instead of a swimming pool as first envisioned, we set our sights to build and operate the first female fitness center for Saudi women. Fitness had busted loose after its introduction and we wanted to ride the wave.

Taking the first steps, Madawi and I met with David and Najib to brainstorm our current and predicted needs of the new building. Although predominately built as a fitness facility, we wanted it to be adaptable for other functions such as parties, art shows, and educational seminars. I requested maximum functionality by asking for a way to turn one large room into two smaller ones and back on demand, plus at least one wall of mirrors for the exercise classes. We would need office space, a locker room, and a weight room if space allowed. Additionally, the two buildings needed an adjoining corridor, which would require some renovation in the existing facility as well. With our wish list in hand, Najib and David began the process of making it happen with a target to begin preparing the lot immediately and beginning actual construction following the kids' summer program as we had done with the kitchen.

By mid-April, the weather was fabulous and enrollment in ladies' swimming, water aerobics, and water safety was at its peak. The ladies were having a ball. Many even told me they had private pools at home, but had never used them because they did not know how to swim. Now, they could use them. Once the ladies learned, they wanted to swim and those that did not have private pools at home began to ask to rent our facility for private parties.

From the start of my involvement with *Al-Hamdi*, the school year swirled with excitement and new challenges. First, Madawi had given me the honor of coordinating a high school graduation celebration for her oldest female, Nora. In the middle of preparations for the gala event, the initiation arrived. *King Fahad University of Petroleum and Minerals*

(KFUPM) *Girls' School* was hosting their "first annual public speaking competition" in the Eastern Province and *Al-Hamdi* was invited to participate.

"Mrs. Teresa," she began as she stood from her chair and proudly handed me the invitation, "will you coordinate our team?"

Amazed that the competition was even happening given the cultural restraints placed on females, I immediately accepted the chance to be a part of this historic event.

"I would love to," I replied, "and we'll do great!"

"To win," Madawi hesitated, "is not important. I am just happy that the girls can participate." She paused thoughtfully, "It's a big step."

I did not need to ask for clarification; I knew what she meant. Little by little, the girls were achieving more recognition and more opportunities than ever before in this gender-biased society, just as their mothers were.

The rules were simple. Each school was allowed three representatives.

I held a school level competition to determine our three. It was a huge event. Content, organization, and delivery of the two-minute speeches the girls prepared to tryout for *Al-Hamdi's* team did not concern me because I knew that I would teach the selected team these skills. In order to do well at this event, I knew I had to find the girls with the best command of the English language. If the student had this quality, the rest would fall into place.

Excitement filled the air on team selection day, as nothing like this had ever occurred within the walls of this secluded private school. Actually, nothing like this had ever happened to any female students anywhere in the Kingdom. We had eleven eager, nervous students from the tenth, eleventh, and twelfth grades try out for a position on the team. Unexpectedly, the competition was stiff. Madawi and numerous teachers judged. When the votes were tallied, three emerged as the best representatives we could send. Ironically, the team comprised one from each of the grade levels: Safa from the senior class; Sylvana from the junior class; and, Fatma, Madawi's second daughter, from the sophomore class.

Excited and eager to begin, the girls selected their topics from the assigned list provided by the organizers of the contest. Safa chose to write on *Diabetes*, Sylvana selected *The Role of Women in Islam*, and Fatma wanted the remaining topic of *Rainforest Deforestation*. Long hours of research, revisions, and practices began. Not only were my afternoons at the school consumed with speeches, my nights fell prey as well. Because their society is nocturnal, it was not uncommon for my phone to ring after midnight beginning with, "Ello, Mrs. Teresa, I have a question about…"

In addition to the three required topics for the first round of speeches set forth by the competition planning committee, a plan was set for a second round to determine placement of the top five speakers of the first round. The second round would consist of impromptu speeches from fifty preset topics, rather than polished prepared speeches like in the first round. Knowing that the judges would look for organization, not look for substantial content in impromptu speeches, I drilled my team once their first round speeches were complete.

"Attention getter, tie to audience, preview, thesis, one or two points, and conclusion!" I would shout as we practiced pulling topics out of a basket from the selected list. "It really doesn't matter what you say," I would reiterate, "even if you feel funny. The most important thing is organization, organization, organization!"

The night of the contest finally arrived. Held in the university auditorium, a huge cheering section turned out from *Al-Hamdi* to encourage our team. Naturally, only females were allowed to attend. After the ***abayas*** were discarded, an hour of socializing followed among the students and ladies attending. As the start time drew near, my team became even more anxious. I encouraged them by letting them know I was proud of them no matter what the outcome. Then with one final thumbs-up to the girls, I took my seat with my stopwatch in hand. The lights dimmed and KFUPM's competitor in the *Role of Women in Islam* speech took the stage. With applause and cheers followed because the competition had begun. Soon Sylvana, a touch nervous, took the stage to represent *Al-Hamdi*. She did a good job and was under her five-minute limit, but she did not stand out from the other five participants in her topic.

Still encouraged that we were holding our own, we watched as the competition moved forward to the *Rainforest Deforestation* speeches. Fatma, with her boyish gate, stepped up to the podium. With a deep breath she began.

"Close your eyes and imagine. Imagine a world without butterflies, a world without..." she continued and the audience was mesmerized. Unlike any other Saudi ladies' gathering I had attended before or after, there was utter silence in the audience. Studying and good grades were never Fatma's forte; however, brains and theatrics were.

Safa was the first to present on diabetes, and the *Al-Hamdi* group cheered as she approached the podium. It was as if magic dust had been sprinkled on my girls that evening; Safa took the place by storm. Clear, focused, organized, and dramatic, her speech stood out and brought down the house yet again. We could hardly control ourselves as we jumped for joy upon her completion; however, we had to regain our composure and endure the final five prepared speeches of the evening.

A second intermission followed and our excitement was uncontainable. As we enjoyed the refreshments provided, we talked, analyzed all of the presentations, and decided that our girls would be in the second round. Finally the judges returned with the final five names, and the crowd was called to order.

Silence fell over the auditorium as the KFUPM competition coordinator approached the microphone to announce the second round participants. As she did, my heart raced, and everything on my body that could be crossed was.

Safa and Fatma were two of the five that progressed to the second round – the impromptu speeches. Five folding chairs were placed in a semi-circle in the center of the stage, and the girls took their seats. Tension and the unexpected silence drifted over the audience. The entire *Al-Hamdi* cheering section set breathless until the speeches were complete. Yet we whispered non-stop as we anticipated the final outcome. Thankfully, our long hours of hard work and preparation paid off. Fatma took second place and Safa took first! *Al-Hamdi* had prevailed.

Given our financial situation, I decided to allow it even though I knew I was pushing the envelope with regard to what would be overlooked and what would not. It was a decision that would come back to bite me. One evening, the private pool party got a little loud and drew the attention of the neighbors. The next day, Nashad, the compound manager of DM16 as well my compound, was telephoned and told "no more" by the authorities. Fortunately, they did not know it was not a Westerner's party. Regrettably, our swimming program had to close after the summer. The risks were too high and the operating costs of chemicals and upkeep became more than the center could bear.

On the heels of a similar February declaration, bin Laden reared his head again in May of 1998 via a press conference in Afghanistan. This time his threats became more pointed and he declared a holy war against US forces on the Arabian Peninsula, most of which were in stationed in Saudi Arabia. Rather than a Warden Message, we received a line-by-line copy of this interview. I assume the company wanted us to know what we were actually facing. Yet, it was still distant.

It was one of those rare, slower paced days when the ladies' program was coming to an end and the kids' registration yet to begin. I was in my office doing some paperwork when I discovered that our center had been invaded. I was startled when Madawi came briskly into my office with her *abaya* flying behind her. She closed the door without stopping on her path to my desk. Towering over me as I sat, she demanded with a glare in her eyes. "Do you know who is in your center?"

I was clueless and "no" was all I could muster to utter.

Touching one slender finger to my desk to emphasize the importance of her words, she continued. "YOU have a DIRECTOR of another school sitting in your classroom! Get her out!"

Completely shocked because I had never seen this side of Madawi, all I could mutter was "yes, I will take care of it immediately." She turned and left without saying another word.

Fawzia, the director of an aspiring copy cat center, entered our shamsiyah by enrolling in a basic business class to see what we were doing and how we were operating. She never revealed her day job or her purpose for being there to reception when she enrolled. For the second time, I saw the same authoritarian, powerful demeanor I had seen in the states when she fired our driver/bodyguard. However this time, her wrath was at me. At that moment, I decided I never wanted to be on the receiving end of Madawi's anger.

Refusing to accept my lame excuse for her being removed from the classes that she had rightfully registered and paid to attend, Fawzia began to call me attempting to gain readmission. Because I side-stepped her requests and comments, her accusations became stronger and her calls increased. Eventually, she began calling my home and at all hours of the day and night. It continued for weeks and got to the point of insanity. Eventually, Madawi had to flex her royal muscle to make the calls cease by "sending someone to her house." What that exactly meant? I'm not sure, but I never saw or heard from the woman again.

As with previous summer programs, we allowed the children to select the classes they wanted to take based on their individual interests and schedules. It was structured so that a child could come and spend the day or simply take one class. We had learned from the prior summer and were ready for the enrollment onslaught, peaking at just over 250 kids in a given week. Additionally, the summer 1998 saw the inclusion of a new workshop. We called it "adventure workshop," which was essentially a field trip from the center every day of the week. We took the kids horseback riding, swimming, and to local museums. It was an instant hit.

In the middle of our summer program, sadness came for our ladies when Mama Ann left the Kingdom to live in America. My father had come out of retirement once because of his love for his daughter and the Kingdom. However, he felt was time to return to their home in Georgia and play golf. After all, he had worked 35 years. Happy for my mother, yet sad for themselves, the TLC ladies held her a *ma'assalaamah* party before she left, showering her with gifts. From the day she left until the day she returned two years later, the ladies constantly asked about Mama Ann.

On the airbase, my father was honored as well when Colonel, now General, Awad presented him with a gold-plated model of the F-15 Eagle. On the way to the presentation, my father's Colonel told him no cameras would be allowed because of the prince, General Awad. My Dad respecting protocol agreed to such. Fifteen minutes later in the conference room, the General shouted across the room to David with his typical politician smile, "You got your camera David?" My Dad and David still laugh when they remember Colonel Abdullah's look of horror. Dad had been on the Peace Sun Program since its inception and witnessed the roll out of the first MDS F-15 in the 1970s. His tenure with the program was unprecedented and the General respected this. Even today, they refer to him as **shabah**.

While heavy equipment and contractors rumbled outside my office clearing the property for Madawi's latest dream, I worked diligently on our fitness, brochures, membership cards, student databases and the like. Lulu became worried about me and started delivering Ben's delightful creations from the palace to my desk. I knew my attention would soon be on decorating and there was no time to waste. With the Colonel's blessing, David's creative financing, and Najib's construction genius, they made it happen yet again. Najib and his crew were skilled at their trade. They began by demolishing the walls of our business office toward the vacant lot, making the corridor, adjoining the old and new, look like it was part of the original facility.

Because the vacant lot was lower in elevation, the passageway between the two incorporated two steps and a small dog-leg shift to avoid the north wall of Saleem and Riaz's room built just outside, which was now sandwiched between the two buildings. Once down the steps, the new business office and locker room were to the right, the weight and massage rooms to the left, and the large multi-purpose aerobics room straight ahead. Our budget dictated cinder block and concrete slab, but we did what we could with décor to give the place a touch of class. The corridor walls for the business office and weight room were glass with mini-blinds if privacy were required.

The business office was simple, but useful and became a hang out for the staff once we added a few overstuffed flowered chairs. To doll up the beige walls, I took a feather duster dipped in a contrasting green color and sprinkled the back wall with random marks. This technique not only looked terrific, but was cost effective as well.

In fashion with any world class gym, the weight room had one wall fully mirrored. The other two walls I painted a pale peach and then dotted in beige with my feather duster technique to carry the décor throughout. Madawi donated her personal weight machine from the palace and purchased our two spinning bikes. David, on the other hand, found a treadmill that had been put out for trash that he was able to have repaired, costing the center nothing to have a treadmill available as well.

Our addition of a massage room was an afterthought once we saw the facility dried in and could get a visual of the space we were afforded. As luck would have it, Madawi had a massage table she donated and an American woman had just arrived on my compound that was a certified massage therapist. It would be another first for TLC in our fall offerings. Unfortunately, it was an unsuccessful first and only lasted through the fall. Apparently, the ladies simply were not comfortable with that type of exposure to a stranger, even if it were a female.

The locker room became our thorn. I wanted something striking to make the ladies feel warm and welcome, yet the budget didn't allow for much. However, with a little creative thinking, it turned out superb. I had the masons take the broken teal green floor tile, left over cuts from installation, and break them with a hammer into saucer size pieces. Then, I had them plaster the pieces to form the vanity and the drop down ceiling above it. Riyaz, the construction foreman, was a master carpenter. He took wood and hand carved doors for the changing rooms that could be turned one of four ways to create a different look. He beamed as I praised his workmanship.

The corridor ended in a T, giving the multi-purpose room glass door entrances. Najib creatively designed the room to accommodate the needs I expressed in our planning meeting. The wall dividing the larger room into two was paneled and covered in floor length mirrors. For this, Najib designed a tracking system recessed in the floor and on the ceiling so the panels could be folded like an accordion against the back wall in a matter of a half an hour with Saleem and Riaz working together.

The footprint of the facility consumed the vacant lot, leaving only one meter (approximately 3 feet) between the building and the back privacy wall. At almost 4,000 square feet, the cinder block building was approximately 53 feet wide by 70 feet deep. The men did a wonderful job and presented Madawi with almost a half a million dollar building for a minimal overhead charge. Naturally, she was pleased.

As a bonus, Najib had enough left over cinder block and two used doors to build Riaz an identical room across from their existing room opposite the outdoor wash area. They were thrilled to have their own space. The rest of the staff was simply happy the endless squabbling between those two ceased.

With only finishing touches remaining with our new facility, I finally got a chance to slow down and take a deep breath before fall term would begin. For the first time in months, I took a few days off to hang out on the compound and work around my house. With it being August most women and children were out of country on holiday, so the compound would be nice and boring which was just what the doctor ordered for me. I needed precious "recharge time."

On the morning of August 7, 1998, I was enjoying a lazy morning complete with a hot cup of cap and my favorite fluffy slippers when I tapped the power button on the remote control. I was horrified at the images of death and destruction that flashed before me. Panicked, I went for the volume button. The American Embassies in Nairobi, Kenya and Dar es Salaam, Tanzania had been bombed. In Nairobi, where the US Embassy was located in a congested downtown area, 291 persons were killed by the explosion and about 5,000 wounded. In Dar es Salaam, 10 persons were killed and 77 wounded. The news reports indicated that twelve Americans died in Nairobi that day. Immediately my thoughts went to Mary, TLC's Taekwondo / Self-Defense instructor, who had taken her holiday to visit her in-laws in Nairobi. I prayed she did not go to market that morning and anxiously awaited word of her safety.

Chapter 15
Fate Unveiled
August 1998 – April 1999

I was thankful to receive word that Mary and her family were safe and unharmed. Even though we had become accustomed to our regular security warnings and armed gates, their significance seemed to be drilling closer to home and more often. Bin Laden's verbal barrage continued to threaten U.S. interests in Saudi Arabia. At least one of these threats must have been note worthy for the U.S. Embassy in **Riyadh** and the Consulates in **Jeddah** and **Dhahran** to close for three days in early October of 1998. For me, this was unprecedented during the seven years that I had been in Kingdom.

With the cooler weather came the fourth fall term for TLC. We were on the top of the wave and I was hopeful for the future. The ladies seemed so happy and energized while there, and always appreciative of any new offering we could share. Hence, I knew for a fact that the latest "first" we were planning would be an instant success. Our computer department by its very nature was primed to mark another first for us and we were about to catapult to the threshold of the 21st century.

There were two industrious Americans on my compound that recognized the potential of the internet and the thirst Western expats had to remain in contact with what we referred to as "the real world." Blessed with extensive computer knowledge and obviously influential INCO connections, these men creatively accessed the World Wide Web and acted as a service provider for our compound.

Utilizing the in-house compound telephone system, any home could access the net for the fairly substantial fee of 500SR per month (approximately $125.00) plus telephone charges, if any were incurred. Although expensive, expendable cash laden expats craved the chance to stay in touch with family and friends, and they gladly passed over their **Riyal**. With a potential customer list of 500 villas, these entrepreneurs made a cool fortune in a matter of no time.

The internet had found Saudi Arabia and TLC was not going to be left behind. Yet, we would have to be creative to pull it off. The only feasible idea we could discern to give the center internet access was to connect TLC to the internet via my villa, thereby accessing the net with the other Western residents. This idea not only allowed TLC to have internet access, it also came with a bonus.

Essentially, every thing in the Kingdom is monitored by the government. It was an unstated rule to always assume someone is listening or watching. By connecting through the compound rather than a local provider, TLC enjoyed faster slow internet and our usage flew under the Saudi radar by not drawing attention to the large amount of usage pouring in and out of a single, in-town building. To make this happen, we used three computers donated to the center via **baksheesh**, compliments of our regular computer supplier, and set-up a control room in the kitchen by the class.

With the idea and hardware in place, the only obstacle that remained involved acquiring physical telephone lines, on the compound and for the center. Now, I realize in Western thought an additional telephone line or two is a rather insignificant issue. However in Kingdom, it is immensely significant. Telephone lines are sought and coddled. With the abundant wealth flowing into the oil rich nation, it is easy to forget that Saudi Arabia is still in the process of upgrading certain things with regard to infrastructure. Even with the finances to support an effort, it still takes time for things to develop and perhaps even longer to be accepted.

In *Al-Khobar* at the time, the telephone infrastructure had not kept up with the needs of the growing population, which caused a backlog for available lines. Even a princess was limited on the amount of telephone lines she could have for her use. The center itself had four lines assigned by the government (one for each of the original four apartments.) However, one of these was our main line for registrations and three lines simply were not enough to accommodate 12 computers simultaneously dialing my compound and subsequently accessing the internet. It was thanks to Madawi, however, that we were able to use four additional lines originally assigned to the palace. The very day our new Internet and Web Building class offerings hit our brochures, the classes were overflowing with students wanting to learn.

Compound telephone lines were necessary for the computer at my house to dial up the compound's internet provider. A simple telephone call from David, under the clearance of the Colonel, to our compound manager provided us with ten lines to use. Nashad, the compound manager, was a bit irritated he had to part with the lines he had little choice because the Colonel owned my compound. Securing telephone lines for the center was a different story.

Our online connection was miserably slow, and the limited, antiquated telephone lines were not the only factor. Due to the country's excessive control of its citizens and what they experience, all internet lines went through **Riyadh** for censorship and then to local providers throughout the Kingdom, which slowed the connection even further. Obviously pornographic sites were blocked, but so were sites such as Victoria's Secret and Oriental Trading Company. But patience, a virtue practiced five times a day, saw us through the extremely long download times. Waiting 15 minutes for the opening page of MSN seemed like a small price to pay for the privilege of accessing it at all.

Our core curriculum continued to offer opportunities for our ladies in English, French, and Italian Languages. Our cooking classes weren't immensely popular, mainly because many of the women did not cook in their homes, but we did have a group of ladies that continued to take whatever class was presented and then ask for more. Safa took her

Arabic cooking a bit further to add an Arab sweets workshop. During these classes, Safa identified a need within the social environment and began to teach social etiquette to the ladies. This workshop became very successful and ran continuously for two years with at least the required minimum of five students each term.

The success of the South American dinner brought Francisca into our haven to teach South American Cuisine. The short, round, wonderfully uplifting lady in her early 60s added a spark to the center when she would insist on "just one more taste." Our ladies that focused on cooking classes loved Francisca and the cooking knowledge she shared. She remained with us for two terms, but then had to decline because it was simply too much for her physically.

The new Fitness facility opened our fall with a bang, offering classes and information that were completely foreign to many of the ladies. Angela offered basic and advanced step aerobics as before, yet we added Terri's spinning and a new instructor, Gloria, to teach weight training and body sculpting. To provide an overall fitness program, I found an American lady on my compound, Shelia who came on board to help with our demand for aerobics classes, and she eventually offered nutrition workshops and individual nutrition counseling.

As luck would have it, the company's latest arrival of American families brought a certified masseuse to the compound and, in turn, the center.

ॐCreating Shamsiyahॐ

Linda, a delightful older lady, offered message therapy in the new massage room and worked diligently to make the program fly. Unfortunately, her efforts were fruitless. With the Exception of western workers, labor is relatively inexpensive in Kingdom and the Saudi women understand economics. For what one hour would cost them to have Linda give a massage would cover the cost of an in-home servant from the Philippines for a week with massages on demand.

    Because exercise wear was not available in the local market, I ordered basic black leotards, bike shorts, and spinning shorts from the states. I then had a local tailor embroider "TLC" in white on each piece. Pat, designed a tee-shirt for our fitness so that the ladies would have something to wear over their exercise gear. Pat's design was perfect in that it included our initials and a sense of exercise, yet not explicit where it would draw unwanted attention. Unfortunately, the ladies preferred to wear sweats and only the tee-shirts sold. Pat's logo, however, was so popular that we eventually had tote bags made sporting the design and they sold like hot cakes. In order to encourage water consumption during exercise, I had TLC water bottles and cups made as well to give to our students upon enrollment.

    The fitness facility and the opportunities it provided was a huge risk for us on many levels with regard to the Saudi culture and Sharia law. In such, we had to require membership so that we knew exactly who was in the center and seeing what we were doing. We simply could not take the risk of a female

muthawen in *The Learning Center*. Realizing I did not know all the ladies or the family names that may be associated with the more radical Islamists, Madawi would check our membership listing daily. The slightest oversight could cause our total demise: closure of the center at best and possibly imprisonment, at least for me, and I am unsure of what the consequences would have been for Madawi.

Initially, we offered three types of membership. Select membership was our basic annual membership. For the annual fee of 500SR ($125), the select member received discounted workout packages, nutrition counseling prices, a TLC water bottle. Basically, our select membership was the minimum a lady could do if she wanted to enter our facility to exercise.

For our upper echelon, we offered two premium packages, which would remove the need for them to ever open their handbags in the center. Our "Gold" and "Platinum" membership packages offered unlimited aerobics, weight room usage, a nutrition consultation and supporting workshops, 20% discount on all massages, a locker, a TLC water bottle, tee-shirt, and fitness bag with logo tag. The platinum package was superior because it also included 36 massages and unlimited spinning. Spinning fell into a different category for our pricing structure because of the teacher-student ratio, typically one on one but occasionally one to two.

Although the gold and platinum memberships were the best value for the money, not one lady bought a package. I tend to believe it was because of their fundamental belief that everything is **Insha Allah** – God's will. After all, only God knew if they would be there in a year to use the membership or if the facility would be there for them to use it. Hence they did not purchase. They did pay for the select membership, however, because it was the only way we would let them in the door.

The students of our *City & Guilds'* program shared the spotlight with the new fitness in the fall of 1998. The first year program students enrolled in the second term of their two-year course of study. As part of the required curriculum for *City & Guilds'*, Carol explained that the students had to host an art show upon completion of the term in order to show the efforts of their first year in the program. So ready or not, we set our sites on hosting the first TLC Art Exhibit and, I believe, the first all female art show in the province.

Madawi's love of art continued to blossom and she felt empowered enough to make another step by taking the power of TLC outside our wall for the first time – but with caution. With Pat's doing the leg-work, Madawi sponsored one of the first, if not the first, public art exhibits in the area. We put our membership and expertise behind orchestrating a show featuring Saudi artist, Abdulaziz Ashour, and held it in an obscure, basement room of the Carlton Hotel in **Al-Khobar**. Naturally, we did not indicate on any publicity *The Learning Center* or any of our names, simply that the exhibit was being held. Keeping with the theme of Ashour's artistic achievements, Pat designed tee-shirt for the staff to wear when it was their turn to keep watch over the exhibit. She also designed advertising posters and postcards for the visitors of the exhibit to collect and have signed by the artist when he was available. The two-day show was a tremendous success for the artist's sales and for the women of the province.

It was not long before Nabila arrived for her scheduled seminars and began demanding more of the center and its staff. It was confrontational from the start. My perception was that with each victory, she sought a new quest. She insisted the center staff coordinate all production of her classroom materials, which was something all of the other TLC teachers did themselves rather than cost the center in office manhours. Our staff had to translate her English programs into Arabic, print, and bind them for her. She drove Amal, Nada, and Maria crazy with her demands of their time and complaints of their efforts. Her demands were not only detrimental to the center financially but, more importantly, damaging to the morale of the TLC team. With each new demand met or "policy altered" specifically for Nabila, the other teachers began to feel more and more like the poor step children and their enthusiasm began to diminish as a result.

Nabila started offering private counseling again and scheduled appointments when the center was typically closed, requiring additional office staff until around 10:00 o'clock in the evenings. Honestly, this would not have been an issue had the center received any compensation for her presence to offset her expense.

When I shared my financial concerns with Madawi and explained the drain on our current staff, Madawi's solution was to hire another receptionist. Unfortunately, her direction to hire another receptionist only served to mutate the problem, rather than solve it. I do not think she considered the fact that a new employee meant additional costs. Yet, Madawi never seemed to consider that telling Nabila "no" as an option either.

As a result, Reema joined our team to accommodate Nabila's needs and relieve the extra workload for the current staff. Reema was a beautiful 20 year old Syrian woman whose father somehow knew Princess Madawi. Simply stated, Reema was angelic. She always carried a smile and saw the good in everyone. Being sheltered her entire life, Reema was naïve when she joined us and blushed often at the simplest of things. In spite of being a "forced hire," Reema turned out to be a perfect match with TLC. She and the other staff bonded immediately and worked together beautifully to make things happen.

Over the years, the TLC office staff provided me with very few headaches and never quarreled among themselves. Loyalty to the center and each other was strong among these women, which was evident in their longevity and performance. Of the six ladies hired to work as office staff during the seven and a half years I ran TLC, four were still working the day I left with only two having quit because they left

Kingdom. Not only were they committed to women's education, they were masters in multi-cultural cooperation. The diversity of our shamsiyah was exemplified as a Saudi, a Lebanese, a Syrian, a Briton, and two American women worked together for a common goal.

They were special ladies with good-hearted, optimistic souls. These ladies worked for peanuts spending more on their cell phone bills than they made in a month. Yet, money was not their reason for being there. They, too, believed what we were accomplishing was something good and something most certainly worth our effort.

This commitment to mission actually flowed throughout the TLC team. On two separate occasions I had to gather these ladies and lay our financial situation on the line. Each time they supported me and our mission by either electing to take pay cuts or giving more of their time, creativity, and talents to increase our cash flow problem and to keep the dream alive.

For the next week, Nabila's demands continued. Because of her unusual hours, she felt it was necessary for her to have a private car and driver rather than use Saleem and the center's van. Nabila also decided she needed a designated telephone line to our front desk so that her students would not get confused with TLC's programs. Our internet and website building classes utilized seven of our eight lines and TLC only enjoyed one on our front desk. The idea of loosing one was unthinkable.

When Nabila made this demand, it was the straw that broke the camels back for me. Believing I could rely on Madawi's backing, I pulled her into the dispute when it got to be what I considered too much. Unexpectedly, Madawi seemed to empathize with my position on the issues, yet supported Nabila's requests. Madawi did, however, offer a car and driver for her personal use. Nevertheless, the rest was left for me to cover with presumed TLC funds. I had no choice but to acquiesce to the demands. In my opinion, however, Madawi's response, although attempting to be neutral, sent a clear signal to Nabila that she did not have to do as the other TLC instructors did. From that point on, it was clear that Nabila had the upper hand and she knew it.

Although Nabila's presence demanded more of the center's resources than her TLC counterparts', her popularity and following among the majority of our students did not. Nabila enjoyed only minimal growth outside the small, pace setting clique, the informal leaders of TLC and the drive behind Nabila's popularity. Even with lower than anticipated enrollment, she had managed to attract the interest of this most influential group. Nabila's keen sense of targeting the decision makers of a group appeared to serve her well as time passed.

The majority of our students stayed in the shadows with Nabila's self-discovery programs and did not enroll. Yet, they became very active in the center because they still wanted to be near the princesses and other prominent ladies of the province and they still wanted the opportunity to learn. Unfortunately, what students she did enroll drained the other TLC classes, resulting in some being canceled because they didn't have that precious five needed to hold the class at cost.

There was no time to take a deep breath between Ashour's show and TLC's first art exhibition highlighting the achievements of our new *City & Guilds* program three days later. This two-day exhibit was the first event held in our newly built fitness edition. It was a gala affair and everyone who was influential in the community attended.

To prepare, Carol and Luwa worked non-stop hanging and labeling the students' work. Surprisingly, the large multi-purpose room did not have enough wall space to display the art we had to share. Creatively, our ladies decided to make free-standing screens that would accommodate art on both sides and fill the large empty center of the room. So that we could utilize them in the future, we built the eight three-fold screens out of wood. Pat designed Arab looking design cuts for the top of each to add a unique flare and distract from the painted plywood. Borrowing Madawi's camping carpets again and adjusting the ceiling track lighting Najib had provided add the finishing touches to a class A art exhibit. I could not have been prouder of our students and staff for their accomplishments with this event.

As if we did not have enough going on at the time, a mystery befell the center. Over a two week period surrounding the exhibit, staff and students alike began to "misplace" things. In three years of operation, we had never had anyone stop by the office to mention they had lost something and ask for us to keep an eye out for it. Before we knew it, we had a fairly long list of items waiting to hit our yet to be formed "lost and found." It became so obvious that the staff could not help but giggle and reference our resident suicidal ghost after a lady would stop by the office, describe her missing item, and leave. It wasn't until Carol and Luwa were breaking down the art show did we realize that two pieces of art were missing. Carol was beside herself feeling that she had lost a student's work. I, on the other hand, knew Carol had not misplaced anything. It wasn't her nature and I became suspect. Plus, I knew that Carol and Luwa had cataloged each piece as they hung and labeled it. I spoke with the staff and together we started putting the pieces together – we had a thief amongst us.

  Security had always been a priority and I was not about to allow a breach from within. So in response, I had David coordinate with Dick, the former fair-haired royal security guard, install hidden cameras in various locations throughout the center. For over a week, the morning videos revealed nothing.

  Then, one afternoon one of our current students entered my office with a shopping bag. She was humble and asked to close the door. Safa and her sister had been students with TLC for over a year, and as she spoke, my heart couldn't help but go out to her. It turned out that she had found every item that had disappeared from the center in her sister's bedroom.

Noura was a kleptomaniac. As she handed me the large bag, Safa apologized over and over again for her sister's actions and begged our forgiveness. All I could do was hug her.

In November, we felt another wave of heightened security in the expat community when Saudi Interior Minister Prince Nayif stated publicly that bin Laden was not responsible for the Khobar Towers bombing or the bombing in November 1995 of the Office of the Program Manager Saudi Arabia (OPM/SANG) facility in **Riyadh**. Nayif did however suggest that individuals motivated by bin Laden could have conducted the attacks. At the time, I did not think much of the public statement. But now, I know differently. We all know differently.

In spite of the income generated from our successful ladies' and fitness programs, the two arts shows coupled with the strain of Nabila's demands and her student drain found our bottom line red yet again. We simply did not have the pockets to cover these expenses, even without my being paid, and it was more than I could personally contribute. Although it was a minimal amount compared to the amount of revenue flowing in and out of the center, I had to go to Madawi again for the additional capital. It was not a pleasant experience.

Looking at the situation from a business standpoint, I felt we were on par for only having completed six terms and established two separate facilities in less than three years. Given that most businesses do take time to start running in the black, it would stand to reason that we would follow suit, particularly since we faced the unique challenges of operating under the legal radar and unable to advertise for more students. Sadly, Madawi did not seem to hold the same view as I. Oddly, as she ranted about the requested $4,000.00, she began to refer to the center as mine – not ours as before. To be perfectly honest, I felt her reaction was a bit much for such a relatively small amount. Even so she gave it to the center, but made it clear she would never again.

As the year came to a close much had transpired regarding our personal security situation. It had happened slowly but steadily, thus making it easy to feel surreal. Because of my experience in Egypt, I was paying more attention, but it would not have significant until long after I returned to the states.

There were numerous threats against the U.S. Military, civilian personnel, and facilities during the year, but none were officially deemed "terrorist incidents" by my government. Bin Laden took the stage by announcing a *fatwa* on the 23rd of February in 1998 under the name "World Islamic Front for Jihad Against the Jews and Crusaders." He declared that it is a religious duty for all Muslims to wage war on U.S. citizens, military and civilian, anywhere in the world. He also proclaimed a desire to return the Muslim lands, specifically the land of the two Holy mosques, to the control of Muslims and "cleanse" them of Western influence and corruption. Many now believe that these statements as well as others were foreshadowing the bombings in the east Africa in the summer of 1998. However in December bin Laden gave a series of interviews where he denied involvement but claimed instigation, and he continued to call for attacks against U.S. citizens worldwide and the overthrow of the Saudi royal family. Surprisingly, the Taliban pressured his silence following the interviews.

In response, the Saudi government continued to reaffirm their commitment to combating terrorism through their policies and statements. Crown Prince Abdullah (now King Abdullah) stated publicly in essence that terrorist acts are not representative of Islam and called for a "concerted international effort" to eliminate terrorism. Over the year, we had even heard of potential attacks that the Saudi government thwarted in pursuit of this mission.

Before the bombing of Al-Khobar Towers in 1996, our privacy wall around the compound was protected by a bar over the entrance and several unarmed, pleasant TCNs to call residents when their guests arrived. Afterward, however, our security wall was protected by two gates, machine guns, and delta barriers.

Yet, we had learned a new way to survive in the desert and soon reached the point where it seemed natural. We went along with our daily routines while the Saudi National Guard boats patrolled our parameter, and we took cookies to the guards in the elevated security huts surrounding our world. We often joked that our children would be ultra-tidy later in life because they were used to having the undercarriage of our suburban checked for "cleanliness," as David would tell them, every time we returned to our secluded compound on the sea. The guards would walk around the vehicle with a mirror on a stick each and every time we returned while a jeep off to the side supported a Saudi military officer and his M-50 caliber machine gun.

Oddly, this scenario did not shake me because they were doing their jobs by protecting the compound. Ironically, I never saw them as protecting me, only protecting the compound, or I would have probably felt fear. Security measures continued to heighten as the company began to escort the school buses – our children – to school and park the buses on our compound, under our care at night rather than in the motor pool across town.

Our Winter Jamboree in 1999 did exactly what it had done before and what we had expected and hoped for yet again. The success of this program never wavered as long as I was running the center and I was always thankful to El-Bandari, my Saudi angel, for the idea.

To someone on the outside looking in, the flow of people through the center gave the appearance that we were making money. The excitement generated by our very existence accentuated this sensation. However, with every "new" we brought on board came increased costs as well. I still hope that Madawi was naïve to this cause and effect relationship when she layered even more financial responsibility on the center.

She insisted I hire Roy, one of her nannies' husbands from the Philippines, to be a second driver & security guard for the center. Honestly, the center did not need an additional employee, but Bandari's nanny, Nancy, would remain in Kingdom for a few more years if he were allowed to accompany her. In addition to Roy, Madawi felt the center should begin paying for all benefits received by Saleem, Lulu, and Riaz rather than just their monthly wages as before. These benefits included medical expenses, contract completion bonuses, and round trip airline tickets to their home countries every two years, which happened to fall right after this decision was made.

1999 saw more milestones as the ladies continued to discover new interests and achieve new goals. I was able to bring the *Microsoft Certified Systems Engineering* (MCSE) program to the center to meet the needs of a relatively small, but energetic group of technologically inclined ladies. However its tenure with the center was bumpy from the beginning. The time demands of offering this caliber of program exhausted two instructors in as many years. Johara, my most educated and professional computer instructor gave the MCSE her all. Sadly, her giving eventually burnt her out and she felt she had to walk away. Yet, we pushed on.

Our spring term saw the graduation of the first year *City & Guilds* class. These women had worked hard to complete the stringent requirements of this prestigious art program, and this was their day in the spotlight. Utilizing the fitness facility, we hosted a lovely ceremony complete with invitations, risers, mics, podium, Persian carpets, and our birch dinning room chairs. Tied all together with flowers and greenery, it was elegant. Following the actual ceremony and presentation of certificates, all of the ladies and their guests met at the westernized Oasis Compound to enjoy sweets in their five-star restaurant. For the entire afternoon the twenty-three women dominated the family section with our laughter and Kodak moments.

Keeping with our mission of socialization, the steamy spring night was perfect for a Mardi Gras themed ladies party. I specifically selected this theme because I knew it would be relatively inexpensive to host. I ordered fancy feathered masks from the states for the ladies to wear with their evening gowns. To decorate, I simply utilized some scrap plywood to cut and paint huge masks for the entry and main party room. I catered the dinner through my compound's restaurant and coordinated the nannies from the palace to serve. In spite of the relatively low cost, the evening was splendid.

I was walking on cloud nine with our achievements and the personal growth of the ladies, only to be disillusioned by a rumor circulating that Madawi was joining with four other Saudi women to form a new educational center. The rumors concerned me, but there was nothing I could do if what was meant to be actually happened. So I focused my attention on the positive instead and prayed for the best.

Chapter 16
Reconnecting
May 1999

Madawi's interest and appreciation for the arts continued to widen. Be it an opera, an art museum, or a musical, she was always up for the experience. Even in play, education was her focus. The school year had been tough on our relationship with challenges at every turn, yet topped with encouragement for us to continue the mission we had begun. Like the frosting of a petite four, our successes masked the transforming cake below. With me directing the center and not at the palace daily, we were loosing touch. Most saw the successes and new horizons for the future that TLC offered, yet we knew that the distance between our parallel, yet different paths had widened within our friendship. Intuitively, Madawi knew we needed our Shamsiyahs. We needed time to rekindle our friendship, encourage one another, and swap a kiss for luck before we could begin again.

As the ladies filed through reception towards their waiting cars, the chatter almost rumbled the walls with who would meet whom later in the evening or who would be taking which class during our next term. Joy was in the air, as it typically was at *The Learning Center*. In the scurry, I looked up from my desk to find Madawi peering in my office door, smiling as usual, yet clearly harboring a surprise.

Stretching her smile further and tilting her head more, she raised her eyebrows to create suspense and began. "The ballet," she enticed with a grin. "Are you up for the ballet this weekend Mrs. Teresa?"

Completely taken off guard by the surprise, but intrigued as I love the ballet, I decided to step into the fun. Raising my brow as well and grinning to beat the band, I questioned.

"The ballet, and how in the world can we get to the ballet this weekend?" I chuckled feeling it impossible as it was Monday and I had not obtained an exit/re-entry visa, which normally takes weeks and would be virtually impossible for me by Wednesday for a pleasure trip.

"We," she emphasized, "don't have to get to it. It is coming to us!" Pausing for effect followed by a chuckle, she clarified, "well, almost." Stepping into my office since the surprise was out, her smile widened and she explained.

"The Russian Ballet is scheduled in Bahrain this weekend. I thought you and David would like to join me, the two big girls, Amina, and Elizabeth for the weekend."

Settling into her favorite overstuffed chair in my office, she let her bags slip to the floor, indicating she was there for a wee visit so we could sort out details. Moments later, Lulu arrived with two cups of cap for my princess and me.

Naturally, I was thrilled with the idea of going and told Madawi, yet I simply could not see a way for me to go given all of the hurtles I would have to jump to be able to depart Kingdom in only two days. Over our cap, I shared my concerns.

First and foremost, I had Mason and Michelle. They were only 5 and 3 respectively, and I had never left them alone without David or my parents to oversee their care by the nanny. Madawi quickly put this concern to rest assuring me the children would be with their nanny at her house, surrounded by many to attend to their needs.

Also, there was the legal issue of our exit/re-entry visas. I saw no way to get it solved in time. From the hand gesture that followed this concern, it was obvious that this did not pose an issue to Madawi. When David puts in the papers tomorrow, have him give them to Colonel Awad," She instructed, dropping her voice to indicate this issue was handled.

Realizing more details existed, yet ones I had not focused upon until the possibility of our getting to go became a reality, I anxiously agreed that we would love to go and began my preparations immediately.

Not even another pretty day could get me down that particularly morning. I was excited about the weekend with Madawi as I, too, felt the need for us to spend some time together. Since things were rather slow at the center, I decided to take the morning and enjoy the children. I so loved this opportunity my profession afforded me.

When David arrived, I was dressed and refreshed, anxiously ready to head to the palace. After bags were loaded and pets hugged goodbye, we all piled into the suburban for our weekend adventure. Being around the Awads was so normal for our kids. Mason and Michelle were thrilled at the idea of sleeping over for two nights rather than just one. They knew their weekend would be filled with trips to the Giant Store amusement park, Toy's R Us' indoor rides, McDonald's and all the fun activities that kids see as entertaining. Consequently, the rapid fire kisses on the fly by into the palace were completely expected, as I watched them scurry into the family entrance while I gathered my handbag, abaya, and scarf out of the Suburban. In the distance, I heard Mohammed, the palace gate keeper and telephone switchboard operator, instruct David to park the Suburban in the garage. As David stepped in his direction to clarify, I decided to let the men handle the cars and I headed indoors for some tea before departure.

After hugging all the servants as I entered the girls' salon, which seemed to be an unexpected ritual that was done every time I saw them on a day I would travel, I moved into the family salon to find Elizabeth and Amina already there and as excited as I was to be going. With my teacup full and sinking back into the salon U shaped sofa, I listened as Elizabeth and Amina talked about what was to come. Amina mentioned the ballet was actually Thursday night, the following evening, yet that was the extent of her knowledge of our weekend itinerary. I typically never knew the itinerary when I traveled with my princess, so I offered no insight. I believe Elizabeth fell into the same category as I because she offered none as well. After an awkward moment of silence and another round of dates, the discussion turned to the topic of ballet in general and we each began to share which ballets we had had the opportunity to see. As Amina talked, I watched her, reflecting on our time together, intently analyzing her while I relaxed and listened. Amina is a beautiful woman, sporting the Arab trademark of silky raven black hair and big black eyes. Her skin is paler than most, yet beautifully creamy against her dark features. Obviously well schooled in Britain, her English is impeccable. She is very pristine, neat, punctual and serious for the most part. Honestly, I believe she loved to be silly but seemed to find it hard to let her hair down. In a nutshell, I could easily describe Amina as a modern day Jackie Kennedy, an intelligent lady in every respect. It was obvious, however, by her posture as she spoke that she was the most thrilled out of the three to be included for the weekend, as her invitations from the princess were rare.

As usual, Madawi came scooting into the salon in a quickened gate, indicating departure. Scooping up my handbag while standing up from the sunken sofa, I fell into line as we headed to our waiting, cooled vehicles. Outside, Madawi assigned cars as was her typical routine, motioning for me and Amina to join her in the Beemer. Seeing Amina as my guest as well as Madawi's, I immediately offered to take the middle seat. I wanted her to be as comfortable as possible for your brief journey. As I bent to step into the car, I noticed David in Nora's Cadillac waiting for the motorcade to file out. This struck me as strange as he usually had a driver as well when we would accompany the family on trips as a couple. Yet, I saw his smile, which put my concerns at ease and my questions on the back burner for later in the evening.

With our backseat curtains drawn, none of us felt the need to veil as Abdullah spun the Beemer to take the lead of our motorcade through the massive gate. Extremely chilled by the air condition, I was happy I still had on my *abaya* and that I was sandwiched in the middle. As our six car motorcade whizzed down the **Corniche**, I took in the view that the middle seat afforded me as Madawi and Amina discussed a lotion of some sort. For me, their conversation faded as I gazed into the brilliantly lit day.

The Persian Gulf was on my left and Khobar Towers on my right with manicured landscaping sprinkled in between. Unexpectedly, I found these images comforting, yet disturbing. The vibrant colors were overwhelming as if they had been taken straight from a picture book. With not a cloud in sight, the bluest of blue sky contrasted the wettest of aqua seas. The rhythmic waves tipped in white shimmered in the vibrant rays of sun, bouncing from the desert wind while we drove along the coast. In the distance, I could see the causeway stretching to Bahrain, a totally different world compared to the Kingdom and our destination for the weekend.

The view to my left gave the feeling of hope and brightness, offering the best feelings of what would come, yet the ones to my right gave me an uneasy feeling of the uglier side of things. Still reflecting assault the towers, where 19 American soldiers and hundreds of Saudi Nationals perished at the hand of hate, stood looming with the sun to their back, enhancing their darkness.

Unexpectedly, the car merged left to enter the causeway. As we did, I noticed our motorcade picked up two vehicles that sped ahead to take the lead, increasing our intimate caravan to eight. It would be these two that would escort us across the King Fahad Causeway to the island nation of Bahrain.

Although the colors of nature still lured me and the grip of physical cold from the overeager air conditioner had me subconsciously rubbing my arms, my attention was shifted as I heard my name mentioned.

"Mrs. Teresa," Madawi's voice suddenly seemed loud. "Tell Amina about the new fitness program" is all I heard before the non-stop discussion began. Our conversation was such that we took no notice of our swaying bodies as the car moved with the pavement. Astonished when the car came to what seemed like a sudden halt, my back straightened to give me a better view and get my bearings to determine what was going on around me. I saw a valet attendant with a luggage cart and rotating glass doors. People were walking all around and the echo of car doors slamming could be heard. How in the world could we be at the Gulf Meridian already? What about passport control, customs and the additional four stops required on the causeway? Where was David?

My gaze and contemplation was broken by Madawi's voice.

"Yellah, Mrs. Teresa, we have much to do." Madawi announced as she bent down to look back in the car for my eyes. "Come." She smiled to calm my obvious anxiety. Shaking off my uneasy feeling and not wanting to be left not knowing the next step, I hurriedly departed the backseat and subconsciously slipped into traveler's mode as I strolled through the gauntlet of open doors ahead of me.

Mr. Abdul was in the lobby waiting our arrival. I stepped up by Madawi as they spoke in Arabic and he handed her some papers. After their business was concluded, he slightly bowed and nodded repeatedly while backing away as he always did when he would leave Amity's presence. With cordial and religious verbal exchanges of goodbye said, he turned and made his way to the exit. Madawi turned and began to pass out room assignments and keys, which ignited the typical, hectic dash of excitement when we all began to move to find our floor and room number.

David and I were given the room across the hall from Madawi. A beautiful king size suite reflecting the finest five star accommodations offered us a marble bath, fluffy housecoats, an incredibly stocked mini-bar, and every bath necessity imaginable. As I plopped onto the bed, David made his routine walk through the suite as he did with any new location. A habit for security he had developed. Frustrating at times, but comforting as well. I opened the discussion to the curious things I had seen that day just when the bellhop arrived with our luggage. I became quiet and the man placed our luggage. He then waited patiently for David to complete his room inspection because he would have never looked to me for payment with my husband present. As David tipped him and escorted him to the door, David commented that he knew what I was going to ask and he smiled because he knew he held the answers, which only served to prompt my questions.

"Why did you drive the Cadillac? Did you follow us? I never saw you. And what about the stops? We never stopped on the way. Just pow and we were there." My heightened curiosity reared as I rambled non-stop and went to my knees. Chuckling, David crawled up on the bed beside me, settling my concerns with a kiss, and began to share what he saw.

"First of all, Mohammed asked me to drive the Cadillac. He said Madawi wanted it here this weekend, which wasn't what got my curiosity. Instead, it was what Mohammed said."

"Said?" I echoed as I rose up from his shoulder to check his face. Was he playing or was something going on?

Sensing my anxiety level rising, he chuckled again and continued. "It's not bad as in bad, but rather strange," he began. "Mohammed told me to take the center on the bridge and not to let anyone pass."

"Take the center?" I questioned. "What did that mean?"

"It is a security measure, Honey. He wanted me to drive over the middle line so no one could pass the motorcade." He answered reassuringly, yet seriously.

A long silence followed and then I popped up yet again.

"But we didn't stop." I uttered with confusion.

"It was the most amazing thing." David began as he sat up with his excitement to share.

"You know in the middle of the bridge where we enter that series of checkpoints?" He clarified with hand motions. "Just as I thought we would begin to slow down, the entire motorcade veered off to the right and this big gate swung open, revealing a direct road with no stops all the way here."

My face showed my confusion and he continued. "It's just a few feet off to the right concealed by the hedges we normally see parallel to the road we have to use with numerous checkpoint stops such as passport control and customs."

"And where did it come out on this side?" I questioned still a little shocked to find out this road existed. After the many times we had crossed the causeway and had ice cream on the top of the Saudi tower, I never knew until now.

"On this side of Bahrain's first check point, avoiding their stops as well," he answered. My mental wheels riving up to full steam, I left the comfort of the bed and began to pace, first with excitement and then concern.

"That is so cool," I began. "Now anytime we come to Bahrain, perhaps we can use the special road and avoid all of those grueling stops along the way." Smiling, I thought of the possibilities and then, fear struck.

"The babies!" I exclaimed. "What if something happens to the children?" The look on my face must have startled David and he beckoned for me to explain my thoughts. "What do you mean, Teresa?"

Pacing faster as my mind raced, I explained. "We did not leave the country David!" I pronounced looking at him intently as if he should know my thoughts instinctively.

"And..." he paused, waiting for the rest of my thought.

"You know how they think." I emphasized. "We DID NOT leave the country according to our passports! If something happens with the children and we have to go back without Madawi, we won't get back in baby!" I was almost frantic at the thought by this point.

"With all the excitement, new road and the security instructions," he replied, "I didn't think of that." Standing at the realization, David's face took on one of concern as well. Immediately, my thoughts turned to my friend to solve yet another concern. "Madawi," I said demonstratively as I headed for the door, "I'll go talk to her now."

The door to suite 522 opened after a long, hard rap. Elizabeth opened the door and smiled at my unexpected visit. I entered to find all the girls who had already found their rooms and assembled in Madawi's suite for the fun to begin. Laughing from something that must have just happened, Madawi looked up from the comfy chair. Through her laughter, her face revealed her surprise to see me there so soon as well.

"Oh Mrs. Teresa, welcome," she greeted. "I thought you would want to rest and spend some time with David before you joined us."

Trotting in with a quick hello to all rather than individual acknowledgements, I went straight to Madawi's side. Her demeanor immediately shifted from jolly to serious as she read my body language, and she turned in her chair to hear what I had to say. After sharing my concerns, Madawi's face went from serious to reassuring with her gentle smile, as she gently touched my hand on her arm chair.

"Oh Mrs. Teresa," she began, "please do not worry. If something should happen with the little ones, you will have no trouble getting to them." Making eye contact, the pause between us confirmed that all was well. However, she must have felt the need to reassure yet again because she knows that a mother's concern for her babies is always pinnacle. "I promise," she stated firmly yet lovingly.

Relieved, a big smile flooded my face and hers in response, and I turned to the girls. "So what's the plan girls?" I declared employing my best Groucho Marks voice tainted with a southern twang, as I leaped into the center of the bed between Nora and Fatma. The laughter roared with my impersonation and the joy of our outing had returned.

We enjoyed a delightful meal at Trader Vics, overlooking the Arabian Gulf. The warm breeze through the open air restaurant heightened our senses to the Polynesian cuisine and the faint swish of the waves along the seashore. David chuckled through the meal as he enjoyed the company of six women.

Afterwards we took a stroll through the downtown souks for a little evening shopping. We meandered through the stores looking at everything from clothes to jewelry and had fun in each passing shop. When something new or unusual was found, one of us would either adorn it, attempt to work it, or dare another to give it a go. Meandering, yet not really stopping, we continued. The last shop we visited was an upscale jewelry store, housing phenomenal pieces typically found in such stores as Tiffany's in the states. One piece in particular caught Madawi's eye. A gorgeous ruby necklace and earrings set gleamed from the casing and she could not help but stop. As she spoke with the shop keeper, the rest of us continued to investigate all of the unusual and expensive jewelry sets highlighted in the shop with each of us pointing out our personal favorite.

"*Yellah*, girls" we heard Madawi utter and we turned to see. There she was beaming with delight as she sported the ruby set in front of the full length mirror, turning from side to side to see the beauty. "*Masha Allah*" she murmured followed by a long silence as we all watched her try it on. Then addressing her audience she inquired, "well?" with a huge smile across her face. We all agreed that it was a wonderful choice as it did look stunning draped around her long, beautiful neck. After pausing to look a bit longer, Madawi turned to the shopkeeper and spoke in Arabic, handing back the ruby necklace. Then, she turned and headed for the door and the rest of us quickly followed. As we made our way to the car, we all chattered about the necklace set and agreed that she should buy it. Smiling serenely Madawi slightly raised her hand and commented definitively, "I will speak with Awad." With that comment, I knew immediately that the set was pretty expensive for her to seek the Colonel's opinion or permission to buy.

Once back at the hotel, we all knew we needed to sleep because we had a big day ahead of us, yet none of us were sleepy. As we reluctantly began our good nights, Fatma could not stand the thought of sleeping so early and cried out, "cards!" We all stopped in mid-sentence and looked at each other for the indecisive moment of silence that followed. In unison, our eyes widened and no words were needed. It was play time! The mood of the group quickly escalated and we agreed to meet in Madawi's suite in a half and hour. After a bit, we all started to straggle into her suite. When David and I arrived, we found Fatma already warming up the cards as she shuffled them monotonously.

Once Elizabeth arrived, we circled up on the floor to determine our game. Card game after card game was mentioned and then dismissed for one reason or another. Unexpectedly, Elizabeth came up with the idea. Grinning and blushing, she asked, "Have you all ever played spin the bottle?" Mine and David's eyes widened at the suggestion and for a brief moment no one said a word. Not sure which path Elizabeth would take this idea, I simply indicated that I had and waited for her to explain. The curiosity was growing among the girls as each of them made eye contact with the others like super sleuths embarking on an adventure.

Elizabeth proceeded to explain that how the game works, including that when the bottle stops spinning, whomever the bottle top is pointing to would then have to do a dare determined by the other players. Silence followed, yet eyes darted determining the level of mischievousness the group would embrace with the final looks falling on Madawi. In that she truly loves surprises and holding the suspense of others for fun, Madawi said nothing, only raised her brow at our suggestion. Looking from person to person around the circle, she finally agreed and laughter mingled with excitement exploded. Fatma overjoyed with the idea of mischief, jumped up and ran for the room service cart to get a bottle. I followed with almost as much excitement to insure she selected the best one for the game. Everyone else took the opportunity to raid the bulging cart for snacks before their challenges would begin. Once watered and fed, we all circled up again in the center of the floor for the game to begin. Ceremoniously, Elizabeth made the first spin and everyone giggled with excitement. Our dares were simple at first with such questions as your most embarrassing moment, yet increased in risk level as the confidence of the players rose. Dare after dare, we laughed, perhaps snacked, and then spun again. Nothing we did was illegal, yet incredibly embarrassing as our dares moved from the confines of her suite 522 and began to encompass the lobby and parking lot as well. Believe me, it is terribly embarrassing to cross a huge, elegant, busy lobby of a five-star hotel walking like a chicken and burping out a few clucks along the way as six pairs of eyes peer over the 5th floor railing to confirm dare compliance. Once Madawi's prayer robe was thrown into the mix with one of the dares, I could sense from her voice that she had enough for the night. Obviously out of her comfort zone, she declared that we should all make a promise to keep our game secret. Ceremoniously, we made our circle a final time, held up our right hands, and swore secrecy to the others that who had done what would never cross our lips. Hence, I honor my pledge.

Our Thursday was a whirlwind of sightseeing. We began with the Bahraini National Museum. Situated at the intersection of the *Muharraq Causeway and King Faisal Highway*, the museum is home to a wonderful collection of exhibits from contemporary Bahraini paintings, sculptures, and ceramics to scenes depicting life on the island 6,000 years ago complete with a burial mound and actual skeleton. We saw a replica of a typical 1930s Bahraini souk, and enjoyed an extensive exhibit documenting the history and prominence of the nation's pearl industry, which was the former source of Bahrain's wealth before the discovery of oil in the 1930s.

Bahrain is a conglomeration of 33 islands and its name is derived from two Arabic words, "***thnain Bahr***" meaning "two seas," which refers to the phenomenon of sweet water springs under the sea that mingle with the salty water around the islands. This phenomenon is believed to be responsible for the unique luster of Bahrain's natural pearls.

Bahrain is a lovely country with lovely people. Offering a fascinating blend of eastern and western cultures as high rise buildings vie for space with more traditional dwellings and historical sites. The external structure of Bahrain mirrors that of the Kingdom in architectural design, Arab symbols, roads, restaurants, and flair for the best the world has to offer. Yet, its soul is quiet different.

Bahrain's population of just over a half million includes a significant number of expatriates from all over the world. In general, I found Bahrainis are more accepting of people who are different and of things or ideas that are unfamiliar. There are Churches beside Mosques beside Synagogues. The Islamic daily prayer calls are observed, yet the secular activities do not close in observance. Women drive. You see people wearing everything from traditional Arab dress and **abayas** to trousers and shorts.

Following a delicious, relaxing lunch at the internationally known Fish Market, we decided to slow down our pace. Fatma and Nora wanted to hit the pool, Elizabeth wanted to get her hair cut, Amina wanted a manicure, and Madawi wanted to rest. Hence we all took off in different directions once the doors were opened for us at the Gulf Meridian. Unsure of what we would do, David and I accompanied Madawi in the glass elevator to the 5th floor. Once we reached our doors, Madawi paused and look to David and I. "It's play time," she smiled, "enjoy your afternoon," and she disappeared into her suite before I could reply.

Wanting to experience the Meridian as much as possible, David and I spent the afternoon walking the extensive hotel grounds. The landscaping of the gardens that buffered the gulf, took our breath as we strolled in the warm breeze under the manicured palms along the stone walk path. Clear blue skies overhead coupled with the warmth of the sun showered us as we walked over the bridge of the massive kidney shaped pool, noticing the service and amenities the hotel had to offer. As we walked, we talked about how lucky we were to have the opportunity to experience so many cultures and beautiful places. Just as we reached the center of the bridge, our conversation was broken by the shouts of our names. It was Nora and Fatma frolicking in the water, shouting for our attention and smiling as wide as their faces would allow. Waving their arms into the air, they giggled with excitement as they enjoyed the refreshing water of the pool. After a brief exchange, I reminded the girls of the time and what time we were to be ready for dinner and the ballet.

"You only have about another hour girls," I shouted over the giggles and splashes of the other hotel guests, "so be mindful of the time." Although I was directing my comments to the girls, I knew full well as did their nannies that I was speaking to them and not the girls. It was the nannies' responsibility to make sure the girls would arrive on time, dressed nicely and ready for the ballet.

 As instructed, we all began to gather in the hotel lobby as 8:00 pm approached. The first ones there found a centrally located grouping of chairs near the baby grand piano, which offered a majestic setting for us to assemble. When Madawi arrived, those of us waiting rose as we knew it would be time to depart. We would have to ride to the Gulf Hotel where we would have dinner and watch the ballet.

 The evening was all inclusive for the limited seating of the ballet. Hosted on the roof of the Gulf Hotel along side the five star swimming pools, we enjoyed an magnificent buffet, complete with all the delicious traditional Arab dishes intermingled with the finest of Western cuisine. From fruits to meats to sweets, we all piled our plates high as we passed through the buffet. I always found presentation of food to be pinnacle in this region of the world. Fresh cut lilies and orchids adorned the elaborate buffet tables and encircled the massive ice sculpture of an open shell cradling a pearl, marking the heritage of the islands. I took and extra moment to enjoy the sculpture as it would not exist in a few hours due to the grueling 95 degree heat.

 Following the dinner, we moved our seats in front of the portable stage located at the other end of the roof. Padded folding chairs were lined in front of the elevated stage, flanked by massive speakers and a navy cloth backdrop. Our view from the front row amazed me as the ballet began. We were so close to the dancers that I could actually see sweat fling from them as they performed leaps and turns across the stage. The heat and humidity was dreadful. I could not help but feel sorry for the dancers as they continued to delight us with their talents. The heat was grueling for the amount of exercise and energy required by professional dancers from Russia. The amount of sweat that found the stage that evening was so enormous that the dancers omitted the last two numbers from their performance for fear of slipping and possibly breaking a bone.

As we approached the lobby, Madawi held back from the group and turned to David. She asked if he would go with Abdullah to the jewelry store from the night before and oversee the pickup of her new jewelry set, and meet back in her suite. Willingly, David agreed and assured Madawi he would take care.

Once we were all comfortable and gathered again in Madawi's suite and David had returned, giggles filled the air. Nora, Fatma, Elizabeth, and I encircled Madawi as she tried it on again, yet this time as the new owner. It truly was stunning on her set against her dark features, olive complexion, and elegant frame. Even though I had seen it a thousand times before, I was still in awe that a princess, one wanting for nothing, could always be so genuinely appreciative of her blessings. Each time, she approached the new blessing bestowed upon her as if it were the first. Satisfied with her purchase, she began to remove the earrings as the requests began. Nora and Fatma wanted to try it on. And once they had, the attention turned to Elizabeth and I who also took a turn to adorn the rubies and feel like a princess too, if only for a few minutes. Amina, on the other hand, refrained. I am not sure if she did because she wanted to appear as if the purchase was no big deal to her or if she was shy and out of her comfort zone. Either way, she did not touch the jewelry.

The trip did the trick and our spirits were renewed following our weekend in Bahrain. Rested, I was ready to keep going. With summer knocking at our door and the fitness program running in high gear, there was no time to slow down and ponder what was brewing beneath the surface.

As our spring term drew to a close, I learned that the rumors I had heard and feared were true. Madawi, in fact, was joining with four other Saudi women to form a new educational center like TLC, but "Arabic." She tried to convince me that it would in no way conflict with TLC but I knew at that moment the end was near, particularly when I learned that Nabila was one of the partners.

She continued to repeat "Arabic center" as she described the vision for her new school and a mirror image of TLC. Yet, the emphasis stayed on the seemingly single difference – Arabic as opposed to English.

"It will be the same, but different, huh" she continued characteristically over a cup of tea in my office. "*Al-I'maar* will be the Arabic side and *The Learning Center* the English," she repeated.

"*Al-I'maar?*" I questioned, never having heard that Arabic word.

"Yes, *Al-I'maar* – the new Arabic center," she responded definitively.

The chain of events began to move quickly, which was highly irregular for anything in the Kingdom. Naturally, they began the necessary steps to begin their business, while Madawi continued to profess there was no conflict of interest.

She told me they would require the use of our apartment D upstairs to hang their shingle and I should have it ready for occupancy by July 1st. Until then however, the five partners would continue to meet in one of our classrooms to plan their new center. Madawi and the other partners' personas began a subtle transformation, which I simply noted at the time as a logical step in the evolution of their personal growth. Unlike before, they would enter TLC carrying their briefcases and pass straight through reception with a quick smile or a wave of the hand. The extended greetings and occasional cups of tea became fewer and fewer. Soon, even the hello and goodbyes became random.

Unexpectedly, Madawi asked me to attend one of their weekly board meetings to clarify their needs before the first of July. Reluctantly, I pushed my work aside and headed for Apartment D. From the moment I entered I felt somewhat uncomfortable, but brushed it off as expected and took my seat at the table. After the hellos and introductions, Madawi listed all that they would require with regard to the facility. With the requirements noted and clarified, Madawi changed gears.

Emphasizing yet again the Arabic theme of *Al-I'maar*, she explained that they had acquired a few educational programs to offer and they would be hiring someone to translate them into Arabic and staff their office full time. Security, for some reason, seemed to be a concern. Who knows, maybe it was thought we would take their programs, or maybe it had nothing to do with TLC. Either way, I was instructed to have the locks changed for apartment D. Suddenly, overwhelmed by an uneasy feeling, my eyes were drawn by Nabila's stare from across the birch dinning table. Throughout the meeting, she had not said a word, but her gaze had been intense. I wanted to understand the intent behind the stare that made me feel so terribly uncomfortable.

Even so, I could not help but relish the look of pride and accomplishment I saw on Madawi's face when I rose to leave and she gave me one of her new, crisp *Al-I'maar* business cards and signed it "with love, Madawi" in May of 1999. My heart could not help but celebrate her latest achievement and be happy for my Shamsiyah, in spite of what I intuitively foresaw for me and TLC.

Chapter 17
Pushing the Envelope
June 1999 – December 2000

Periodically throughout the years, I was asked to help with Madawi's girls' school. Typically, I was asked to help with special, one-time events, but I had never been given a regular class, until now. Madawi felt good about whom she was and the personal growth she had achieved. She had been exposed to new ideas that had made her life more complete and she wanted to begin to do the same for the girls. In such, she asked that I develop a program designed to teach the sophomores and juniors at *Al-Hamdi* basic communication concepts. Safa, our Iranian educator, would teach the seniors the basics of etiquette to compliment my efforts. Finally, after seven years with Madawi, I was inside the walls of *Al-Hamdi* to really teach and utilize the benefits of my master's degree, not just coach speeches, choreograph and teach dances, or other fun, frivolous things.

At what appeared to be somewhat of a parent teachers association meeting one evening in late spring, Madawi gave a persuasive presentation to the mothers of *Al-Hamdi's* students explaining the benefits of my teaching the class and the information I had to offer. She further explained that my portion of the program was a segment of a larger wellness program she wanted to implement in the upcoming fall. The mothers were elated with what was to come, and I was shocked later in the year with what I discovered regarding the wellness program Madawi referred.

In spite of our internal issues, TLC was riding the wave of success within the mindset of its students, but the water was becoming shallow as we neared the shore. Fitness was in full swing as the end of our spring ladies' term drew near. The students were enjoying their exercise so much that they did not want to stop simply because the term was concluding and kids would be in the building. They requested with such conviction, I couldn't say no and we scheduled to keep the fitness classes going until the end of the kids' summer program in August.

As instructed I had the locks changed on apartment D for Al-I'maar and they set up their offices mirroring TLC's below. They found a lady that fit their requirements to translate their purchased English programs. Haifa, a Christian Arab from Lebanon, started within the week as Al-I'maar's secretary, transcriber, and receptionist. They took two of our strictly limited, hard to come by telephone lines for *Al-I'maar*'s sole use, used our copier and supplies, and TLC paid their power bill. The financial drain on the center became steady, in spite of the successes we had in other areas of the center.

Only a few weeks after Haifa began, Madawi stopped my office. I was surprised to see her standing at my door that June afternoon just as I was loading my bags to head off early for the compound. Ignoring my preparations, she literally plopped into her overstuffed chair, enjoying the after effects of a good aerobic workout. Naturally, in came her tea because Lulu always knew everyone's moves.

She was careful to choose her words as our idle chit-chat turned to business. It seemed as if the ladies of *Al-I'maar* were upset that Lulu had entered their offices to clean. Believing the changing of the locks had not pertained to me or Lulu, I was somewhat shocked at the request for Lulu to clean only when Haifa was working. With no other business to address, I anxiously explained that I had to leave and hurry to the compound to pay my deposit for a weekend shopping trip that the compound ladies were coordinating.

"Oh fun!" she exclaimed. "Where are you going?"

"To Iran for five days. The compound ladies have organized the trip so we can shop for carpets!" I answered excitedly. I loved shopping for Persian carpets, and with four of the five worlds finest carpets immerging from Iran, I simply couldn't pass up the adventure.

"Iran, why?" her demeanor immediately changed from the jovial tea sipping friend of a few minutes prior. "There are plenty of carpets here, Mrs. Teresa."

"Yes, but not as inexpensive as in Iran," I replied with a smile and a wink because Madawi knew this to be true.

"Well I just don't see why you need to shop there." She continued, "There is so much going on, where will you find the time?"

"Oh, don't worry, Madawi," I answered believing her concern for my professional efforts. "I'll have all my ducks in a row before I head out." I added with a smile and the conversation was dropped. We exchanged goodbye kisses and I flew out of the door to Saleem and the waiting van.

In an attempt to turn the historical wave and avoid beginning our summer program with a deficit, I decided to utilize the fitness facility on the weekends for private parties to create a new revenue stream. Stateside, this would have been considered a sound business move. Yet in Saudi, it could mean our death as a center. We had to be careful. Riaz was our gate guard, Saleem our driver, and Roy swinging between the two where needed. However, with this new endeavor, I felt it best to work Saleem overtime on the gate when he was not driving. After all, he was a Kenyan *Maasai* warrior and I knew he would watch over us. He always had.

While Riaz, Roy, and Saleem kept an eye on the outside, Lulu handled the party. She directed the men with table set-up, cleaned before and after, and was there throughout the party to assist in any way she could.

In addition to the facility rental fee, a student could take advantage of our party coordination services if desired, but not required. Drawing on the expat community, I could coordinate themed party cakes, clowns, magicians, and even party characters like Batman, Mickey Mouse, and Barbie. To compliment, Pat would offer party theme ideas or completely coordinate the actual decorations for an additional fee for her time and creativity. Every lady that took advantage of this new offering, paid for everything to be done for them. Like the children, she could walk in before the party and be surprised as well.

I knew I was pushing the envelope yet again, but felt I had no choice. We hosted birthday parties for all ages and graduation parties for girls. As anticipated, this effort was successful in generating revenue, but it brought more problems than the extra revenue helped. It drained the staff, resulted in excessive wear and tear on the fitness facility when party participants would get out of control, and it drew attention to our existence when neighbors of the center began to report they had heard party music coming from our building. The program had to be dropped for fear of bringing down TLC.

Even though TLC was still illegal and operating without any form of business license, we were becoming more publicly visible. Actually, I was a bit surprised that we stayed as invisible as we did for so long. I assume because we had been in existence for almost four years that people just assumed we were legal. But we never were even to the last day I stepped foot in the center.

Al-I'maar, on the other hand, had chartered for a business license and the three influential Saudi women of the original five were listed as partners with the princess. Consequently, *Al-I'maar's* business license processed quickly unlike the one that never came for

ॐCreating Shamsiyahॐ

an educational learning center run by an American and staffed predominantly by Christian instructors and staff. She never did tell me why even though I asked periodically for years. Perhaps I was holding her back unknowingly.

Yet some validation of our existence and achievements came our way. In June of 1999, *The Learning Center* was featured in the *British Wives Association's* bi-monthly magazine, <u>Desert Roses</u>. It was a nicely done, full color magazine that was distributed to the several thousand British Aerospace employees in Kingdom. I was stunned that Madawi agreed to the exposure because she had never agreed to any type of publicity in the past, although I was continually approached by Arab and Western organizations alike. Madawi was obviously feeling empowered enough to allow us to go public, even if in a limited capacity. Other than the handful of Western ladies strewn around the world that had a glimpse of our hidden beginnings as instructors or staff, this article, and a well-known former US Senator's wife are the only testament I have to corroborate what I recollect in these pages.

Summer Spectacular 1999 ran the course as other programs before it. The kids continued to flood through our doors and we continued to make it happen. With fitness continuing into the summer, Madawi came every other day to exercise, but no longer opened her wallet to pay for her sessions. I would guess she had paid more than her share for lessons, yet it was costing the center 100SR per session, three times per week for MaryAnn's time to spin with her one on one. Now I feel sure she never gave this a thought and meant nothing by it. However as director, I had to consider it.

June soon passed and it was time for me to pay my final fees for my Iranian trip with the compound ladies, and coincidentally another afternoon when Madawi unexpectedly stopped by my office. Once she learned that I was on my way to pay my fees, she closed my office door before slipping into her overstuffed chair. Somewhat shocked at her suddenly somber demeanor, I forgot my urgency to leave and sat back down to hear what my Shamsiyah had to say.

Still in **abaya** and ignoring the tea, Madawi began. "I tried to talk you out of going to Iran, but you have not heard me."

My mouth began to gape as she spoke. I had no idea what she was aiming, yet I was pleased to see it coming out so assertively.

"I do not want you to go to Iran, Mrs. Teresa" she uttered with the straightest of faces yet gentlest of voices, and then upped the stakes and hardened her tone to drive home her point before I could respond. "I will stop you at the border." From her tone, it was clear that she meant her threat and I knew she could do it.

"But Madawi…but…why?" further words evaded me.

"Mrs. Teresa" she paused. "They will kill you."

My look must have said it all and, after a pause, she concluded.

"They teach people to hate you and they will kill you in the market. I do not want you to go." With the completion of her proclamation, she turned and left my office.

Obviously the regional terrorist climate had deteriorated more than I assumed or I don't believe Madawi would have forbid me as she did. Once she did, however, I had a choice and I decided not to go to Iran. As much as I wanted to go, I felt it best to follow the advice from my friend who I knew would never want harm to come my way. Interestingly, the young American English teacher they had hired from the states to replace me tutoring at the palace did not make a year in Kingdom. She chose the Iranian trip.

In no time, *Al-I'maar*'s tentacles extended from their three back offices to consume all of apartment D, including our old fitness room and, out of default, our new kitchen. Nabila began to use the old aerobics room for seminars, which caused strife in scheduling between the kids' summer program and on-going ladies' fitness. We had to juggle all rooms available to run all three programs simultaneously, with room assignments totally based on number of participants to accommodate. Hence loosing any precious space became an issue. It was nearly impossible to file ten eager, young campers by the door of a serious ladies' seminar without being noticed. Unfortunately, our cooking classes became the casualty and our new kitchen sat empty.

Through all of the chaos surrounding the kids' coming and going, I got to know Haifa since she was the only one from *Al-I'maar* that stayed in the office with regular work hours. She was a delightfully insightful lady with whom I enjoyed many interesting lunches and afternoon teas. Unfortunately at the end of August, she came into my office in tears. She told me of the discrepancy in her pay because she was a Christian rather than a Muslim. She was told that her pay for the same job would be lower because she was not Muslim. She said that it wasn't Madawi that said this to her, but she wouldn't tell me who. That particular day was Haifa's last with *Al-I'maar*.

With the summer program complete, we maintained a minimal staff so that the ladies could continue their exercise. Otherwise, no other programs ran and I was free to work on our upcoming fall term and my assignment to enter *Al-Hamdi* in October.

Spawned from the popularity of our internet classes in the spring, I decided to follow a new stateside trend and open an internet café in the fall of 1999. It was another first on our list of first, yet this one was risky and I had to be cautious. Because of the law, it was limited to usage by our current students and their daughters and only open in the evenings. We developed a small menu of snacks such as chips & salsa, popcorn, and sodas available at an additional, minimal cost and served by Lulu. In the short term, our internet café saw success, probably because it was new and unfamiliar. But it only took a few short months and the availability of net access to hit their homes for its popularity to begin to dwindle.

When our doors opened in the fall of 1999, I witnessed the beginnings of an ominous trend for TLC or the emergence of a very important logical step towards empowerment. Even though TLC offered the core courses our ladies had become so accustomed, we were able to offer more new and exciting ones as well. Unfortunately, our ladies' registration was only tepid because many were taking the new *Al-I'maar* seminars offered in our old aerobics room, which began to drain TLC's student fee income in addition to the overhead it created.

In an attempt to broaden our horizons and our life raft a bit further, TLC began to offer English tutoring and TOEFL preparation to kids simultaneously with the ladies' programming. We held the sessions in the remote language classrooms and during after school hours. Enrollment in the program wasn't outstanding, but it did serve to contribute a little to the overall running of the center. Fortunately, the presence of the children was not disruptive to the ladies and we were able to continue.

In November, TLC hosted its 2nd annual art show, the "1999 Group Exhibition of TAC Artist," which ran simultaneously to a "TLC sponsored"/*Heritage Gallery* Show open to the public in downtown **Al-Khobar**. I was never asked to be involved with the gallery's show and only learned of its existence when Pat wanted me to proof the invitations she had designed. Attendance at our show was halfhearted at best. Yet, the ladies flowed in and out of *Heritage Gallery*. The most influential princess in the province publicly supported the show and encouraged attendance in an article featured in the *Saudi Gazette* newspaper. It was a huge coming out for many local artists and it was good to see Madawi beam as the evening progressed so elegantly.

However, simply looking at the brochure made for each exhibit reflected the state of affairs. The brochure for the "TLC sponsored" *Heritage Gallery* exhibit that Pat designed and coordinated was professionally bound and included a color cover and 6 two-sided pages of color art inside. Obviously money was behind this endeavor because those brochures were expensive and Pat's expertise and time were not cheap either. Whereas all TLC could afford was a single sheet 3-fold brochure we produced in house. Knowingly or not, Madawi was beginning to lose touch with TLC, outgrowing it perhaps. It was at this point I began to pull from my personal finances on a regular basis to help keep the center's cash flow going during the valleys between our peaking successes. Conversely, on the peaks, I would pay myself back and/or at least get paid my wages and the cycle would begin again.

Following the shows and the distance I felt as a result, I was pleasantly surprised but somewhat shocked when Madawi requested that I put together a proposal for a few communication workshops. These workshops would subsequently be translated into Arabic and presented by Arabic speaking facilitators through *Al-I'maar*. She asked that I include my fee for their development and that I have it to her by the end of the year. Obviously, I had no love loss for *Al-I'maar*, but I eagerly jumped on board to submit the proposal. After all, it was educating women that was my ultimate mission. Whether it was in English or Arabic was insignificant to me as long as it was so.

Unexpectedly, Madawi asked me to attend a ladies dinner at the *Heritage Museum* in **Dammam** the last weekend in November. No details of the evening were given to me ahead of time. Actually, it was almost an eerie cloak and dagger routine, but even so, I sensed she needed her Shamsiyah and I went willingly. To my surprise, I found the entire museum closed for our event and the facility full of American women with the *Young President's Organization* visiting from the U.S.

This evening was incredibly significant in that I believe it was the first semblance of tourism in the Eastern Province of this closed country. From what I gathered, several influential Saudi businessmen wanted to host the organization and solicited the help of their wives to entertain the wives of their guests. The American ladies told me they were given an abaya and scarf once they made their way down the gangplank of their luxury cruise liner harbored in **Dammam** port. They were then loaded on a bus and brought to us. No shopping or sight-seeing was being allowed and they would return to the ship that evening. One of the ladies was from Atlanta, which is near my hometown. I gave her Ann's telephone number and they met for lunch.

I was thrilled to see the evening held in the new museum along the sea. From the day I arrived in 1991, I had felt that the Kingdom needed to acknowledge and remember their past. It was so appropriate to host these ladies in such a fine display of the history of the Kingdom and its people. The Arab music played as we enjoyed traditional Arab cuisine in the folds of a tribute to their heritage.

As our fall term drew to a close, our ladies' participation had dwindled further following Al-I'maar's offerings and came to almost a standstill by December. The Fitness, Kids', and Art programs were holding their own financially, but offered little back to cover the deficit still felt from Al-I'maar's presence and maintain its own general overhead. As a result, I reached again to the cycle.

Perhaps she knew her Shamsiyah needed a break or perhaps she did not want to go alone without hers, but Madawi invited me to attend a business women's conference in Dubai, UAE with her in early December. David and I had already made arrangements to take the children to Petra, Jordan with a group from the compound for the U.S. Thanksgiving holiday, which made for a little scheduling nightmare that was overcome with creativity. Because I needed an exit / re-entry visa to get in and out of Saudi for each trip, there would be no time to get a new one after returning from Jordan and before needing to fly to Dubai. So, rather than fly home after Petra, I simply flew onto Dubai to spend a few days with Nora while David flew back to Kingdom with the children.

Following her graduation from *Al-Hamdi*, Nora had started attending the *American University of Sharja*. Madawi and the Colonel had set her up in a beautiful private villa and sent her nanny, Susan, and driver, Romelo, with her. She was currently in her first year of study and doing superb. She beamed when she showed me "her" jeep, which she could now drive at will under the supervision of Susan or Romelo.

Unlike at our children's museum conference experience in Minnesota, Madawi was enthralled with every session offered in the Dubai Business Women's Seminar. She listened intently and made notes. It was strictly business for her. However when we were not occupied with a seminar, we enjoyed delicious restaurants and shopping just like old times. I remember taking a moment to be grateful of my blessings as the warm evening breeze lofted from the Arabian Gulf and into the open-air restaurant of the *Chicago Beach Resort*. And then again later when we walked the pier for our evening stroll and we caught up on everything in each other's lives, sorted through some issues, and set our paths again. It was a wonderful trip.

Unlike Saudi Arabia, the United Arab Emirates (UAE) allows other religions to practice their faith within their border. Although limited as compared to the states, the UAE does have stores that openly sell Christmas items to Christian citizens. I went wild in the store when I found the items, and Madawi stood back and watched me shop for almost an hour as if she were happy just to see me so happy. I walked out of the store with two box loads of decorations. So excited to have found the items, I beamed as we got into the Mercedes and the driver loaded my goodies into the trunk. After thanking Madawi again for bringing me by the store, it then hit me as to how I was going to get all of the stuff I had bought back into the Kingdom.

"You bought some cute, funky bunky things, Mrs. Teresa," she began chuckling as we got into the car.

"I know Madawi," I replied enthusiastically, "and at such good prices!" Then I paused deciding how to approach the topic of my dilemma.

"But," I paused again trying to formulate the right words, "how will I get these home?" I questioned.

As always, Madawi had the perfect solution.

"Do not worry, Mrs. Teresa," she said in her calm, stately way. "I will ship them for you."

"Really?" I questioned with surprise and then responded with joy. "I would be so grateful."

"*Mofie mushkala*," she replied with that special raised eyebrow and side smile of hers. "*Yellah*," she said to the driver and we were off.

Because Madawi wanted to spend some extra time with Nora, I flew back to **Dhahran** before she did after the seminar concluded. Two days after my return, a knock came on my villa door. It was a palace driver, delivering the two boxes from **Dubai.** As promised, Madawi came through for me yet again.

Because of Madawi's request, I submitted a proposal for a three segment training program to *Al-I'maar* on the 11th of December. In a sense I was somewhat perplexed with there request. Yet, I did my best to put together a program that I thought would be beneficial to *Al-I'maar*'s mission for the project: raise awareness in the areas of personal and business communication among their clients. To incorporate versatility, the program included three full-day segments that could be offered as one three-day program or three individual seminars. The first segment addressed basic communication skills and they increased in complexity to conclude with the third segment targeted specifically to business owners addressing internal and external communication skills.

In addition to the actual training program, the proposal included my training *Al-I'maar*'s Arabic speaking trainer to facilitate the program, a hard bound copy of the program, two computer disks containing master copies for future reproductions, and a trainers' guide manual that I would also develop as a companion to the program. Because it had been so long since I had sold a training program, I called my former university professor to ask what I should charge. She offered a different ways it could be packaged and a price range for each. In that the program would be duplicated time and time again, she suggested a flat program fee. Following her guidance, I decided to quote 20,000 SR ($5,333 U.S.) for each individual segment or 55,000 SR ($14,666 U.S.) on the program in its entirety. Within a few days, I received an unexpected written reply indicating that the proposed program was too expensive. It's curious how a packaged training program which can be duplicated and offered multiple times, allowing for revenue and further personal development for more women can be seen as too expensive, when in November of 1997, a 24-hour workshop and 20 seminar hours went for over $4,000 more. My proposal was never returned and it was never spoken of again.

 Unexpectedly one afternoon after our return from *Dubai*, I was called to attend a meeting at *Al-Hamdi* where I was to meet with Madawi. When I arrived, I found Nabila on the sofa in Madawi's office. She said nothing but hello and goodbye for over an hour while Madawi and I discussed her wishes for me. She wanted me to continue teaching my communication program and add the 12th graders to my schedule as part of a new wellness program Nabila would be overseeing for the school. Basically, the same as what Safa and I had implemented in the spring, yet it was now a part of a wellness program that Nabila was directing. Social Etiquette was pulled into the new program as well, adding the tenth and eleventh grades. It seemed as if nothing changed but our new teaching days, grades, and times, but in reality, a lot had changed.

 My parents left retirement for a third time in February of the new millennium and returned to the winds of the Kingdom. My father's employment with another American company brought him back to *Al-Khobar*, but they were assigned to live on another

༓ Creating Shamsiyah ༓

Western compound, *The Oasis*, which was about 2 miles south on the **Corniche** from mine.

Because they had left exit only previously believing their retirement to be permanent, their paperwork had to begin again and Baba John arrived 90 days before Mama Ann. They were frustrated to no end and missed each other desperately. To help alleviate some of his sadness, Madawi invited all of us to come to her coastal shamsiyah for an evening by the sea. With the Persian carpet buffering the wet evening sand, I sat with the Saudi women as the younger ones danced to the latest American top 40 tunes. About thirty of us in all, we sat, ate, laughed, and danced as the evening continued.

Daddy had driven me to the picnic and was still on the property, but he didn't want to intrude out of respect of the women. Consequently, Madawi found him by the servants fishing on the pier. What made her search him out, I do not know. From the distance, I saw them sitting there, side by side, like father and daughter. Legs hanging over the edge and chins to the heavens, they talked. After about a half an hour, they returned together to the carpet. As Daddy approached, several of the older ladies reached for their scarves to cover, yet Madawi said something in Arabic and they stopped. When they reached us, Madawi spoke in Arabic again and introduced my father to them, calling him "Baba" John.

My Dad, being quite the poet, could not let a tender moment like this pass and decided to write a poem commemorating the beach house, her umbrella, to her. I helped him get it framed and he gave it to her a week later at the palace.

From the early morning sunrise,
To the desert setting sun.
The solemn prayer at evening,
When all days' work is done.

Comes the pleasure of Shamsiyah
My treasure by the sea
This beautiful place that God has blessed
Is there to comfort me

With cooling breeze and shading trees,
Where all worries surely cease
It takes away my troubles
And brings me inner peace.

I will always love Shamsiyah
And the happiness I have found.
The laughter of my children
With cookouts on the ground.

Now when my life is over
And time has passed me by,
I am sure that I will find
Shamsiyah by and by.

When he finished reading it for her and handed her the frame, she hugged his neck and then placed it on the bookcase in the family salon. You could tell she loved them both.

From her very first experience with the concepts of communication in our original villa, our more

ॐCreating Shamsiyah ॐ

humble beginnings, I believe Madawi sensed their importance. These skills are valuable tools for an effective leader and she absorbed them instinctively. Consequently, she felt it was important to expose the teachers of her children, of her school, to the concepts as well. I developed a two-day workshop covering the basics. *Al-Hamdi* paid TLC per participant for the program, which included materials and a catered lunch each day. We held the workshop in one half of the fitness facility's multi-purpose room complete with a podium, hand-held microphones, overhead projectors, and LCDs. The other half offered the space to provide lunch with five star seating for the participants.

Originally developed in English, Madawi requested that we translate it to Arabic for her teachers that were not bilingual, which were the majority. Seeing the point to this, I thought it was a grand idea and I set to work to make it happen. I assigned Reema to translating the participant's manual and I put me on the mission of finding a woman that could facilitate a workshop well and speak both languages to boot. Finding her with basic knowledge or understanding of the human communication process was not even considered. However through a friend of a friend, Amal found someone and she asked her to come in to see me. Ghada, a mid-thirties Lebanese lady, entered our doors. She was perfect from hello. She was spunky and enthusiastic. She was bilingual and held a degree in communication from a university in Beirut. Perfect. We began her training on the specific workshop the following day.

I was encouraged in the spring of 2000 when I negotiated a partnership between TLC and Executrain, an internationally recognized computer instruction company. TLC would provide the facility and computers, its staff, and its name, which had become well-known and trusted in the area. Executrain, however, would provide the instructors and actual instruction. I was elated at the idea of having them on board, feeling certain that they would help the center recover from *Al-I'maar*'s drain and move TLC into the future. Conversely, I was devastated when we had to halt the classes because we were not licensed. We were only able to offer the classes for a few months, until our legality became an issue.

In another attempt to level the cycle, I achieved another goal I had set for the center jumping numerous hurdles like I always seemed to do. I brought the popular stateside Franklin Covey programs to TLC in the hopes of boosting revenue. Sadly our registration was only tepid because class times conflicted with other seminars being offered. Simultaneously, I proactively closed the café since it had not shown a profit and was becoming an additional liability and security risk.

My emotions were split when *Al-I'maar* secured its own facility and moved from TLC in late spring of 2000. I was proud for the ladies and their personal growth. I knew the courage and determination it had taken to see them this far. I knew the progression had begun and I was happy for them, especially my Shamsiyah.

Yet, I felt ominous relief. I felt like the heaviest burden had been lifted from my shoulders and that the threat to TLC had left. Unfortunately, it had not left but only changed locations. Many of the women that used to flood our doors, I never saw again. I had Saleem drive three revolutions of the city block so that he could creep slowly each time in front of their facility. It was dark. They had a sign. I could say nothing as I looked at it and Saleem turned down his music. I never was invited inside.

The centennial year for the Kingdom of Saudi Arabia fell between 1999 and 2000 on the Western calendar. It was a glorious year marking the 100th year of the country under the rule of the House of Saud. Celebrations were everywhere, all year long. The Eastern Province marked this momentous occasion by erecting symbolic wood *dhows*, banners, and other representative icons of their heritage throughout the city. Special gold coins encircled in silver were minted to mark the year as well. Everyone was joyous and celebratory of the country's progress, and this excitement pervaded every occasion that year at *Al-Hamdi*.

The ninth graduation party I attended in the spring of 2000 exhibited a different tone and homage than previous years. Whereas Western and basically American themes had dominated previous ceremonies, the Kingdom's centennial brought about a subtle, yet fundamental change in the attitudes of the teachers, the students, and Madawi. Sparking a sense of nationalism and pride, this historic year yielded change in what was important to them all. Subsequently, I was not asked to help with this graduation. I only operated my spotlight that evening because I was the only one who knew how.

The evening began as usual, and again, I was in the second row, dining room chair and I would hop up and scoot to the back of the room when the spotlight was required. In spite of the usual events marking the beginning of the graduation, there was a very different feel to the night. At the time, I did not see these differences as negative; rather, I saw them as a positive step toward acknowledging and praising their heritage. Since my first visit to **Hofhuf** in 1992, when I saw how the Saudis had shoved their roots to the wayside in exchange for Western ways, I had encouraged healthy nationalism. I was proud for them and proud that they were finally taking pride in themselves, their country, and their heritage.

With the exception of the English class presentation in which it was necessary to speak English, all performances that evening were completely Arabic. The performance was not anti-American, just pro Saudi. Throughout the evening, the girls exalted the beginnings of the country through traditional dances, songs, and attire. The students symbolically revealed how the House of Saud came to power, how they united the divided tribes, and then illustrated the good things that were felt by the people after the change of regime. The food flowed, as did the Saudi pride. Even though I was a Westerner looking in and not truly a part of their world, I felt pride as well. Little did I know, little did I see how things were changing for me. I missed how this was a sign of what was to come. Consequently, I never expected what would happen at the final *Al-Hamdi* graduation I would witness.

By summer, our fitness revenue began to drop as similar facilities started opening in the area. Another mainstay for the center was sliding off the map. Fortunately, the kids' summer program would begin in a few short weeks. The stress was mounting and I needed help. Fortunately, she landed. I could not have been happier to see my mom that evening, even if we were late to pick her up at the airport at no fault of our own. I felt relieved and as if my energy calvary had arrived. Mom joined us in late May of 2000 and sadly missed the graduation by mere days. **Masha Allah,** she arrived just in time for the summer program.

We both knew it, but we both knew it was the only choice. We pushed the kids' program to lengths we had never gone before. In addition to the typical program classes like Arts & Crafts, Painting, Cooking, and Exercise, we added "Crazy Tuesdays." A weekly outing for all class participants from ages 5 to 14, boys and girls. We rented a bus each Tuesday and we took them on a new, surprise adventure – a field trip. We visited the *Saudi Aramco Museum* which documents the discovery of oil in their nation and its significance on the culture. We saw soft drinks bottled and learned about manufacturing at the local Coca-Cola Bottling Factory. We took them horseback riding and even ice skating! Yet, the one that stumped us up was swimming. The children had missed swimming so since we had to shut down the lessons at DM 16. Who would have considered the issue we faced by taking them to Mama Ann's compound, *The Oasis*.

On our designated swimming Tuesday, I followed with my Dad behind the two buses loaded with almost 100 children and some moms. We pulled ahead, however, to reach the gates of *The Oasis* compound first. He and Mama lived there and their section of the compound had a private pool just behind their villa. Mama had observed that no one ever swam in the daytime, assuming the residents were working at that time. So we scheduled a Tuesday adventure to go swimming. Before the gates would open, Dad spoke with the guards confirming this is what we had organized with them the day before. With a nod of his head, the buses flowed into the walled community.

Realizing this was a risky move we crossed all our Ts and dotted all of our Is. From the gate guards to the life guards, we had it covered – we thought. Just when all was going well and only the sounds of happy children splashing could be heard, a roaring scream came from the other side of the pool! A mama of one of the teenage girls had just seen a TCN construction worker on the third floor of the building next door looking over at the swimming pool and subsequently her daughter. Instant chaos followed as we loaded the children and spoke with the guards. The lady was somewhat hysterical, and sadly, the worker was

ॐ Creating Shamsiyah ॐ

probably taken to jail for having eyes as good as *Superman's*.

To say the least, the swimming was finished. However "Crazy Tuesdays" continued and we even opened a five day "adventure class" in the few remaining weeks. It was a tremendous hit, yet exhausting to continually think of five new places to adventure and how to get there each week, but we managed. As a result of this new offering, the program's immense popularity relieved the center of its financial deficit and current burden for the time being and I didn't have to go into my pocket.

Whereas Mom was invaluable to me through the children, Daddy was in other ways. He was my emergency driver, confident, and lunch buddy, particularly before my Mom arrived. He would telephone me at the center in the mornings and we would decide what our future lunch would be. He would then swing by the selected restaurant, pick up our food, and enjoy lunch with me in my office with the door closed because of uncovered ladies in reception. I actually think he got a kick out of our sneaking him in and out of the center.

One particular afternoon, Amal joined us in our secluded picnic spot for pizza, but slipped out again when the telephone rang. I was facing many challenges and took the opportunity to share them with him for his advice. After all of that was said and done and after he encouraged me to continue the mission of my passion, he pointedly advised that I never put my own money into the center. Having already broken his advice, I simply replied, "yes, sir," as is the Southern way.

Unfortunately, with the end of the summer program, came the end of my parents' tenure in Kingdom. The ladies cried as they patted their hearts and said good-bye once again to Mama Ann. Their presence from February to July was my life raft. Without their assistance, I could not have kept the center afloat.

My world was changing around me and, even though I could not identify it, I could feel it. The continual rumors of attacks on expats coupled with the company giving us our own personal mirror on a stick with a flashlight to check under our cars for bombs while at the *souks* unnerved me.

Feeling threatened more than ever, I traveled stateside for the summer to buy a house for us to have when the end came. Upon my return to Kingdom, I put a picture of the house on my desk for inspiration. Madawi saw the picture and foretold the future, remarking that "people in Kingdom always buy the house right before they leave for good." She put down the frame and left my office in a somber spirit, neglecting to say goodbye.

Obviously Madawi saw what was happening to the center and rationalized that this situation could still be a "win-win" when she suggested that TLC begin to concentrate more on kids and teens than on ladies. As a result, I offered the first kids/teen after school program in the fall of 2000 to run simultaneous with the ladies' classes. This was the first time we had ever had the two operating in the center together at this level. Before it had simply been a few students studying English or TOEFL in a remote language classroom during after school hours when most ladies were sleeping. However, this time they would be passing in the hall and holding class in adjacent classrooms.

With Madawi's encouragement, the TLC staff and I stretched our imaginations in an effort to keep the center going. We began to test the gray area. In an effort to thwart the financial cycle, I pushed the envelope perhaps a bit too far with three of our five fall kids' programs. English and French training harbored no issues, but didn't have many students enroll either. The other three, however, filled almost instantaneously.

Following the wave of our summer success with "Crazy Tuesdays" and "Adventure Camp," we offered a "Tuesday After School Club." Not as adventuresome as the summer and held within the confines of our walls, the Tuesday club classes studied art, computers, and international cooking with a different country highlighted each week in all three areas. At the end, we held an open house for the parents to view what their child had experienced in the program. The problem herein lied in my allowing 13 and 14 year old boys to register.

Simultaneously, our fall brochure offered a program to attract teenagers as well. "The Teen Thing" was designed to allow young ladies eleven years and older to experience make-up application and skin care, modeling, social etiquette, and photography. To culminate the program, we solicited a local boutique to provide the outfits in exchange for advertising for a private fashion show held for the moms. This program alone grazed the edges of that gray, undefined area, but posed no real threat.

The unforeseen problem arose when we held the classes on Tuesday, when the young men from the Tuesday club were in the center. As I was fully aware, there is a clearly defined point when girls and boys can attend the same class or even the same location for that matter and I pushed that limit without even thinking. Had it occurred to me before hand, I would have made changes in our schedule to avoid it. Unfortunately, I didn't realize until we it the very first Tuesday as the flirting began in reception. From that point on the staff and I ran ourselves crazy to keep the two apart, simply praying the eight weeks would exhaust before we did.

Allowing this, even if accidentally, was a mistake that easily could have resulted in immediate closure of TLC by the authorities or *Muthawen*. Not only could I have been deported, which would have been the best result I could have hoped, the strides we had made for the Saudi ladies would have digressed if not ceased all together. We had to go to unbelievable lengths to keep this from occurring once we realized the possibility existed.

Unexpectedly, however, it was the dancing classes that almost closed our doors and brought the authorities to my fax machine. Knowing that ballet, tap, and jazz classes had enormous potential as I had witnessed with *Jadawel Jazz*, I decided to offer classes to girls ages 6 to 14 years of age. Yet "dancing" was illegal in Kingdom and I should have remembered that fact before I distributed brochures advertising it.

The unexpected ring of the telephone startled me during the quietest time of the afternoon at TLC. Lulu had gone to the palace to get something to eat before the kids arrived for the after school program and I was alone. As I reached for the receiver, the fax kicked on startling me yet again. As it unrolled, I watched, stunned and unsure of the handwritten Arabic script that covered the page, but completely sure of the fax tag printed on the top: Al-Khobar Police Department.

Franticly I called my Shamsiyah even though I had not felt comfortable disturbing her as of late. Without saying hello, I was clear and succinct. "We have a fax from the police department and the only three words I can read are *'The Learning Center'*." With her signature "ooooh" and the click of her cell phone, she came immediately and appeared before me in less than five minutes. Standing in front of my desk with her *abaya* still on, she made no sound and her face showed no emotion as I watched her eyes read each line of the fax. Expecting some discussion or a plan of action, I was shocked when she casually folded the paper in half, tucked it in her hand bag, and announced, "I'll take care of this." Later she told me it was the word "dancing" that prompted the fax. Fortunately, the men at the police department understood when she explained that it was simply my error in translation because, of course, we would never offer "dancing," only "exercise" for the children. Subsequently, the charges were dropped.

Interestingly in the fall, Madawi insisted we begin offering our classes in English and Arabic instruction, which included our new Franklin Covey program. Until now, she had always wanted only English. Perplexed, but committed, I called in Ghada. Started Reema translating and we began preparations.

As our fall continued, TLC hosted its 3rd annual art show and saw the graduation of more *City & Guilds* students. Yet, it was simply not enough. Things were deteriorating, so much so that we did not even have the capital to repair a simple belt on a treadmill that David had scavenged for free when the fitness facility originally opened.

In a last ditch effort to draw ladies from the doors of *Al-I'maar*, we hosted an "International Dinner Evening" for our fall social. Incorporating the theme, we made it a potluck for obvious reasons. Turnout was tremendous, but when the next week came, they went back to *Al-I'maar* to share classes with the influential and Nabila.

The late fall of 2000 brought another speaking competition our way. KFUPM had not held the second annual public speaking contest in the 1999-2000 school year. We laughed, attributing the oversight to their not doing so well in the first. The logistics of our participation in the second competition followed the same pattern as in 1998. Yet, this particular year *Al-Hamdi* did not fare as well. The selected girls worked very hard, but unfortunately, I did not have the same level of natural speakers, fluent in English, as I did for our team in the first competition.

However, our lack of placement success is not what is important with regard to the second speaking competition. It was the global events at the time, which marked the beginning of the anti-American, pro-Islamic sentiment that are so important to note. Two events immediately preceding the second competition set the tone for the speech topics and subsequent events at *Al-Hamdi*.

In September of 2000, Ariel Sharon, now prime minister of Israel, entered the Islamic Holy sites of the Dome of the Rock and the *Al-Aqsa* Mosque on *Al-Haram al Sharif* in Jerusalem with thousands of Israeli police, bodyguards, and supporters. Intended as a provocative demonstration of Israeli sovereignty over Jerusalem, his presence in the Holy sites infuriated the Muslim community worldwide. Behind **Mecca** and **Medina**, the *Al-*Aqsa Mosque is considered the third Holiest site in Islam.

Only three weeks later, on October 16, 2000, Israeli police fortunately turned back members of the Temple Mount and Land of Israeli Faithful Movement, supported by Sharon, from entering the same sites. Had their infiltration not been halted, I believe a holy war of incalculable magnitude would have erupted. These events were seen by the Muslims as an incursion on their Holy places, and in my opinion, are what triggered the current Middle East insurgence.

The sentiment of the Muslim outrage was reflected in the girls' assigned speech topics during the second public speaking competition. There was no discussion of solving global issues like *Rainforest Deforestation* or informing the audience on *Diabetes* as before. Rather, the evening encompassed pro-Islamic reaction and encouragement to stand against the invaders of their Holy ground.

The sweet success of our first fall kids' program was not untainted by a bitter shell. Problems began to arise left and right. From day one, accomplishing anything in the Kingdom took more effort than was required to do the same in other countries. Roadblocks were a daily part of life both physically and metaphorically, but I had learned to adapt and adjust to accommodate while still achieving my desired end. However, by this time, they became more and more prevalent and I was running out of energy and rarely saw my Shamsiyah. I was thankful we had survived the kids' fall program without incident or closure and I vowed to never cross that line again.

Our personal security situation deteriorated throughout the year as well. Americans and other Westerners were targets of more local terrorist attacks that never made the news. We heard of an American couple in **Riyadh** that prompted a memo suggesting we keep our windows closed while driving in town. The couple had a bomb thrown through their open window, killing them both on detonation. Rumors flew about a man whose legs were blown off when an explosion occurred in his tire well.

ॐ Creating Shamsiyah ॐ

The weekend of my son's birthday in November, a Thursday actually, Madawi telephoned to see how things were going with my party preparations. I sat on my bed and chatted as we laughed about it being his first sleepover and that I wouldn't get a wink of sleep.

"I can just see it now, Madawi," I giggled. "Me shaking David all night to jump up and drive these boys home!" I chuckled in anticipation of the big night.

Slightly laughing, she then casually mentioned, "Oh, it won't be that difficult. It's just on the compound."

"Oh no, Madawi. These boys are from many compounds. They are his little friends from *Dhahran Academy*." I added for clarification, "They do not live on my compound."

After a moment of silence she added, "Have David wear **guthra**, huh."

"What?" my excitement dissipated as I felt a cool breeze flow in my open veranda door.

"Just have David wear **guthra** if he drives them tonight, huh." She said rapidly and then concluded. "I will see you soon, **Insha Allah**, **yellah**." The phone went dead. Still feeling the breeze, I sat bewildered with the receiver in my hand.

Chapter 18
Ma'as Salaama
May – June 2001

I do not know the day or the time, but it happened in January. We hoisted the children into the suburban and buckled their car seats. Then I went left and David right. I was a bit frustrated that shopping day because we had forgotten our mirror. As I finished a complete revolution around the suburban and checked the passenger tire well once more, I was about to stand upright when I heard a scream. It was Michelle, laughing in glee at something her brother had done. Relieved, I looked across the hood of the vehicle to see David stand upright as well and reality hit me. I was putting the two people I love most in the world in a vehicle and then walking around it to look for bombs. It was time to leave.

To be honest, I think I had lost hope that I could make things right for the center again. I had given it my all and I was simply exhausted. Stripped of everything I had established to make the center work, other than the volatile children's programming, I was void of new, feasible ideas. It was time to let go of what I could not save and make sure I protected what was my divine blessing to save.

On the security front, things were worsening for us. More attacks against Westerners occurred downtown, yet rarely made the news, particularly if there was only an explosion with no fatalities. On simple trips to the local mall, we were spat upon by young Saudi boys even though we were appropriately wearing *abaya*. Obviously, the welcome mat was a bit worn.

I truly believe the events that led to this moment unfolded as they did and when they did for a reason. Perhaps it was the next logical step in Madawi's personal growth and the growth of the other Saudi ladies or perhaps not. Either way, however, I felt as if I had fought long enough and it was time for me to fade away and let them move forward without me.

In February of 2001, I told Madawi I was leaving Kingdom for good. We were in her office at *Al-Hamdi*. After I began I wished that I had prepared my thoughts more thoroughly and I wish I had not surprised her. Sadly, it was a short exchange. I explained that I would leave after the center's spring term in the hopes of making the transition smooth. I wanted time to find a new director and train her, transfer the books to an accountant, and help coordinate kids' summer program. The center was like a third child for me and I wanted to do everything I could to make our separation as smooth as possible. I wanted every form, every policy, and every procedure in place to make sure TLC had the best chance possible for success.

My commitment to the girls ran just as deep. I had worn my scarf and abaya to enter the gates of *Al-Hamdi* every Tuesday afternoon. My mission was to share new information that had never before pervaded the walls of the school. By staying until June, I would be able to complete that mission.

In March I began taking the necessary steps to transfer the center financially and find a new director, my successor. I asked Madawi for an accountant to transfer the TLC books. I wanted to have time to show them to him, give documentation if necessary, and then be available for a few months to answer any questions that may arise upon further investigation. She avoided the topic numerous times. Finally after I pushed to the point of being a nuisance, I met the accountant, Mohammed, in May. We met on several occasions, and by June Mohammed and I parted ways when he indicated that he had completed his work and that everything was in order.

My decision as to whom I would recommend to direct the center was grueling. There were so many things to consider. Eventually I hired Ghada as my replacement. From the ladies available, Ghada possessed the majority of the requirements I thought necessary for the new director. She was a business-minded, Christian Arab woman from Lebanon that was bilingual and held a bachelor's degree in communication. I knew she was energetic and outgoing, but I was never convinced that she would nurture the center as I hoped.

During this time, my staff did not waiver, nor did the servants I knew and trusted. The Saudi women, however, seemed to become more distant from me, particularly once it was public knowledge that I was leaving.

From the servants at *Al-Hamdi* via my nanny, I learned that Madawi was facing major business problems that she had not shared with me. The details were sketchy, but the scuttlebutt indicated that the headmistress and her husband had stolen millions from Madawi. The Lebanese Muslim husband and wife had managed *Al-Hamdi* for some twenty years. I am sure Madawi was devastated if the rumors were true. And if that weren't enough, the whispers told that the manager of her computer store left for his supposed vacation, but in fact stole everything in the store. His crime was not found until he did not return. Both events placed a pit in my stomach and an ominous feeling in my heart.

As is the life of an expatriate, moving from place to place is normal, but requires good records when the time comes to seek future employment. Almost every instructor that left the center requested a letter from me validating their work to include with what they called their "CV." As Americans, we know this as a resume and the letters as our list of references. Because a move can easily take you to another country and the prospective employer may have no way of reaching the former, letters are written which validate that you worked the work you claim. I always wrote the letters when the teachers requested, whether we had had an outstanding work relationship or not. It was a matter of record.

For this same purpose, I asked Madawi for a letter of recommendation, or at least a letter of validation to the work I had done whether she thought it was good or bad. She refused both. Following the confrontation, I stood in a tiny bathroom located in the back corner of the upstairs in the school, looking out of a window the size of a peephole, and feeling as if I were trapped. Slowly, tears ran down my cheeks while I silently prayed to be out of there. Madawi's behavior towards me dramatically changed after the facts of the headmistress and the Egyptian manager came to light. Now I often think what she must have felt and what internal struggles she faced. Perhaps she thought if her own people, Arabs, would treat her like this then most certainly the Christian American would.

I was later told that if she had signed my recommendation or letter of validation, she would have owed me *gossi*, a Saudi contract completion bonus, for the years I had worked for her.

It was my last *Al-Hamdi* graduation in May of 2001 that revealed how life in the Kingdom had changed, how the sands had shifted. Unlike previous years, I got my own driver to take me to the graduation. Unlike previous years, the hellos when I entered were somewhat cold. They were not rude, just robotic. In retrospect, I can see that anti-Western sentiment existed, subtly just below the surface. I did not get the overstuffed chair or even the dining room chair. I had to fight to even get a chair. I finally sat in a regular folding chair that was stuck on the end of a row over by the wall, placed there by a caring servant that still had feelings for me and continued to treat me as before. As the evening began, the tone was set by the very first act, an extremely pro-Islam and anti-West display that continued throughout the evening. As a result of global events, a sense of supremacy filled the ceremony as they exalted Islam and its beliefs.

Our ladies' program drew to a close and as usual, we were facing the cycle again. However, our registration for the summer program was looking good and I had no worries as in years before.

It was late in the evening of May 7th when the telephone rang. It was Ghada, who was now acting director of TLC. She said that Madawi had asked her to call me and that I should be at the center for a staff meeting the following day at 1:00 p.m. I had not seen Madawi in several weeks and a sense of foreboding flooded my being. Alert, I questioned my need to attend. I was busy packing my household items for departure and only acting in an advisory capacity to Ghada and the staff at this point. Why did I need to attend a staff meeting to work on a term I would not be present to witness? Ghada was evasive and only repeated my need to attend. It was only the second time I had ever been called by someone else to meet Madawi. The first time had been when Abdullah, the palace operator, called for me to go to *Al-Hamdi* when I found Nabila over a year prior.

The feeling I had stayed with me through the night and woke me with the dawn. When David was leaving for work, I told him to be ready to come immediately for me if he got a call after 1:00 p.m. My little inner voice was screaming. I was scared. Why? I had no clue, but I just knew this was not going to be good. The feeling was so intense by noon that I almost did not go. But I knew I had to show. Madawi had been my friend for ten years, but she had been a princess her whole life and I fully understood her position and the power she held. To openly defy her request for me to be there was not an option.

Just before 1:00 p.m. Madawi entered the center in *abaya* and carried a briefcase. It was strange for her to be on time, much less early. Tall and striking, she paused briefly at my office door to let me know she was ready to begin, but her face showed no emotion. She continued down the hall to the classroom in the art department without saying a word. I entered behind her to find the conference room filled with a dozen of my teachers surrounding the table. I had arrived shortly past twelve and I didn't even know they were in the building. It was quiet and they were all looking at me and the empty chair by the door, across from Madawi.

For the next twenty minutes I endured future accusations and humiliation. When I heard her begin, "Do you think simply because I am a princess you can use me like a money tree?" I was stunned. Her furrowed brows and verbal tone were like nothing I had ever heard from her before. My mind began to race trying to determine what was happening and why she was so angry. As her barrage continued for what seemed like an hour, but in fact was less than five minutes, I could not focus or feel.

The only thing I heard her accuse me of doing "wrong" was that I had not repaired the treadmill. The same one David had scavenged for free when we opened the facility. Otherwise, her anger seemed focused on the future. Not having been involved in our standard financial rollercoaster ride, it probably shocked Madawi to see us nearing the end of the spring term and not as much cash in our account as we needed to pay our instructors. After all, I feel sure she hadn't experienced this feeling with her personal accounts.

While she continued, I saw her mouth move, but I heard no more. I began to taste the distinctive taste of blood in my mouth. I had unconsciously bitten my cheek so as not to verbally rip her to threads in my own defense, but then my mind flashed my children before my eyes and I continued to bite. When the wrath finally stopped, the room went quiet and an awkward silence ensued.

My shock held back my tears as I starred straight into her soul. I wanted to throw in her face all the personal sacrifice and heart I had given her dream. Yet, I could not. Like an unexpected, sobering slap, I remembered where I was and who was across the table from me. I remembered that with a simple command from her I could be thrown into jail and the reason for my imprisonment would be insignificant.

Mohammed was already to his feet by the time I reached my office, professing his innocence and asking my forgiveness. As tears swirled with mascara streamed down my face and Mohammed continued his confessions, I called David. When he answered, all I could say was "come now."

Knowing I had about fifteen minutes before he could possibly arrive, I began grabbing my personal items while the tears continued to distort my vision. I pulled my framed degrees and art from the walls and stacked them by the door. All the while, Mohammed moved about the room with me, declaring he had told her over and over that I done nothing wrong. He said she simply refused to listen. When I could stand it no longer and hold nothing else, I made my way out of the front door to wait the remaining few minutes outside. Walking away with my memories sliding from my arms and my path blurred by my tears, I could hear Mohammed repeating that he was sorry.

While I stood just inside the outer gate, I thought I would hyperventilate before David arrived. I could not believe what had just happened. By the time the suburban pulled to a halt on the other side of the wall, I was shaking uncontrollably. He tried to ask me questions and help me with my things, but I rambled through my tears and threw my bags in the suburban. We did not speak on the way home.

I was relieved to see our villa door and thankful to find my bedroom. I curled up in the middle of my bed until the sky turned black. The tears had stopped and all I could do was stare. The trays of food came, hardened, and were removed. The tears didn't come again until that evening when I reached my mom in the states and told her what had happened.

Throughout the evening several of the instructors that had been witness to the meeting telephoned me. Nada, Amal, Carol, Angela, and Mirna shared with me their perceptions of the day while offering condolences. From what they said, they believed that

Creating Shamsiyah

Madawi thought they would be upset to know there was not enough money to pay their wages for the spring of 2001. They also felt she was shocked to know that they knew of the current financial standing and that they knew they would get paid as they always did. They knew the cycle and explained it to her. Sadly, she never knew I had no intention of asking her for assistance to cover spring of 2001, just as I had not the majority of TLC's terms.

In the days that followed, my staff literally freaked out and called me several times an hour with questions. But in their frenzy, they continually offered and showed their support of me. After a few days passed, Carol called and told me the TLC ladies wanted to have a good bye party, a *Ma' as Salaama* party, for me, but she wanted to make sure it was okay with me first. With mixed emotions, I agreed.

From a few close friends I learned the compound rumor mill was spinning out of control. Feeling unable to hold two fronts, I became reclusive. I did not leave the villa for days at a time. There was no goodbye party for me from the Westerners. I could not help them anymore and association with me could be misconstrued

As I dressed to go on the evening of May 22nd, I called my true, lifelong shamsiyah – my mom. I cried because I did not know if I could walk into the center again for my own goodbye party. I had no idea if I would have to face Madawi again or not. And if I did, I had no idea what I would say. I was scared to death.

But with her encouragement, I went with my head held high.

Surprisingly, Madawi had all the food catered from the palace for approximately 200 guests. She paid for everything, but she did not come. I caught myself looking for her all evening, hoping she was just late.

My breath was literally taken away as Nada opened the fitness door with a giggle. She was so very proud, as she had a right to be. She and the other gals had done a beautiful job with the decorations. The windows were draped in peach silk with coordinating table linens. Overflowing baskets of flowers accented the u-shape seating and buffet, while candles filled the air with the smell of sandalwood.

After a delicious dinner and some formal words, we morphed into children as if attending a birthday party. Before I knew it we had slipped off our high heels and circled up on one of the Persian carpets. Everyone vied for a spot to see as I opened the mound of **ma'as salaama** gifts. While I unwrapped, different ladies would share different stories. Some embarrassed us with things that had happened and we laughed until our mascara ran. Others remembered serious times when they claimed I made a difference. Their words and the loved they held made me know that what we had accomplished was good. In spite of everything, it would have been good to have Madawi hear her praises, too.

Although my Shamsiyah wasn't late, I did find a small, unique wood box and a card on my desk after

ॐ Creating Shamsiyah ॐ

most of the guests had left and I was waiting on Saleem. The earrings were exquisite, gold with semiprecious stones. The note, written and signed in her own hand, read "Big and gold hearts only exist in Magic-Kingdom. Safe trip and happy life for the dear kids. Madawi Fahad." In spite of my deep understanding of the Saudis and their culture, I was unable to determine the meaning behind her words. Amal, Nada, and other close friends sat with me in my office as we read it over and over. We were all perplexed.

 In preparation for departure, I spent my last forty-five prayer calls getting our things in order. In the spring, I had offered my costume inventory and my spotlight from *Jadawel Jazz* to Madawi for *Al-Hamdi* for a very reasonable price. When she declined, I made the same offer to *Dhahran Academy* and they jumped on the opportunity. I had already had the costumes delivered and only the spotlight remained. But Madawi still had it at *Al-Hamdi* because we used it for their graduation in May and I needed it back. The *Academy* wanted to buy it and I wanted to sell it since I had dug into my savings for TLC. Plus, they were about to close for the summer and needed to conclude the business transaction. Spotlights were hard to find in the Kingdom and outrageously priced if you did, so naturally both schools would want such a piece of equipment.

 Along with my final grades for the students in my *Al-Hamdi* classes, I sent her a letter through Saleem asking if she would send my spotlight to my villa or did I need David to go by with the suburban and get it. Three days later I received a written reply stating that the return of the spotlight was not an option. In essence, she felt I owed her for the telephone charges incurred for the center's internet access through the compound and she was keeping my spotlight in lieu of those charges. Sadly, she also added that the kids program had not done what I had expected. I still wish I could have been there.

One week before my flight, David's father became ill unexpectedly and he had to leave the country immediately. His father died before he reached the United States. Suddenly, I was left in a male dominated society where I could not drive. I was responsible for packing out an entire home of ten years of memories. I was left to deal with the problems we encountered with our nanny's American visa. It was nothing illegal and easily resolved through personal interviews at the Embassy. Yet, I had to hire a taxi to drive her to **Riyadh**, a four hours drive away, twice to resolve the issue, so it was expensive and more irritating than anything. By the time it was solved, I discovered the nanny's travel letter was out of date and Madawi had already left the Kingdom for summer holiday. I did not feel that I could call and inconvenience her over this, or perhaps I had no idea how she would respond. Either way, I decided not to call. Rather, I asked the TCN working in the compound office to duplicate a previous exit letter with a new date, which gave her permission to leave the Kingdom with me. He gladly assisted.

Stifling would be the only way to describe the heat that night. It was the night I left Kingdom for the final time. I was anxious, which caused my heart to race and my breathing to labor. Saleem seemed to move in slow motion as he heaved our luggage into the van while the children's laughter seemed surreal and distant. But, he was doing his best, and I knew it. Yet, I could not stop pacing nor dam the flood of emotions that ran through me. Deep appreciation and respect temporarily thwarted my fear while I watched him work.

Earlier in the day, Amal shared with me what a risk that dear man had taken for me and my children. Calling regularly to ask just "one more thing" regarding the center, Amal broke her word to Saleem by telling me that he had intentionally disobeyed Princess Madawi. It was the very day I ran from the center in tears that Madawi told Saleem he could no longer drive me, adding that "he had a new Director now." Yet, bravely and unselfishly, he disobeyed **Amity's** instructions and, for almost three weeks continued to drive for me without saying a word about his defiance. A true **Massai** warrior, Saleem was there for me through my last hours in the Kingdoms in spite of risking his livelihood at the very least.

To temper my anxiety, I decided to check the villa one last time. Like a rapid display of digital movie clips, a decade of memories flashed before me while I took my final walk through our villa. Only the company-issued furniture and household items remained either against the wall or neatly folded on the kitchen bar, just as they had been when I had arrived ten years earlier. From room to room I strolled, burning my memory for a lifetime as I knew it would be the last.

    I saw the murals in the children's rooms and thought of all the magnificent ones Mel had painted for me over the years for nothing short of peanuts. I saw a younger Nora and Fatma laughing with glee in the middle of my flour laden kitchen after an English lesson on recipes and measurement conversions had gone astray. I remembered our elaborate birthday parties that Madawi's girls couldn't wait to attend. I thought of our annual Halloween party on the compound when the girls, their nannies, and every servant child of the palace joined us in costume for pizza on the floor and trick-or-treating into the night.

    In the living room, I could still see my four year old Michelle climbing up and down "Auntie Madawi's" back as she repeatedly bowed to Mecca. And then her motherly smile as she claimed it hadn't bothered her in the least. I could see Fatma standing before me, practicing the speech that won her second place in the first female high school level public speaking contest in Kingdom at KFUPM. Yet, the patio swing did not move as I remembered the way Madawi would always slouch in it a bit when we slowly swung, sipped tea, and chattered under the ever clear night sky.

    Packed so tight that none of us could move, the van rolled along the highway with Saleem's favorite Arabic music resonating the roar of the engine

ॐCreating Shamsiyahॐ

laboring in the heat. We seemed to drive endlessly through the black of night, rarely passing another car on our way to the *Dammam International Airport.* It was "o'dark thirty," thirty minutes past midnight, and the stars twinkled in the heavens over the desert as they had done for me a thousand times before.

Even so, I simply could not wait to be out of the Kingdom and away from all that had happened. I was nervous and in "red alert." I was not going to be caught off-guard again, so I assume that I looked for the unexpected because I had not seen it coming before. I was truly fearful of what lay ahead of me. I was still in shock from all that had happened. I had no idea if I had unknowingly committed a faux pas and I was unsure of any ramifications. I still didn't understand.

Unfortunately, I wasn't fluttering in and out of the Kingdom in royal style with my princess, expecting everything to be first class. Rather, I was quietly leaving, with kids and baggage in tow, through the dark of the night. Leaving as if the past ten years had never happened and the things that I had accomplished had never occurred.

Inside my footsteps echoed against the massive marble floor, making me feel subconscious as if everyone were looking at me. When we approached the ticket counter for our boarding passes, I stepped slower to gain my composure. "Only a few more challenges and we would be airborne," I reassured myself acting as confidently as I could. As I should have anticipated, the check-in portion of our journey was exhausting. "For ten years it had been that way so why should this night be any different?" I thought with exasperation. "Oh, Teresa, get a grip," I urged myself. To my despair, these attempts to reassure myself were truly ineffective, yet I had to continue.

Once on the plane, I looked around suspiciously as the nanny heaved the heavy carry-ons into the overhead compartment, neglecting my regular routine of helping the children settle into their seats, their personal space for the next fourteen hours. Nervously, I took my seat by the window still clad in my ***abaya***. Although I heard the children comment about this and that, I cannot recall the details because my attention was elsewhere. Soon, the engines began to rumble, and the flight attendant announced to cross-check doors. I knew then we were almost home free, and my heart began to beat more rhythmically. I was running but not from fear, rather from heartache.

As I felt the thrust of take-off push against my chest, my hand unconsciously touched the glass. For one last look, I pulled myself up against the forward thrust of the plane to see out of the window as we made our assent. I saw the defined area of the city lights skirted by the darkness of the barren desert. As we rose higher and higher, the city lights became more distant and took on the shape of celestial bodies. They twinkled for me as stars do. Again, my hand went to the window as if I were trying to hold on. And then, I felt it. A single tear ran down my cheek, as I said the final goodbye to my home and the way of life to which I had become so accustomed.

I would assume this is where I should conclude by tying the events of a decade together into a nicely packaged message. The problem is I can not. There could be so many explanations of why events unfolded as they did and numerous alternatives if simultaneous scenarios are considered.

Given the world we find ourselves, most would love for the conclusion to be that our two religions pulled us apart. It would make for a juicer ending. However, although I am unsure which scenario we actually played out, I do not believe it was this one. Out of mutual respect, Muslims and Christians can work together for a common vision and enjoy successes. We are a good example. For almost seven years, Madawi's visions coupled with my leg work made things happen for our ladies through *The Learning Center*. Future generations will remember Madawi for placing the umbrella in the sand because what we did was good and not against anything that either of us held dear.

It could be argued that our business and, subsequently, our friendship was the target of a hidden agenda held by an ambitious woman who did what she needed to do to achieve what she wanted to achieve. Illegal? No. Unethical? Perhaps.

Possibly we grew apart as we grew from within and our missions took different turns. Or, it could be as simple as issues typically associated with mixing business and heart. But then again, could it have been a heart that turned the events?

If I were to hold fast to my faith and believe that everything happens for a reason – by God's will, then I would have to believe that what happened did so for a purpose. I see the Saudi women stepping up as their sisters did years ago. The Saudi "feminist movement" I refer is just that …the Saudis. It will reflect them and their values, not those others. They are intelligent women that have a lot to offer their communities and could be equated to a healthy return on a society's investment.

Just as I can not tie up the past, I can not predict the future either. *The Learning Center* provided the women a safe haven where they were among friends to mould, develop, and grow personally as women, while experiencing ways of thought that are necessary to move forward. What will they do with the knowledge our shamsiyah provided them by a woman who carries the torch of those that went before her? I do not know. But I do know that no matter what path they choose to follow, it will be their path – one that respects their culture and honors their religion, as is their way. It is my belief therefore that what the future holds is God's will or **Insha Allah** as Madawi believes.

I do know however that it was because of my Shamsiyah that my path through Kingdom was as it was and that my efforts today are as they are. And I know the same is true for her because I was recently reminded, "good work with good hearts keep going wherever we are."

Glossary of Arabic Words

Appendix A

The Arabic language is a phonetic language. Words should be enunciated as written.

Abaya – the traditional long, black covering for women worn to hide one's figure
Afwan – "you're welcome"
Al – preceding a name indicates "family of"
Allah – Arabic for "God"
Allah Aakabar – essentially "there is but one God" in Arabic and is said to lead the call to prayer five times per day
Al Hamdulila – "praise be to God"
Al I'maar – literally translated means "department" but selected as the pseudonym for the Arabic center referenced
Al-Mana Hospital – the major local hospital used by most westerners in the Eastern Province
Amity – "your highness" when referring to a female
Amir – "your highness" when referring to a male
Ashufee baden insha Allah – ***"I will see you later, God willing"***
Asr - The late afternoon prayer call, which is one of five daily prayer calls practiced by Muslims. This prayer occurs around 4:00 p.m. / late afternoon
Baba – father
Bata – an old shopping district in the heart of Riyadh
Baksheesh – basically means "kickback," yet not considered illegal in Kingdom; rather commonplace
Bedouin – the nomadic people of Saudi Arabia
Bin – "son of"
Bint – "daughter of"

Bisme Allah - "thank you God for the blessing"
Bukkra - tomorrow
Champs d'Elysee – a famous street in the heart of Paris, France, that stretches from the Arch d'Triumph to the Louve Museum.
Corniche - a scenic road that parallels the *Arabian Gulf* the length of the Eastern Province
Dohr – The midday prayer call, which is one of five daily prayer calls practiced by Muslims. This prayer occurs around 11:30 a.m. / late morning.
Dhows – traditional Arab boats, hand made of wood
Dubai – one of the United Arab Emirates on the Arabian Peninsula
Eid Al Fitr – the three-day holiday which directly follows the Holy month of Ramadan to celebrate the breaking of the fast
Eid Al Hada – the three-day holiday that follows the Hajj to celebrate the annual pilgrimage
Empty quarter – a region in the southeast corner of Saudi Arabia that consists solely of desert
Fagah – a small potato like vegetable that grows wild in the desert
Fajr – The sunrise prayer call, which is one of the five daily prayer calls practiced by Muslims. This prayer occurs at sunrise each day.
Fatwa – a Muslim legal opinion
Faux pas – French for "mistake"
Ghawa – "coffee"
Guthra – the traditional red and white headdress for Arab men
Habebee – sweetheart, baby, enduring term
Hajj – the annual pilgrimage to Mecca dictated by the holy Quran observed by Muslims from around the world at least once in their lifetime.
Hajji – a term used to refer to individuals in Kingdom for their required pilgrimage to Mecca.
Halawah – a mixture of honey and lemon cooked on the stove and then chilled before using to remove body hair.

Hiyah – a segment of the Committee for Public Morality, the religious police that handle dealings with westerners

Hummus – a dip made of chickpeas, seasoned with garlic, lemon and tehina and eaten with pita bread by scooping the dip

Igal – the black band that goes on top of the men's traditional Arab headdress

Igama – the required Saudi Arabian work permit for expatriates in the Kingdom. It is your "lifeline," your identity. There is a large fine applied if you loose it or are ever stopped at a checkpoint or roadblock without it. Pictures of the man's family are included in the back.

Il est dommage –French for "It is a pity."

Imam – a scholar of the Quran

Imshee – "walk" or "follow"

Insha Allah – "God willing" or "if God wills." Muslims use this phrase constantly in that their belief is so deeply rooted in the idea that God controls everything.

INCO – an acronym meaning "In Country Company Number," which is assigned to each expatriate employee, marking the date he enters the Kingdom for the first time.

Isha – the sunset prayer time

Jamboorah - a small kangaroo like rodent that is indicative to Saudi.

Kayf Haalak – "How are you?" to a male

Kayf Haalik – "How are you?" to a female

Kebsa – a traditional celebratory Arab meal consisting of goat and rice

Kolasse – "finished" or "stop"

La - "no"

Maasai – famous as herders and warriors, they once dominated the plains of East Africa. Now however they are confined to a fraction of their former range.

Ma'assalaamah – "goodbye"

Maghrib – The sunset prayer call which is one of five daily prayer calls practiced by Muslims.
Marbrook – congratulations
Marhaba – "welcome"
Masha Allah – a thankful, complimentary comment
Majlis – an open court held weekly by the King and Governors in the Kingdom
Mofie Muskala – "no problem," a very common phrase that westerners learn almost immediately
Mubarak – an Arabic term used to offer good wishes on a holiday.
Mumkin – literally translated means "possibly" but is used in conversation to mean "please"
Muthawen – the Islamic religious "police" in Saudi Arabia
Nam – yes
PUBH – an acronym meaning "peace be upon him" and used whenever a reference, either written or spoken, is made to the Prophet Muhammad (PBUH)
Quran – Holy Book of the Islamic Faith
Ramadan – the ninth month of the Islamic calendar in which Muslims fast as one of the five pillars of their faith. This is an extremely Holy time for Muslims.
Riyadh – the capital city of Saudi Arabia, located in the Central Province
Riyal – the name of Saudi currency notes
Sambusha – a triangle pastry filled with either feta cheese or seasoned meats
Shabah – "old, wise man" used in a fond, respectful manner.
Salla – "prayer time"
Shammal – sand storm
Sharia Law – ***the laws that guide citizens of Saudi Arabia based on their religious beliefs***
Shariah – ***the judicial body in Kingdom***
Share'a Al Khabbaz – a famous shopping street in Hofuf

Sharja – one of the United Arab Emirates on the Arabian Peninsula
Shawarma – a wrapped sandwich
Sheesha – a water pipe usually filled with dried fruits and spices
Shiite – a sect of the Muslim community that does not directly follow the teachings of the prophet Muhammad (PBUH)
Shukran - "thank you"
Shula – a popular, older indoor shopping mall in Al-Khobar
Sideeke – literally means "friend," but used by expats to refer to a homemade alcohol.
Souk – "store" or "shopping area"
Souk Al Khamis – "Thursday Market"
SR – the abbreviation for Saudi Money called "Saudi Riyal." Used like the dollar sign for American money. Saudi Arabian currency is tied to the U.S. dollar and has a standard exchange rate of 3.75 SR to the dollar.
Taif – a city located in the Southern Province
TCN – an acronym for "Third Country National," which refers to individuals working in Saudi Arabia from third world countries
Thobe – the traditional Arab attire for men, long and usually white
Tieeb – "okay"
***Qadis*-** Islamic judges
Ulema – The Islamic authorities in the Kingdom
Wahid – "one"
Ya mama – actually means "mama," but is used when speaking to anyone you care about as an endearing term.
Yellah – an Arabic term with diverse meaning depending on the context. It can mean "hurry," "come along" or "do something"
Zakat – the act of giving alms, which is done to fulfill the third pillar of faith in Islam

ॐ Photographs ॐ
Appendix B

Saleem with a prop from the first *Jadawel Jazz* holiday performance.

Our first dance holiday performance

Horseback riding through the Valley of the Kings in Luxor, Egypt.

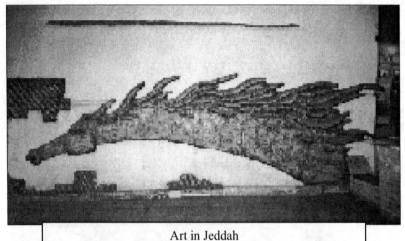

Art in Jeddah

The artist used what was available to create three-dimensional creations encircling an inner court yard walls snuggled in the heart of downtown Jeddah

The New Learning Center
Opened in November of 1996

Painted by Pat on our
Drawing classroom wall

TLC's Painting Classroom

Our Computer class and Internet café

Our Appreciation Dinner

Sunset with Baba John at *Shamsiyah*

Our gift

South American Dinner Social

New administrative office in fitness facility

Corridor from TLC to new fitness facility

Weight & Spinning room

A staff birthday party with eight nationalities celebrating together

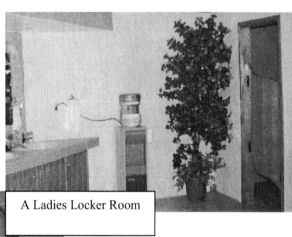

A Ladies Locker Room

TLC's First
City & Guilds
Art Exhibit